Advance Praise for
Moving On: Grief in Ministry Transition

"What a taonga Silvia Purdie's book is! Her artful weaving of stories, poems, prayers, and research crafts a kete fit to hold the emotions, spiritual, psychological and physical challenges, personal and communal impacts, and practicalities inherent in ministry transitions. Personal stories express the breadth of culture, ethnicity, and ecclesiology in Aotearoa New Zealand and candidly tap into themes of identity and vocation, home and belonging, community and relational entanglements so common in ministry. Scripture finds voice in poems and liturgies that name the realities of transition, grief, and loss, yet engender hope and the possibility of new beginnings. Here is deep, hard won, hope-filled wisdom that is accessible, realistic, and practical. It is reassurance for those who are in the midst of transition – others have navigated this terrain and emerged richer for it. *Moving On* is above all a timely contribution to the training and sustaining of all who minister in these changing times."

Rev. Dr. Karen Kemp,
*Senior Coach/Lecturer in the Centre for Church Leadership
and School of Theology, Laidlaw College – Te Wānanga Amorangi*

"What a wonderful treasure trove drawn from deep wells of lived experiences, Biblical reflections and helpfully instructive insights, all masterfully interwoven by Silvia. This is no detached theoretical handbook, but a living, breathing testimony to Silvia and many other practitioners doing life in the dust of the arena of ministry, surviving to tell a 'graced story.' So much has spoken to my own journey – oh how I wish I had read this previously, through my own journeying on the ministry path. But perhaps the famous adage is relevant here, that 'when the student is ready, the teacher will appear.' I sense the teacher, the guide that has walked the path and survived to tell the story, has appeared, and this student is listening!"

Donald Scott,
*Spiritual director and co-ordinator of Te Raranga church leaders network,
Christchurch (previously Senior Pastor, Northcity Church)*

"*Moving On* presents sage pathways for making room to grieve amidst ministry transitions. Seasoned with the wisdom of first-hand leadership experience, Silvia Purdie weaves perceptive insights, tender stories, spiritual practice, and thoughtful conversations into a real-world guide for attending to the particular rupture(s) emerging from transitioning ministries. I commend *Moving On* to anyone grieving or journeying alongside those mourning ministry changes, for through this helpful volume you will discover afresh that you are not alone and your grief matters."

Dwight J. Friesen,
Associate Professor of Practical Theology at The Seattle School of Theology & Psychology, author of numerous books, including: 2020s Foresight, The New Parish, and Thy Kingdom Connected

"It is said that no matter how effective a politicians career has been for most it inevitably ends in defeat. Sadly for far too many in pastoral ministry their experience has a similar feel. In this comprehensive overview of ministry endings Silvia Purdie very helpfully addresses the grief and pain experienced by many in ministry transitions. It also raises questions about the adversarial culture that has been allowed to develop in too many church settings, that is a far cry from the Family of God picture of the New Testament writers."

Murray Robertson,
Pastor Emeritus, Spreydon Baptist Church (now South West Baptist Church), Christchurch

"What a fascinating and insightful book about ministry transitions. I found it to be very engaging with its mix of reflection, interviews, poetry and practical ideas. I was moved by people's honesty about difficult situations they had found themselves in and how they processed that, grieved and moved forward. Coming from our own context of Aotearoa New Zealand makes it easy to relate to and I am sure the stories it contains will resonate deeply with readers. Silvia has skilfully woven together our human stories with the big story of our Christian faith; of being people of the resurrection, which gives us hope. I believe it is a book which will be helpful to ministers and congregations alike."

Rev. Rose Luxford,
Moderator Designate, Presbyterian Church of Aotearoa New Zealand

"The beginnings to new ministries are well defined: there will be a service, someone will be invited to preach, flowers should be provided for the minister's spouse, perhaps gifts for their children, pleasant words will be spoken, always full of hope and good times ahead. For the new ministry family there may be the excitement (and trepidation) of a new home, new community, new school and new opportunities. But departures are less well-defined and likely to be painful, even if there is the joy of (say) moving into retirement or shifting to a more desired location (let's be honest, a lot of ministers want to shift from the country to the city). Familiarity is being disrupted, local friendships unsettled, and there may be a little or a lot of unfinished business about to be left behind, perhaps never to be concluded in a healthy, healing and timely manner.

In *Moving On: Grief in Ministry Transitions*, Silvia Purdie assembles an impressive cast of writers to weave a set of stories, build a treasury of wisdom and provide a toolbox of liturgical resources in order that many aspects of ministry transitions can be engaged with. Any movement from a ministry appointment is a loss, a wrench away from a community of love. Even in the most difficult ministry situations, to leave is to lose loved ones, and so there is grief in ministry transitions.

There may be anger too. The pain of transition in ministry is faced here. The honesty made public through this publication is helpful. I commend this book as a ministry in its own right – a service for God's servants so that we may transition better."

+ Peter Carrell,
Anglican Bishop of Christchurch

"*Moving On* is an eminently practical, honest and theoretically sound book that is so topical for today with the significant amount of change that is occurring. Many people will enjoy its relevance: while written primarily for clergy and the church it also speaks to people facing transition in their jobs, retirement and life events like illness and bereavement. It is impressive in the breadth of viewpoints, research and case studies presented. It does not give superficial answers or strategies but wrestles with complex situations. Best of all, it is very readable!"

Rev. John Hornblow,
Deputy Mayor of Palmerston North 2004-2010

Moving On

Grief in Ministry Transitions

Silvia Purdie, editor

Philip Garside Publishing Ltd.

Email Silvia at: silvia.purdie@gmail.com

Paperback International edition 2022: ISBN 9781991027252

Also available
New Zealand paperback edition: ISBN 9781991027085
Paperback print-on-demand USA: ISBN 9798353743422

PDF: ISBN 9781991027269
ePub: ISBN 9781991027276

Philip Garside Publishing Ltd
PO Box 17160
Wellington 6147
New Zealand
books@pgpl.co.nz — www.pgpl.co.nz

Cover illustration:
Painting of the Kahuterawa Stream in Linton
by Lynn Ramage

Contents

Foreword – *Maja Whitaker*

Dr Maja Whitaker is Lecturer in Practical Theology at Laidlaw College. She recently moved from Te Tihi-o-Maru Timaru to Ōtautahi Christchurch with her husband and young family.

• • •

The invitation to read *Moving On* was remarkably serendipitous for me, providing as it did the opportunity to reflect on our family's own recent transition out of a decade of pastoring. We had embarked on a new adventure in a new city, and the sheer busyness of that shift (with four children in tow) had meant that we hadn't intentionally paused to properly reflect on what was going on in our own hearts. As pastors we are accustomed to attending to others' griefs and shepherding them through their transitions, but when it comes to our own, we are (or at least I am!) more in the habit of barrelling on full steam ahead, too busy with the future to deal with the past. I knew that I had to let the dream of ministry in that location die, but I didn't know that I had to grieve it intentionally and prayerfully.

This is where Silvia's work, and the contributions that she has gathered, are so helpful. The contributors in this volume come from an array of cultural contexts and share from both theory and deep experience. They have given me both permission to slow, reflect and grieve, and language with which to do so. In particular, my western impetus to close that chapter and move on to the next has been gently rebuked by the reminder from more communal cultures to both celebrate and preserve our bonds with that which has passed.

For myself, the transition out of a previous ministry context had been coming for some time, gradually building with both discontent at what was and glimpses of anticipation about what might be. There was a lengthy lead-in to prepare the church, the family and the practicalities. We held a growing sense of excitement about the future, but at the same time a growing sense of exhaustion. We had a few connections with fellow pastors who were also leaving ministry positions for a range of reasons. They all echoed the sentiment that "it feels exactly as good as you think it's going to" when the weight of pastoral responsibility comes off – and, for us it did… for a short time at least. The mental load of the shift soon consumed any sense of lightness, and for some months it concealed the deep wrench and loss that lay beneath.

For us, pastoring was less a job and more a way of life that our whole family was involved in – perhaps *too* involved in at times. My personal sense of identity was enmeshed with pastoral roles and expectations, but the identity challenge brought about by the transition was also felt by the whole family. Who are *we* now? Children who have grown up in the church, living at the centre of church life, are often nested in loving relationships – a whole complement of aunties, uncles, grandparents, brothers and sisters. They too have experienced the relational challenges as people join and leave the church, making room in their hearts and in their homes for the parade of strangers made welcome. This break is a whole new positioning of their identity in community, and they need to be allowed to mourn that. However, it also brings a welcome relief as the weight comes off the parents and family time opens up again.

Our weeks are no longer shaped around church events, groups and meetings, and the new sense of relational space is refreshing, but also destabilising. Friendships that were once so scaffolded by that structure need to be renegotiated. Relationships that were enmeshed with pastoral responsibilities need to be untangled, and it is no easy process to discern which relationships you wish to carry on in your new context (as far as it depends on you). In some cases, working this out is a smooth mutual process. In others, you find yourself cut off or clung to in ways that you hadn't expected.

Looking back over a decade of ministry with these people in that place, it feels like watching a movie roll of highlights and lowlights. There is much joy, but there are also many experiences that leave you cause for grief: rejection, unfulfilled dreams, disappointment, potential untapped. It's not uncommon to find that you carry greater vision for a person's life, greater faith for how they could flourish in both being and vocation. Of course that vision can easily slip into paternalism, but there's a sense that you can see what could be. And with leaving that ministry space behind, I have felt some anger at God at what I felt He didn't do – even anger at others for how they didn't cooperate with what I thought God wanted to do in and through them. Most of all, however, there are profound doubts about whether you were sufficient, and regret for those many times when you most obviously were not.

We feel a profound sense of gratitude for the enormous privilege that it has been to shepherd other followers of Christ and to lead them, week after week, into worship. Truly this is a high calling, whatever the rest of society says about it. In many ways, our own moving on has been characterised by an ease for which I am grateful. The decision and the process was mutually discerned, and for myself there was a clear sense of call to a new expression of ministry, with job security in that.

For many others the process is much more fraught. One may feel pushed out, or directly asked to leave, and the relational fall-out is heart-breaking. Ministries are downscaled and even fresh church plants can 'fail.' Despite the messiness of these situations, I retain a firm conviction that God is always calling us – perhaps not to pastoral ministry or to any official role, but instead to rest or retreat, either as a midway point to something new or as a final landing place.

This sense of calling can empower us to embrace the flexibility required to allow our story to take a dramatically different turn. When you've poured your life into a people, responding to what you are necessarily convinced is a divine mandate, it should be no surprise that laying this down either willingly or under compulsion is no simple process. It requires attentive listening to our own hearts and the ongoing support of both friends and the wider church. *Moving On* offers both a gentle and substantial resource in aid of this.

Introductions

Grief in Ministry Transitions

"Whether the ministry was a good experience or not, you grow with people, and leaving weighs heavily on you. It hurts. The grief is very real in leaving a ministry. It seems to go with us, and it affects our thinking about other ministry experiences. I think why it's hard, why it's a painful, why it's heavy, and why it doesn't leave us, is because ministry is what we are called for. It is our job description to be a Minister of Word and Sacrament. Our heart and soul is committed to it. We give it everything."

The Moderator of the Presbyterian Church of Aotearoa New Zealand,[1] Fakaofo Kaio, is describing the grief of ministry transitions. This grief has a lot in common with other forms of grief, but it is also distinctive. For Fakaofo this is because of the personal, spiritual and emotional investment that ministers make in their work: "we give it everything."

Any ending of a ministry involves a unique and complex mix of grief for all involved. The pastoral relationship ends, and all that it was must be reworked and re-storied as it moves from present reality into memory. Grieving our endings takes time, but often we rush on into the next thing. It takes friendship and support, just as we leave our community. It takes honesty, but few people want to hear it. The vulnerability of grieving can conflict with ministers' self-understanding as the one who cares for everyone else.

Ministers are professional experts on grief. Holding others through endings, dying and bereavement is a core part of the job. However, attending to our own grief and transitions is easier said than done. It helps when we apply what we know about grief to ourselves and our own families. Grieving well releases fresh energy and joy, to be available to new communities and contexts. Grieving releases us more fully into God's life-long call, through different seasons and expressions of ministry.

Ministry is not just a job. It is understood by those who do it as a divine calling. It can be far easier for us to hear the voice of God in a call to a new beginning than in the ending and the leaving. Does the ending deny the validity of the call? 'Did God change his mind?' 'Did I fail my call?' The theological and discernment questions around ending and leaving are difficult, especially when a minister comes to the decision that she can no longer stay. Grief plays a major role in these questions, not just for the minister herself but for her spouse and family.

This book reflects upon the experience of the pastor as he or she works through the process of 'moving on' from a ministry. It explores the complex and compound nature of grief, especially when a ministry has been conflicted and when the decision to leave was difficult. It offers a wealth of experiences from a breadth of cultural contexts, from nearly 40 contributors. The grief of ministry transitions is addressed in prayer and liturgy. There are tools and resources as well as discussion about church processes and polity related to endings such as resignations and retirement.

Moving On includes both lay and ordained ministry. While most contributors are ordained ministers there is also discussion of the role of church elders and employed staff. It challenges the church to be a good employer and to realise that the endings matter as much as the beginnings.

Transitions are, by definition, transitory, while a book is permanent. These stories capture a moment in time for the contributors; many are painful moments characterised by discomfort and uncertainty and a reaching out to God for healing and peace. Please be aware that for each of these contributors, life continues; they may now be in a very different place, and more transitions will come.

Our stories are our own. I have tried to avoid blame or any cause for offence in relation to the events and experiences described here. People are not named unless they have contributed directly to the book.[2] The names of places and parishes from the past in contributor's stories are replaced with a random initial, other than in the brief introductions prior to each chapter.

Moving On: Grief in Ministry Transitions emerged in conversation and relationship. Most chapters are based on interviews. It is a work of pastoral theology, starting from the assumption that as we attend to our own life experience, including the hard stuff, we encounter Christ. Chapters have an uneven texture, with my own voice appearing and disappearing as I have sought to reveal the conversational nature of this work and at the same time enable each person's words to ring true. The book is well sprinkled with the wonderful poetry of Ana Lisa de Jong, which she has offered with amazing insight and generosity.

Layers: a Cross-Cultural Conversation

Shrek: Ogres are like onions.

Donkey: They stink?

Shrek: Yes. No!

Donkey: They make you cry?

Shrek: No.

Donkey: If you leave them out in the sun, they turn brown and start sprouting little white hairs?

Shrek: No! Onions have layers. Ogres have layers.

Donkey: Oh, you both have layers. Oh. You know, not everybody likes onions. Cake! Everybody loves cake! Cakes have layers.

Shrek: I don't care what everyone likes! Ogres are not like cakes.

Donkey: You know what else everybody likes? Parfaits! Have you ever met a person, you say, "Let's get some parfait," they say, "Hell no, I don't like no parfait"? Parfaits are delicious!

Shrek: No! You dense, irritating, miniature beast of burden! Ogres are like onions! End of story! Bye-bye!

This moment from the movie 'Shrek' has rather worked its way into our culture as a container for complexity. Human experience, like onions, has layers, and the delightful contrast between ogre and donkey suggests the diversity of human responding to pain. The contributors to *Moving On* speak of the layers of their experience of ministry transitions.

Some layers are shared and foundational: the raw emotion of loss, the hunger for connection and human community. The chapters ring with courage in speaking from the heart, from the hope that this vulnerability enables others to reflect with courageous honesty on their own stories.

Culture adds complex layers to human experience. Many of those contributing to this book are part of the Presbyterian Church of Aotearoa New Zealand, and they represent the cultural diversity of this church which includes Māori, Pacific, European, Asian and African ethnicities. Hearing people from cultures different from our own enriches us, and also reveals what we do not see because we take things for granted. Fundamental relationships are viewed and felt differently. The Western view of 'professional' ministers who come, do a job, and leave, is not shared by communal cultures such as Cook Islands and Māori, where ministers and congregations share a continuing belonging.

Those who have crossed cultures and nations in their response to God's call on their lives bring a distinct layer of grieving for another place and way of doing things, even while fully committing to their new context. Ministry is never in isolation from culture, marriage, and families, both nuclear and extended. Even within this country, major changes, such as leaving the military, create a culture-clash.

These contributions share the conviction that God is part of the conversation, and the assumption that the Bible is a central layer in ministry. Each of the interviews and articles reveal ongoing dynamic relating with God, 'who was and is and is to come' (Revelation 4:8). Contributors reflect on past calling, present hearing and look forward confidently to God's presence in the future. The pain, even trauma and heartbreak, in these stories, can be profoundly confronting but yet is held within this conversation with the living Christ.

Contributors explore layers within the Bible and expect scripture to inform experience. Across our diverse cultures the Bible resonates in both common and unexpected ways. Henry Mbambo expresses his dislocation from family in terms of the grief of exiled Israelites for "the songs of Zion" (Psalm 137:3). Sarah Beisly describes the immediacy of Gospel stories in a Kolkata back alley. Fele Nokise re-examines culture and theology in the light of human pain. The prayer liturgies in Section Four invite spiritual and emotional connection with scripture stories and metaphors, expecting the Spirit of Christ to be present and alive in the points of contact between ancient text and contemporary situations.

The final layer explored in 'Moving On' is the institutional one. Ministry, as discussed in these pages, happens in the context of church and under the authority of the church. Collectively we create this thing called 'church' and share responsibility for its healthy functioning. Central to this is our collective ability to be the body of Christ with freedom and grace. As we welcome one another into leadership and release one another from leadership, can we be ruled by the Spirit of peace, act with generosity and speak with truth and love?

Ultimately the whole 'onion' (or 'parfait'!) belongs not to us but to the One who made us, called us and shapes us. We are not our own but Christ's. This complex layered narrative of loss and love is offered as gift, to the wider church, and to God.

This Heart – *Ana Lisa de Jong*

(Living Tree Poetry)[3]

> My heart is like the onion's skin,
> shedding layers with the breaking.
> My heart is pressed as the garlic bulb
> until it releases its scent.
>
> Yes, my heart is a growing thing
> that pushes beyond its restraints.
> The shell must give yet
> a thousand times
> for this heart to expand.

My starting point

So what layers of culture and assumptions am I aware of in myself? I am a fifth generation Pākehā New Zealander, from English and Danish pioneers who settled in Aotearoa. My childhood included several major transitions, between Fiji and Kaikohe, Ruatoria, Gisborne and Tonga. In and out of very different cultures, breaking friendships, losing homes, learning to adjust and make new friends and feel at home somewhere new. The hardest was the move from Tonga to Lower Hutt, age 12, combined with my parents' separation. It took me a long time to figure out how to be a 'normal' Kiwi teenager, and to recover from being bullied.

The church was always part of the story, from the Fiji Indian church of my earliest memories, to family camps with the Gisborne Methodists, to worship in the Royal Palace chapel in Nuku'alofa! My teen years were rescued by the Waiwhetu Methodist Church in Lower Hutt, and I went into youth ministry from that strong base. I have been richly blessed by widely diverse experience of church life, worship, fellowship and mission. Through every turning point and new adventure Jesus Christ remains my Rock and my Way. Nothing can separate us from the love of God in Christ Jesus. What fascinates me is how this security is in dynamic tension with life's 'trials and tribulations.' As a pastoral theologian I am drawn into the uncomfortable conversations, toward the points of pain, for I trust the way the Spirit of Jesus gently opens up our pain and pours in light and healing.

Tough Honesty

I have been an ordained Presbyterian minister for over a decade. In that time I have held, and left, three pastoral appointments in parishes in New Zealand, each quite different from the others. Each I have resigned: one to take up another appointment, one was a difficult decision, and one because my army chaplain husband was posted to a new part of the country. Each ending was very different, and each was a significant part of my ministry and personal formation. Each was an experience of grief.

Yet when I went looking through my books on ministry for insights about the grief of ending a ministry, it was not there. I found much in my books on the beginnings of a ministry, the process and dynamics of call, and much on sustaining in ministry, often with an explicitly stated intention of preventing pastors from resigning their ministries. But I found practically nothing on the tasks and challenges of leaving. Why?

One brutally honest answer came in an article about ministry in an Asian context:

> "The failed pastor's family and close relatives undoubtedly will suffer embarrassment, shame, and emotional duress. In an Asian community, becoming a pastor surely calls for a big celebration; but, on the contrary, if one quits the ministry it becomes a major embarrassment."[4]

In our culture, too, we celebrate the beginnings with much fanfare, but the endings we are far less comfortable with, especially where there is any hint of 'failure.' Some leavings are honoured, e.g. retirement after a long and outwardly successful ministry. Other leavings are far more difficult and wrought with 'emotional duress,' even shame.

Church culture (mine at least) is conflict-averse, to the point of non-honesty; awkward silences are the order of the day. As I was 'moving on' from a conflicted parish context I was asked by denominational leadership to "end well." I heard this as an request that I not upset anyone, not say uncomfortable things.

For me, this was contradicted by what my supervisor was saying, and what I knew that God was saying, which was to challenge my need for acceptance and affirmation and my desire to keep the peace. I was devastated to discover how deeply committed I was to the idea that if I tried hard enough everyone would approve of me. God needed to crack that open, and grow me bigger than that. Part of that was dealing with my residual pain from feeling bullied and rejected as a child.

The church, too, can be guilty of bullying and abuse. It grieves me that many who leave ministry do so feeling gutted. To attend to these endings with honesty is to stand with Jesus in a place of persecution. Only Jesus holds the way to healing.

Grief is a strange place. I am no longer in it, though some memories still carry the taste of it. It is a surreal landscape in which things hang awkwardly and loom weirdly. It is pointy and gloomy and cold and lonely. To walk with death and failure is part of our calling, though never a path we choose. The insights of grief theory were, to me, helpful. Any loss takes us on a journey, and the only way out is through. There are no short-cuts, but there are guides and companions through grief. These do not lessen the pain to be felt, but do keep us moving so that we don't just go around and around.

I hope that this book is a companion for those in ministry, an encouragement to have the hard conversations and to not be afraid to go deep into whatever it is that God is calling us into, even the darkest paths of pain. For Christ is risen; "God's mercies never come to an end, they are new every morning." (Lamentations 3:22b-23a).

Dedications

To my fabulous husband, Chris, who has been there through it all.

My heart-felt thanks to all those who have contributed to this book. These are not easy conversations, and each person has been courageous in sharing their story.

Special thanks to my dear friend Lynn Ramage. Your painting of the Kahuterawa Stream in Linton is the art work throughout this book. It is a love song to this land, to belonging, to creativity, to friendship – and to God. We treasure the memory of you sitting on the rocks near our home with your feet in the water, using one rock as your easel. We still keenly feel your absence, and also your presence.

> Korōria ki te Atua, ko ia te Tīmatanga me te Mutunga, te Karanga me te Kāinga.
>
> Glory to God: Beginning and End, Call and Home.
>
> Āe, ahakoa haere ahau i te awaawa o te ātārangi o te mate, kāhore he kino e wehi ai ahau: nō te mea kei tōku taha koe; ko tāu rākau, ko tāu tokotoko, ko ēna hei oranga ngākau mōku.
>
> Even though I walk through the darkest valley, I fear no evil; for you are with me; your rod and your staff – they comfort me.
>
> *Psalm 23:4[5]*

A Theology of Transition – *Alistair Mackenzie*

Alistair Mackenzie is a Baptist pastor, theology lecturer, mission consultant and spiritual director. He is a global pioneer in exploring the theologies of vocation and work.

His book *Soul Purpose* is a rich resource for vocational discernment (it can be read online or a free copy downloaded from https://www. theologyofwork.org/book/soul-purpose). Chapters 11 and 12 in particular are devoted to discussing ways of navigating through transitions.

I asked Alistair about his experience working with people in vocational transition, and his theology of transition: "Where is God in those moments when we have let go one thing and we're not sure about the next thing?"

• • •

The way we approach transitions is shaped by a number of factors. Ministry transitions happen for different reasons and these reasons significantly influence what we find ourselves wrestling with in the midst of transition. We need to discern again: 'Who am I? What are my gifts? What is my calling?'

Self-awareness comes as we ask ourselves hard questions. What prompted this transition? How much of this crisis is self-imposed through my own foolishness? What circumstances beyond my control have overtaken me? Do I sense it is time to move on as a natural result of growth in my maturity or stage of life? Am I realising that this church community requires a different style of leadership as it moves into another phase in its life? Do I leave, or do I learn to operate in a different mode?

To navigate our way through a transition it is helpful to identify as clearly as we can the past, present and future aspects of the issues we find ourselves confronting.

What are you being challenged to let go of as you move forward? What do you not want to lose, and must make sure you take with you? Examining the past helps us to clarify this. Letting go inevitably involves grief. Clarifying what we want to take with us involves some careful evaluating. Not everything we might want to hold on to is good for us. But we must also be careful not to cast aside what will be important for us.

In the present it is important to understand: 'In the light of what has happened, what am I learning from this? What are my practical circumstances? What emotional state has this left me in?' Also: 'What help do I need, to both support me here and now, and to assist me to chart a helpful course ahead?'

Realising it is time to move on is often a very difficult experience of not seeing clearly. We know far more about what we are leaving behind than where we are going. We feel the grief of what we are being forced to let go of, without the compensation of knowing what is ahead. For me this has usually been the case when I have confronted changes; I had a strong intuitive sense of when it was time to go, without seeing what the next thing was. I have rarely transitioned directly into something new.

A Bible message I have found encouraging in the midst of my transitions is Proverbs 3:5-6: "Trust in the Lord with all your heart, and do not rely on your own insight. In all your ways acknowledge him, and he will make straight your paths."

How do we clarify the road ahead? What will shape the way we move through a transition? What pieces need to be in place for you to make those decisions? In my experience, a lot of people look for a clear plan or a particular job, but I'm not sure this is the most helpful way to think about it. In my work mentoring and resourcing people in discernment, I encourage thinking about: 'What do you know about who you are, what you value, and what you would love to be doing?'

You may have seen somebody doing work that you are attracted to. Or it may be a compelling sense of: 'These values are really important to me.' Or a deep longing surfacing from within you. Or perhaps you are starting to grow a clearer understanding of your distinctive strengths and gifts. Amongst all that you don't yet grasp, what are one or two things that do seem clear to you?

Act on what you know. A good future is more likely to be built around acting on what you can understand rather than feverishly pursuing and worrying about what you don't understand. That passage from Proverbs 3 encourages us to trust that God is with us. Learn to live according to the glimpses of light you see, one step at a time, rather than feeling overwhelmed by all the unknown.

How do we manage our fears and anxiety about the future? How do we best prepare ourselves for this future? And who are the committed companions we need alongside us as fellow travellers?

I encourage people to recognise that when our circumstances change our faith is challenged too. Is the faith that I have held on to until now sufficient to sustain and orientate me in the midst of these new challenges? What remains the same, that you can hang on to in the midst of transition? And what you are being forced to let go of?

The Bible emphasises the importance of frightening transitions – we don't take this seriously enough. God is at work in the midst of threatening circumstances and uncertainty. The Bible is a narrative of the people of God continually being thrown into uncomfortable circumstances where they have to rethink their faith, sometimes very seriously. I love the words of Psalm 137:4, "How do we sing the Lord's song in this foreign land?" This is a recurring refrain in the Psalms and for all of us in the midst of confusing transitions.

The Bible is full of stories about people in transitions that they would never have chosen for themselves. Again and again they are forced by God to rethink who they are and where they are headed. Whether it's Adam and Eve being kicked out of the garden, or Abraham pushed to leave his homeland, or the people of God led out of captivity in Egypt through the Exodus experience, or later on dragged off into captivity in the Exile. As well as the challenges of suddenly changed circumstances, the Bible also introduces us to a succession of prophets who are raised up to disturb the people of God just when they are getting comfortable with the way things are! If ever there was a book full of resources for transitions, it's the Bible.

Exodus and exile are particularly relevant for this generation. We experience exodus as a pilgrim people on the move, looking for signs of the presence of God in the wilderness. We experience exile when we feel like marginalised aliens in a place where other people are creating the culture and making the rules. We live in a period of massive cultural change which is impacting on every area of life. It is begging for wise and creative leadership. The disturbing effects of this are felt in church life and leadership. People look to the church for stability only to find themselves threatened by changes there too. In times like this, even the best leaders wonder if they are up to the task.

A theology of transition digs deep into themes of journey and pilgrimage, captivity and exile and exodus. I like Walter Brueggemann's interpretation of the Psalms: so many of the Psalms give voice to the cries of people in distressing circumstances. The Psalms move from comfortable orientation, through disorientation, and on to reorientation. This is a perfect description of the transition from what was, into a period of upheaval and waiting and uncertainty, and then a reorientation towards new beginnings. The Bible narrative equips the people of God to be prepared to face challenging transitions at different stages of life.

Transition – *Ana Lisa de Jong*

(Living Tree Poetry)

An exchange always asks of us
to lose as well as gain.

No object can be picked up
with full hands.

While the new might be a gift,
the old will leave its residue

no matter our willingness
to release.

But at the time of exchange
we will find we are ready

when we understand
the ebb and flow of life.

Nothing that we've lived,
either good or painful,

remains the thing it was
when it arrived.

It will have made its mark,
like patterns upon our palms,

and we will carry it with us
deeply inscribed.

And everything yet
that we do or love

will be infused
by the things we've left behind.

But with an openness of heart
we will find our embrace

is something stronger
for the moulding of the years.

And now the new works of our hands,
though something freshly made,

will be blessed
by the passages of time.

Endnotes

1 At the time of writing, in 2021.

2 A notable exception is the name of Rev. Perema Leasi, QSM, whose passing in 2019 is honoured and reflected on. Some contributors have chosen to name their partners and children. Any other people named are published authors.

3 Copyright information for this poem, and all of Ana Lisa's poems reprinted here, is at the conclusion of the book.

4 Simon Nagarajan, "Restoration of Pastors Who Left the Ministry in an Honor/ Shame-Based Society Like Singapore." *Presbyterian*, vol. 45, no. 2 (Fall 2019): 184.

5 Bible Society of New Zealand, *Paipera Tapu* (2012).

Section One:
Grieving Endings and Changes in Ministry

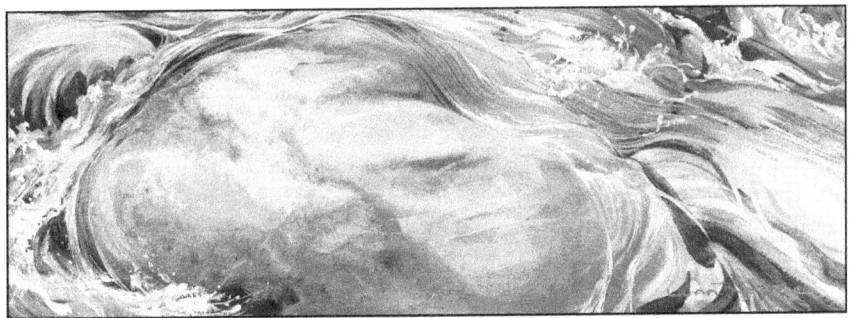

The Tasks of Grief [1]

Grief is our response to loss. Loss happens to you. Grieving is what you do about it. Anything we have loved requires grieving when it is lost, so grief encompasses a wide range of situations. Most of the research and writing about grief and loss relates to the death of a person we love; the terms 'bereavement' and 'mourning' apply specifically to this. However, an ending of a ministry involves the ending of relationships and roles, and theories and models of grief can assist ministers, and their families, in ending a ministry.

One approach to grief describes it as work to be done, work of heart and mind and soul. Specific challenges can be identified within this work, which can be called the 'tasks' of grief. I am an achievement-oriented person, so I am drawn to theories of grief that speak of human agency, achieving things. Tomas Attig writes:

> When we grieve, we can and do control our responses to our losses and give direction to our coping. As we address the tasks of grieving, we have many choices about constructive and meaningful things to do and say. The point of choosing to grieve and addressing the tasks is to put together the pieces of our broken lives and to find ways of living purposefully and meaningfully again.[2]

William Worden proposed four tasks of grief:[3]

1. To accept the reality of the loss,
2. To work through the pain of grief,
3. To adjust to an environment in which the deceased is missing,
4. To emotionally relocate the deceased and move on with life (and reinvest in new relationships).

I have adapted these for grieving the end of a ministry. I split Worden's first task of accepting the reality of loss into two. One task relates to the minister's decision to initiate or accept an ending (inner acceptance). The second relates to the ending of a host of relationships and roles (outer acceptance). The mix of emotions may be unique, but the task of experiencing them is similar to other forms of grieving. Adjusting to the loss requires pastors to come to terms with the ministry that is over, and make it part of their personal narrative in a healthy way. I describe this as the task of 'telling a grace story of the ministry.' Worden's fourth task of 'relocating' our emotional energy into new relationships becomes the challenge of reinvesting in a new ministry context (or other work or retirement). For the end of a ministry these tasks may be happening well before the final service, and may continue long afterward.

The tasks for a minister leaving a position are:

1. To fully decide to leave
2. To end many relationships and renegotiate a few
3. To work through the pain of grief
4. To tell a grace story of that ministry
5. To reinvest in a new ministry.

1. To fully decide to leave

The first task in ending a ministry is to move from ambivalence to decision; to get to the point at which the cost of severing roles and relationships becomes outweighed by the benefits of something new. This could be sudden or take many years. There may be a build-up of 'push' factors or a new opportunity too good to turn down (a 'pull factor'). The decision may be solely the minister's, or there may be a complex process involved. Tokerau Joseph describes it: "You connect the dots and then you make the decision. And sometimes the dots are not always clear. You don't always see clearly but I have learned that you make the decision and you live with it."

This culminates on the day the congregation is told that the minister is leaving. Once the news is public there is then a process of the community coming to terms with it, to 'accept the reality of the loss.'

The process of coming to a decision, or accepting the inevitability of leaving if it is imposed, will include 'anticipatory grief.' I remember feeling intense sadness as I led a worship service the Sunday prior to announcing my resignation; I struggled not to weep. By the time of my final service I was more emotionally detached. Anticipatory grief prepares for the loss to come.

There are parallels with the challenge of coming to terms with one's own physical dying. Elizabeth Kubler Ross famously described this process in terms of denial, anger, bargaining, depression and acceptance. As a minister attempts to navigate a way forward that might enable him to stay in a difficult ministry space, this will likely include aspects of negotiation, with spikes of anger and lows of sadness. Where this leads beyond denial of problems to acceptance of an inevitable end to the ministry, this brings the pastor to the point of announcing that she is leaving.

Near the end of his life Moses had to confront the reality that he would die on the wrong side of the Jordon River. How harsh it must have been for him to come so close to achieving the goal which he longed for but could not reach. With his last dregs of strength he climbed up a mountain where he could see across the valley into the promised land (Deuteronomy 34). Before he did, however, he commissioned a new generation of leadership (Deuteronomy 31). He experienced anger, and fear for his people, but was able to speak God's truth and God's blessing right to the end. He accepted the reality of loss and enabled his people to re-envisage community life without him.

2. To end many relationships and renegotiate a few

When a person we loved dies we grieve for the lost relationship. But ending a ministry means severing and grieving many relationships, leaving an entire community.

The minister is the one who leaves; the congregation get left behind. This creates an imbalance of power, placing the responsibility for managing the process of ending in the hands of the minister. As their pastor I was the person who was there to support them through difficult times, including their grief; how do I support people through the pain of letting go when I am the one causing the pain?

In the situation where a minister resigns, rather than retiring or being called to another position, the ending is odd. The best advice I received was from a wise older minister: "Don't expect anyone to talk to you about it," he said. This was harsh but accurate. From the moment I resigned it became the elephant in every room. In a moment of exasperation I complained to one of the elders, a competent professional man, that no one had said anything to me about me leaving. He simply replied, "I don't know what to say." The fact is, we Kiwis are lousy at difficult conversations. It takes a rare parishioner to ask their minister why she is leaving and really want to hear the answer. It's too hard. It's too personal. It feels like maybe God is leaving, or God has let us down, and the less said the better.

What does it mean to truly 'end well'? In his advice to ministers, Steven Moore writes, "the first lesson in ending well is to be generous in your praise, quick to offer a blessing, and thorough in your expressions of appreciation to those you leave behind."[4] This indeed is my experience. But it is not all my experience. What does 'ending well' look like when the praise and thanks are hard to find? There is a tension between 'going quietly' and saying what needs to be said. Ending relationships well requires honesty as well as blessing, but only as much honesty as people can receive 'well.'

People say "Stay in touch." It may be a genuine desire for ongoing relationship, or it may be them struggling to come to terms with the reality of the ending – 'denial' in classic grief terms. Some relationships may continue and evolve into a mutual friendships, but fewer than I had expected. Even close colleagues seemed to quickly adjust to my absence. I had to learn to not be surprised when people don't 'stay in touch.' It is not easy to forge a post-ministry friendship. The power dynamic between ministers and parishioners gets in the way. For some there is a sense that one 'shouldn't' continue a relationship, that it violates an unwritten ethical code. Each time I have left a ministry there have been a few people that I genuinely wanted to stay in my life. But who is responsible for initiating contact? If we meet, where? Going to visit them in their home feels too much the same as when it was a pastoral visit. I try to put the onus on others to call me if they would like to meet up, but they say they don't want to bother me. It's complicated.

Some denominations insist on a 'clean' ending of a ministry; leave and don't come back to visit for at least a year. Clergy (and their spouses) who remain involved in congregation can undermine a new ministry appointment.

The grief of saying goodbye is beautifully portrayed in Acts 20:36-38, as the elders of the church in Ephesus face the reality of a final parting with Paul. These verses describe the strong emotion and closeness of 'grieving well' together. There was "a great deal of weeping by everyone," hugs and kisses, and all they walked together down to the wharf to wave him off. For his part, Paul enabled healthy grieving by making space for it, setting up a meeting to say goodbye properly. His words in Acts 20 echo Moses' final messages at the end of Deuteronomy. He speaks from the heart, sharing his own emotions. He warns them of trouble to come; "be on guard" (Acts 20:28). He does not 'beat about the bush' but is clear about the "chains and afflictions" that await him (Acts 20:23). Paul places the grief of parting within the context of who he knows himself to be in Christ: "I count my life of no value to myself, so that I may finish my course and the ministry I received from the Lord Jesus, to testify to the gospel of God's grace" (Acts 20:24). Paul invested himself fully in each local community he ministered in, but his core identity and calling was broader than any one community or place.

3. To work through the pain of grief

Grief can be an emotional black hole. It sucks in energy, leaving us less able to care for others, even struggling to care for ourselves. It is also very physical and can make us sick. Grief is unique and varied, but there are also common themes: I'd put sadness, fatigue, anxiety and anger in the top four.

Grief is a process of adjusting, as Margaret Holloway puts it:

> The person and the old life have gone, and a new existence must replace it. The process of grappling with this new life is … the real 'work' of grief, characterised by both disorganisation, as the bereaved person struggles to adjust and make changes necessary to survive without the person who has died, but also periods of depression and sometimes despair.[5]

The ending of a ministry is a form of dying, especially when it leaves future ministry uncertain. Grieving for a role, a community and a home involves the work of 'review', remembering relationships, being reminded of what has been lost, and allowing oneself to feel the "raw pain of grief."[6]

Not everything that pretends to help really does help. Any addiction we are prone to will assert that it is the answer to the pain of grief. I had to notice when I was drinking too much wine, or playing too much solitaire on the computer. Addictions and bad habits may be costly, on our own wellbeing as well as on the people around us.

Because grief has such a wide range and variety of symptoms, and can last for a long time, it can be easy to not recognise our distress as grief. It can be a major factor in physical illness and fatigue, in emotions as varied as frustration, irritability, guilt, loneliness, lost-ness or insecurity as well as the obvious sadness. Thoughts can get stuck in loops that go around and around. Grief can come out as social withdrawal or hyper-functioning, or looking for intimacy in the wrong places. It can lead us into solitude or prayer, or make these more difficult. Recognising and attending to these with courage and honesty is the task of grieving.

One theory talks about grief as a 'dual process.'[7] On one hand we are doing the emotional work of feeling the loss. One the other hand we are adjusting to a new environment, trying to figure out who we are without the person who has died or the role we no longer hold.

For ministers who begin a new ministry appointment immediately after finishing their previous one, there is little time or recognition for grief. This dual process can be acute and unbalanced. The danger is that the demands of a new job and community may override a minister's emotional needs. There is a price to be paid for ignoring grief; suppressed grief can show up as illness, compassion fatigue and a cumulative 'brown-out' lack of passion or joy.[8]

It is also important to note the effects of the end of a ministry on the pastor's spouse and family. Traumatic grief is notoriously tough on marriages. Marsha Frame studied the effects of moving towns on (male) clergy and their wives. She found that many ministers had support systems which gave them resilience, but their wives had less support and were most likely to suffer negative consequences. "Many research results which focused on relocating spouses found them to have lower well-being than their husbands ... manifest in depression, sadness, loneliness and alienation."[9] Supporting one's spouse through grief requires patience, care and encouragement, just when capacity for these is diminished.

One cannot write a book on grief and ministry without bringing Job into it. The book of Job stands as the ultimate chronicle of loss and crisis of meaning. The visceral experiences it describes mark the terrain of grief:

- sadness: "my eyes have grown dim from grief" (Job 17:7)

- restlessness: "I cannot relax or be still; I have no rest, for trouble comes" (Job 3:26)

- suicidality: "[I] wait for death but it does not come. [I] search for it" (Job 3:21)

- overwhelm: my grief "would outweigh the sand of the seas!" (Job 6:3)

- spiritual pain: "my spirit is broken" (Job 17:1)

- isolation: "all of my best friends despite me" (Job 19:19)

- hopelessness: "my eye will never again see anything good" (Job 7:3)

- fatigue: "I have buried my strength in the dust" (Job 16:15)

Central to the grief process of Job is emotional honesty: "I will not restrain my mouth. I will speak in the anguish of my spirit; I will complain in the bitterness of my soul." (Job 7:11). Through his pain Job continues to be in relationship with God; God is both subject and audience for Job's grief, perhaps even therapist. The central theme of the book of Job is the capacity to hold on to the goodness of God "God is wise and all-powerful," (Job 9:4) in the place of human suffering; "even if He kills me I will hope in Him" (Job 13:15). The 'Why?!' question which saturates the book of Job finds no answer in human ethics. In the end Job's moral framework of rights and wrongs falls into silence and repentance in the presence of the living God (Job 42:6). God is God, loss is loss, and grief can come to an end.

4. To tell a grace story of that ministry

We used to think that the goal of grieving is to relinquish old attachments, to 'let go.' This has been challenged by more recent grief theories, and from non-Western cultures for whom a continuing bond with a deceased person is considered both normal and desirable. The goal of grief is no longer seen as letting go of that relationship, but of transforming it, continuing a sense of connection in a new way, in their physical absence.[10]

Perhaps those of us in ministry never truly 'leave' a church where we have pastored. Maybe we leave part of ourselves behind and carry that community with us in some form. The way we grieve determines the form we carry it in, and we do this by the stories we tell. A narrative perspective suggests that "the stories we tell ourselves not only speak of the lives we live, but in fact 'author' them. Stories are not mirrors of reality; they constitute, map, and shape our lives over time."[11] People who leave a church with unresolved grief may carry a story of bitterness, regret, blame or failure.

It is interesting reading Paul's letters with this in mind. There are moments when Paul expresses real hurt and anger, such as at the end of 2 Timothy when he writes about two people in particular whom he feels betrayed by (2 Timothy 4:10, 14). Paul then declares in a sweeping statement that "everyone deserted me" (2 Timothy 4:16). Given the list of names in verse 21, clearly not everyone did desert him, but his personal narrative includes the devastating experience of feeling utterly abandoned. But through this, Paul's close spiritual relationship with Jesus leads him into trust in Christ's bigger story, in which Paul sees himself as "being poured out as an offering" (2 Timothy 4:6). Complaint finds its true home in redemptive suffering.

The grief task of 'emotionally relocating' what we have lost is a process of re-working our internal relationship with it, once the external relationship is over.[12] Where there is anger or guilt, the task is to invite Christ into the story; to keep telling the story until the narrative changes in God's perspective into one of grace. Forgiveness, of both self and other, is neither quick nor easy. It demands a determination to forgive and to bless, even in the face of abuse or rejection. It requires support, and excellent godly competent listening. I would go so far as to say that for we mortals it is "impossible, but with God all things are possible." (Matthew 19:26, NIV).

5. To reinvest in a new ministry

Grieving releases the energy trapped in tangled ambivalence of the past, freeing us to connect in new ways with new people. Henry Cloud describes this as 'metabolising' past experiences, as we metabolise the food we have eaten in order to release the energy from the nutrients. It is a process, often an emotional one, but it leads forward into the new.

When you feel grief, you are saying, "I am looking this reality right in the face and dealing with it, the reality that this (whatever *this* is) is *over. Finished.* Grief also means I am getting ready for what is next, because I am finishing what is over." ... So if your last experience has been properly metabolised, you are ready. You have learned, made the changes necessary, added whatever you need, and are wiser and more prepared. Facing your grief, working it through, and letting it equip you is a significant part of a good necessary ending.[13]

Cloud points out that it is difficult, even dangerous, to invest energy in new projects and relationships while we are still working through old grief. We can't invest energy we do not have. This depletes us even more. I believe this is a real danger for those of us in ministry. We expect ourselves to bounce back quickly from loss or disappointment. The church has a very high expectation of resilience from its clergy. So we put on our roles, smile and preach; but if this is slithering on a layer of unresolved grief the cracks will appear, and likely those closest to us will pay the price.

The risk is that we become less open to risk. People still recovering from trauma feel unsafe, and find ways to protect themselves from being hurt again. In ministry this might look like being less willing to be open and intimate, less self-confident or more need to control. How do we learn to trust again? I am determined to grow, in Christ, through pain, so that I may be more of the person he made me to be, not less.

The grief tasks of adjusting to a new environment and reinvesting in a new ministry require gentleness, first and foremost. We must learn to be kind to ourselves, to rest, to say 'no' to some expectations, to prioritise our family and our own health, even as we find our way into new roles.

Spiritually the task is to be real with God and let God be God with us in new ways. I have known wonderful moments of Christ's in-filling. Yet grief is mostly a 'desert' time where rocks hurt our feet and we feel a bit lost. It may not be immediately obvious, but wisdom is waiting in the desert, wisdom to discern where God is leading us next, together with the courage for the journey.

Nehemiah had a 'plum job' as the king's cup-bearer in Babylon. It was comfortable, high-status; he enjoyed the job and the favour of the king. Why would you ever leave such a great post? However, when he heard of the state of Jerusalem he was deeply moved, and in prayer found a depth of grief and passion which impelled him to act (Nehemiah 1). Nehemiah's prayer moves him from despair into a new mission. In his pain, fear and sadness he turns to God, "the great awe-inspiring God who keeps His gracious covenant who those who love him" (Nehemiah 1:5). As he recalls what he knows of God he recites scripture, remembering the ancient prophecy of Moses in Deuteronomy 30:1-5 that God would one day gather his people out of exile. The prayer moves into the present moment as he asks God to be with him as he decides to resign, and plans to embark on a very dangerous project. Nehemiah experienced himself as "graciously strengthened by my

God" (Nehemiah 2:8). He was able to bring all he had learned and achieved in Babylon to the task of rebuilding Jerusalem.

The Work of Grief – *Ana Lisa de Jong*
(Living Tree Poetry)

> It's the work of grief
> to walk two paths.
> To live the present tense,
> and travel the route
> our hearts would take
> if choice were ours.
>
> It's the holy work of grief
> to acknowledge the cost of loss.
> To weigh up what's left,
> treasures in the hand
> now spent.
>
> It's the sacred task of grief
> to bear witness to grace,
> that comes on silent feet
> to spring-clean rooms
> of residual dust.
>
> And it's the sacred role of grief
> to reroute us on a road
> now taken shape
> upon the remains
> of former gifts.
>
> Grief's task is not done,
> and often
> the fallowed earth,
> newly turned,
> brings with tears
> an Eden remembered.
>
> But grief,
> the shadow side of life's jewels,
> shows us how to regroup
> and outlive loss
> by turning
> to the light.

Fire, Cloud and Calling – *Fakaofo Kaio*

Very Reverend Fakaofo Kaio was the Moderator of the PCANZ, 2018-2021. I was honoured to talk with him about how he sees the challenges facing ministers, through the good and the not-so-good. He speaks about the fires of pre-existing conflicts and the cloud of feeling you have let people down, underpinned by the enduring claim of God's call on our lives.

• • •

I have journeyed with ministers through both good and not so good endings. It can be very disheartening. Some have left the ministry and some have returned. The challenge is what you do with the experience, how you deal with it.

Ministry can be hard, and difficulties are not necessarily the minister's fault. A new minister might come into a community which is not ready and prepared for a new ministry. There is a fire burning and you walk into it. There are a lot of problem issues and it explodes. Seldom does that work out. We have lost ministers through bad experiences in the process, there's no doubt about it.

I remember one friend, there was conflict going on in his parish and also in the wider community. I went to visit him and he looked like he'd been in a fight! He was hurt and really struggling. I said, "Do you want me to come another time?" and he said, "No, I am really grateful you're here. I'm just catching my breath." The next time I spoke with him he sounded better. He told me later that walking into a parish in strife was a good thing because he was neutral. He was not part of the fights, he didn't take sides, and he was able to lead them as a community.

That turned out to be a good case. But in some cases our ministers do not survive. We are not necessarily taught how to deal with a troubled parish, or a parish that does not want to move forward. We are taught how to go amongst people and preach the gospel. But if you do not get the response, the transformations and growth you hope for, if you do not feel it is worthwhile, then you can lose heart.

When you come to a parish, whether it is a peaceful community, a community that's on fire, or a community at a crossroads, the first year is a honeymoon period. You are getting to know them, they are getting to know you. You work on things you both enjoy. But then there is a period we call 'the rubber hits the road.' Expectations come up, the church wants more from you. This is the working together, give and take. If the minister is happy with what is agreed upon they will persevere. But if there is not agreement the minister may think, "I'll give it a try, give it a go, and if there's no change I will move on." It can be lonely. It can be quite hard, especially when you see colleagues thriving with growing churches.

When I was in this phase I grew as minister and I grew as a person. I said, "OK Lord, what do you want me to do?" So I included other ministry in the area, such as Bible in Schools, which grew and was well supported. Ministry can be a cycle over seven years before a new page is turned. I experienced the boom and I experienced the waning down, then experienced the boom again. Changes happen. Then a new challenge burns in your heart. When I received a new Call I felt it was time, because of signs that told me: 'time to move.'

Whether the ministry was a good experience or not, you grow with people, and leaving weighs heavily on you. It hurts. The grief is very real in leaving a ministry. It seems to go with us, and it affects our thinking about other ministry experiences. I think why it's hard, why it's a painful, why it's heavy, and why it doesn't leave us, is because ministry is what we are called for. It is our job description to be a Minister of Word and Sacrament. Our heart and soul is committed to it. We give it everything. And we open our hands, we open ourselves wholly to the community. We show grace by doing that and hopefully the congregation shows grace in their response. They could hurt us, they could embrace us, they could work with us. When we leave, whether it was a good experience or not, it will niggle at us, it will weigh on us, because we gave it everything.

Even if a ministry is only for a short time it is still meaningful ministry, because you went in with the intention of committing your whole being to doing the Lord's work. How it turns out is sometimes out of your hand. You gave your all, whatever happened. There is always learning out of that, from both positive and negative experiences. We must not measure our life's service to the Lord against other people's ministry, long or short. Others have a different context.

When somebody has an experience that didn't work out and they leave, you need to walk with them and let them do the talking as they learn to deal with what happened. You walk alongside them, I do anyway, as a friend and a colleague. I encourage them to continue some form of ministry, to do what is on their heart. They will have questions: "Why did I persevere with this? What did I do wrong?" If they ask me "How would you deal with that?" I bring it back to them and ask them what they would do, what they have learned. They have to find themself again and recover their confidence. It's good to have a friend, someone whose motive is just to ensure that you are well.

This is what I say to all ministers: God trained you. You left home and you were trained and equipped and prepared and resourced by God. Then God sent you. Do you think God will waste that by not using you? I think God will use you. As you are sent out by the Spirit of God to places and parishes, you are sent there as God's messenger, to do this work. If it is not a pleasant experience you have to regroup and say, "Lord God, what happened?" But God will still use you till the day you die.

In Pacific Island contexts we take ministry wholeheartedly. When you are doing well, your family is lifted up, your whole whanau community is acknowledged and praised. Your family is looked upon as messengers of God. But when a ministry does not go well and ends abruptly, a cloud hangs over you, and not just you but over your whole family. If it goes pear-shaped the whole family take a hit. You have let down your whole village. It goes back to our island culture, where they say, "Where is the sign of God?" My family have sacrificed for my ministry, prayed for me, been part of my ministry. If I did anything that is not in the right light of ministry it would bring a cloud over myself and it would affect them also. Pacific leaders in ministry, in parliament or in business, know the reputation they are carrying, of many behind them, many holding them up, praying for them. So they try not to bring that cloud over them. They try to do their best to honour those people. It is a huge responsibility.

When a ministry is terminated or cut short, other people need to understand that they don't know the full story. They were not there. It matters for the person involved to not lose heart and think, "Oh, I'm letting people down." We are called by God, trained by God's people, and sent by God's church to do the work. When it does not work out you may have to leave, but be humble and gracious. When somebody genuinely wants to know what happened you can sit down and explain. But when people are just nosy, or gossipers or judgmental then it is not worth it. Just say: "Well, that is life, things happen." You have to decide what is beneficial for everyone and move on. For me, when I walk away from a fight I will not ever boast. Whether I was victorious or lost I will be gracious about it and speak highly of the people involved.

When a ministry is concluded abruptly or unexpected there is always a visitation from presbytery representatives to investigate. Their report must always be supportive of the leaving minister. For a minister to leave with nothing and no help is not good. When the person leaves it is not the end of their life. They may have a break and come back again. Ministry should start and end well regardless of what happened. I think that is an area the church needs to do better. We need to do it well so that we honour our call to serve, and respect it as a life-long call. This sets a good example for the next generation of leaders. The reputation of the church should be upheld by showing that we value life. We value and respect the call of God. The burning bush is about God saying to Moses and saying to us: "It's not about you. It's about Me."

We didn't choose the ministry. We didn't choose to be servants of the Lord. God called us. And this was tested along the way through prayer and by the courts of the church. Once they assessed us – "Yes, this is a real Call" – they trained us, they resourced us, they invested in us. So the way we were prepared, called and equipped and sent out to do the work, that's all part of the ending of a ministry. We are reminded that we were sent there by the Spirit to do the work of Christ. When we are sent somewhere else we will give it everything. We will journey on to another ministry carrying disappointment or hurt or carrying wonderful memories. We carry that. That's life. As we record in our minds what it was about we can see a lot of learning for ourselves and how it can benefit other people.

In our context, you are called for life. Just because you retire from parish ministry does not mean you stop being a minister. In fact we can still do a lot of the church activities as ministers when we retire. The majority of Pacific Island ministers I know move to a different community and worship there when they retire, and take a back seat. They don't assume authority and they are very respected. It is still a grieving process, letting go of that role until we are invited back.

The reality is that one day we will not have this need of the people for you, where they seek you out, they listen to you and they treasure your words. One day you'll be talking to no one! That is a transition we have to be prepared for. We may have the masses seeking us out, but then next thing it is just the birds and the air seeking us out! We have to be grateful and say: "Lord God, I came into the world as a nobody. I leave as a nobody. But I have been blessed to be called Somebody by you."

Your Loss is Our Loss – *Tokerau Joseph*

Rev. Dr. Tokerau Joseph is the minister of Mairangi Bay Presbyterian Church, Auckland. He shares a Cook Islands perspective from his experience of leaving two parish appointments. Tokerau has written two theses on cultural dynamics within the church, both of which are available online through the University of Otago: 'Ethnic Flames of the Burning Bush: An exploration of ethnic relations in congregations of the Presbyterian Church of Aotearoa New Zealand,' and 'Cracked coconuts: an exploration of why young Cook Islanders are leaving Cook Islander congregations of the Presbyterian Church of Aotearoa New Zealand.'[14]

• • •

Silvia: In the church we are really good at talking about beginnings. We put a lot of energy into discerning a new appointment and setting up the ministry settlement and blessing that. Then when it ends we are not quite sure what to do.

Tokerau: I think you're right; there's hardly anything written about this. There's plenty in the general scope of grief, but it is worthwhile looking at grief in terms of transitioning from one ministry to another.

Silvia: I think we have really high expectations of our ministers being very resilient. I am sitting with this question about when ministers have had a difficult experience and ministry ended with some heartache. How do you then begin a new thing? What does it take of the heart and the energy?

Tokerau: It's one thing to transition from one ministry to another, but actually leaving ministry, opting right out, can be a traumatic thing because our idea of ministry is calling. It brings into question the whole aspect of God's call on your life, and your relationship with God.

When I left my first parish, B Pacific Island Church, it was hard, even though I was only there for five years. I had been awarded a postgraduate scholarship on the condition that I had to use it within five years or lose it. When I started at B they knew of my aspiration to do further studies. As the years went on and it got closer to the five years, this idea of studying and the postgrad scholarship came to the fore – and the conversations were not easy. The parish understood me wanting to study, but the ministry had developed and was flourishing. Leaving was hard because everything was going well. It could have carried on, it could have been even better.

There were people who were upset. There was grief in leaving. But it was alleviated by the fact that I felt the parish was supporting me.

Silvia: I've experienced a Cook Islands farewell. It was amazing, so colourful, expressive and emotive, so much singing and gifts, all the gifts representing so much time and love – very different from a Pākehā farewell. A parish lunch with sausage rolls doesn't compare with the vitality of a Cook Islands feast!

Tokerau: There was a farewell by the parish as a whole, then a farewell by each individual group, then a farewell by just the Cook Islanders group. So in the end we felt, "Let's just go now!"

Silvia: You can do a lot of the grieving in that process so you are not left with a bundle of grief to be dealt with down the track?

Tokerau: That's right. All of my grieving happened during those times, so by the time it was time to go I felt ready. I was able to take a deep breath and say, "Thank you for the journey." All those goodbyes were expressing gratitude and appreciation. They were saying, "Now go with our blessing on this next part of your journey." It helped that I wasn't going to another parish but was leaving to pursue academic study that I felt was part of God's calling in my life.

Silvia: And wrapping up your family in that as well, not just you as an individual?

Tokerau: Indeed. It was hard because we left our eldest son because he had started work. Leaving our son behind was really hard for me.

Silvia: Were there other forms of loss?

Tokerau: The scope of grief was wider than just the parish. It was my involvement in the wider community, leaving all of that behind. And with my extended family, because the majority of them live there.

I had another ministry transition which was different because I left one parish to go to another. I spent 14 years at J; after that length of time the bond is very close. I actually felt that I was betraying them by going to another parish.

But I had known for over a year before I left that change was coming for me. I had been processing that for nearly a year.

Silvia: How did you know? I talk about the first task of the grief of ministry transition is to come to the point of decision. You do a lot of anticipatory grief, but often that is quite a hidden thing. What got you to a decision to leave?

Tokerau: I knew there was change on my horizon but I was not sure what that change was going to look like. The aspiration was always there, the idea of moving on to a different type of ministry – in the back of my mind, that one day I would pursue something else. The seed was already there.

Silvia: That is part of how God works, right? He puts in us these seeds, these aspirations or a sense of who he is shaping us to be. And sometimes the seed doesn't fit the context we are in.

Tokerau: You weigh up all the circumstances for you personally, through devotions, supervision and counsel with retired ministers. You connect the dots and then you make the decision. And sometimes the dots are not always clear. You don't always see clearly but I have learned that you make the decision and you live with it. You 'go with' the consequences of that. But even when we made the decision and made the move, even then we still had questions, we still had 'what ifs?'

Silvia: You said the hardest thing was a feeling that you betrayed them in some way.

Tokerau: Yes, to be honest, that is how I felt at one point.

Silvia: Was it a sense that you were breaking a promise? Why 'betrayal'?

Tokerau: In the fact that I had been there for so long. We had forged a really strong relationship. And not just within the parish but what I was doing in the wider community, with the university, the presbytery and a community group. We had done so many good things. Just when things are looking on the up and up, then I come down with: "I'm leaving." The people were going: "Hey but …!" In their minds we hadn't finished. My contribution was part of their vision, part of their hopes and dreams. So me cutting it and moving on – I remember thinking, "I feel like I am betraying them, because I have not been able to fulfil their hopes and their dreams." The fact that I was going to another parish was saying: "I'm leaving you lot for that lot. I have committed to you for 14 years and now I'm cutting that tie." It is a relationship thing. You are leaving one relationship for another and it is a sense of betrayal.

Silvia: *How do you understand that theologically, looking back?*

Tokerau: It was helpful having conversations with retired ministers who had been through that, and in my supervision. I worked it through theologically as journeying with God. I use the 23rd Psalm; there are times when you are by the still waters and green pastures, and then the journey will lead you through the valleys. Through it all God is part of the journey.

Silvia: *Almost God pushing us into the hard things?*

Tokerau: Yes. That is when God uses the rod and staff.

Silvia: *The rod and the staff used roughly? That feels uncomfortable!*

Tokerau: Even though the Psalmist says "they comfort me" it still has to be used. It is used to defend against predators but also on the sheep, to get them back on track. It is used and you deal with it. That's how I felt about leaving J.

And even the first month or two here in Mairangi Bay it was a mixture of excitement for a new context but at the same time ... my body was here but my mind and heart was still somewhere else. It took a while. I think it was quicker for me to adapt than for my wife and our family. I got into work and switched focus while they were still getting the house organised, getting school organised, familiarising with the community.

Grief takes time. You work through the challenges as they come. You cross each bridge as you come to. Some bridges are easier to cross than others. Some bridges are longer than others! It is a journey that you have to take, but it is not always easy.

Silvia: *A bridge is a good metaphor, that sense of leaving a place of solid ground and on to a space in the middle. Bridges are different: a good solid bridge or a little rope bridge that you're hanging onto for dear life. It might feel unsafe before you get to the other place. Grief theory talks about accepting the loss and adjusting to the new environment. But adjustment and acceptance are easier said than done. You can't just say, "That's it, I'm adjusted now."*

Tokerau: I agree. Some adjustments take longer than others. Keep on walking across it trusting you will get there in the end. A key thing is to keep moving. If you don't keep moving it can make your transition more difficult. There's a tendency to look back, which is not bad but it can affect how you move forward.

We went back a couple of times to J for family functions and for bereavements, and each time I felt less connected with J, because I was feeling more connected in my new context. The new context was the place that I started calling home and *F* was becoming less home. Now when we go down I'm happy to see people again and it brings back wonderful memories, but it's not the same.

Silvia: One of my topics is renegotiating relationships. In the Pākehā church there is a strong expectation of severing relationships. In the Cook Islands churches you have been in, do you have a continuing role with the church after you left?

Tokerau: When I started at *B* I was still fairly young, it was a church that I grew up in. So they never refer to me as a former or past minister, they say "our son."

Silvia: The love is still there. Even though you're not the minister anymore they still own you as their son. Wow.

Tokerau: Those ties are still very strong. So now if they need help with something they call me and say: "Hey, are you available? We've got a situation, would you available to give us a hand?" And if I am available I say "Yes." The channels of communication are still very open.

It felt a bit awkward the first couple of times I went back to *J* for a service, to see the place I used to stand, and instead to just sit in a pew. When they asked me to take the service part of me wanted to say, "Hey, you've got a new minister." I am wary not to interfere.

With both *B* and *J* the relationship is a very good, a strong relational connection that has never been broken as far as I'm concerned.

The way I left has a part to play. There were key people in the parish with whom I had conversations about my future. They were very supportive of whatever I wanted to do. It was still hurtful to say "I'm leaving," but they were not totally surprised by it. Having three months' notice gave me time to talk with more people about it, to talk with groups. So by the time it came to leave we had worked through most of our grief.

I had about a month break before starting at Mairangi Bay, which I think is important. The minister needs to have the space to breathe, to familiarise with the new environment. I am so glad that I took that space. I negotiated with the new parish: "I need a gap, some space" and they were accommodating for that. So it worked out well for me.

Silvia: So it comes down to the graciousness of the church and the church valuing what you need?

Tokerau: It is helpful to have open conversations and approach it with genuineness. If we put our cards on the table, if we want the best for the ending, the transition and the new beginning, and be honest about what we want, people are happy to come to the table and try to make that work.

Silvia: Do you have recommendations for how to do it well, to let go properly and start a new ministry fresh?

Tokerau: It is very helpful to have some key people to talk to, in the parish you are leaving and in the parish you are going to, and some key people who are in neither but are a sounding board for you. People you can truly confide in and who can be honest to you as well, so that it's a two way street. Before I told the parish at F there were three elders that I told first. I sought their advice and I expressed to them: "This is what I'm thinking of doing. Can you pray with me?" They helped to affirm my move. And then together we were able to tell the Session.

Silvia: That is a tribute to your style of leadership, that you built up those kind of trusting relationships where you were able to be vulnerable and say, "This is who I am and where we're at."

Tokerau: It is better to have people work with you than against you. It's a lot harder if you can't get people with you. Each minister has to discern the kinds of people that they can have an open and workable relationship with, so that it helps the process rather than hinders the process. I don't know the formula for that. All I know is that each of us will know.

Silvia: One more question: talking about the Cook Islands process of farewell, are there some parallels between how a parish would farewell a minister and how they would do a tangi or funeral? Do you think culturally there are similarities between death and other kinds of farewell?

Tokerau: In both bereavements and leavings the idea of support is there. It is having a time to be together but also with practical things. There is always a gift that is offered.

Silvia: There is a parallel in the giving of gifts, tangible things.

Tokerau: When I left, gifts were given to me and my family. And people wanted to have a meal with us as part of the farewell. Before Cook Islands funerals the body will be at home and different groups will come to offer support, words of encouragement and a gift. They are there with their presence, they are there with their gifts, they are there with their affirmation. And they will have a meal together. If I were to hold these two up together, the bereavement and this transition for ministry, those are the parallels. There is a time to be together. There is giving of gifts. And there is the sense of, "We are sad for what is happening but we affirm you." And they pray for you. That's what I see.

Silvia: In the Pākehā church we are more avoidant. When there is a death there is support but you don't want to intrude. So people might stay away perhaps or be uncomfortable discussing it. It can be even more awkward when a minister has resigned. It's quite a cultural difference.

Tokerau: Yes, from my experience I would agree. Cook Islands church families and groups approached me to say, "We'd like to have our time with you." And that is similar to a bereavement because the groups come and say: "We would like to have a time with you, for your loss, for what's happening. Because what has happened to you affects us as well."

Silvia: What does that say about understanding loss in the Cook Islands context?

Tokerau: There is a phrase that Cook Islanders always say at bereavements. When a group comes there is a common phrase: "Your loss is our loss." Theologically it affirms how we understand the Body. What affects one part of the body impacts other parts of the Body. "No kotou te tumatetenga, no matou te tumatetenga." Your bereavement is our bereavement.

Silvia: That is profound. Thank you Tokerau.

Never Forgotten: Death in Active Ministry
– *Caroline Mareko, Uili Teó and Mana Leasi-Paese*

I are deeply honoured to share these contributions, from the Porirua Pacific Islanders Presbyterian Church (PIPC), reflecting on the death of their minister, Rev. Parema Leasi in 2019.

Lealamanu'a Aiga Caroline Mareko, MNZM, Justice of the Peace, has been a member and elder of Porirua PIPC parish for over 50 years. Caroline has served as Secretary, Sunday School teacher and as the Elder representative for the youth. She worked alongside the late Rev. Perema Leasi in the Porirua community advocating for the Pacific community in education, housing, employment, social justice, health and wellbeing.

Uili Teó is a life-long member of the Porirua parish, and an Elder of the Church and since 2020.

Mana Fa'ailo Leasi-Paese is Reverend Perema Leasi's eldest daughter. In this section she courageously reflects on the terrible experience of her father's death, and her insights about grief. Mana is currently working in Toitū te Waiora Workforce Development Council as a Research and Insights Analyst. She is the eldest of five children and is married to Daniel Taleni Paese.

• • •

Caroline Mareko

Rev. Perema Leasi – never forgotten and remembered with so much love. It was a sudden ending to an awesome and very blessed ministry at Porirua PIPC church. To this day it is still difficult to fathom that God took a dedicated servant into his House, too soon from our perspective but maybe not for Him.

I remember the day clearly. I was sitting in a management meeting at work and my brother is constantly ringing me, knowing full well that I can't answer his calls. Then a text on my phone lit up telling me that Rev. Perema had collapsed and that emergency services were trying to resuscitate him. I left the meeting to ring my brother. He tells me that people at the PIC House are trying to get hold of me. I tell him I'm on my way. I get my car keys. One of my colleagues who attends church comes with me. I tell her what is happening. She is shocked and starts to cry. We drive the 3kms to PIC House – the longest trip ever. My brother rings me as we are half way there to tell us that Rev. Perema didn't make it. We start screaming and crying the rest of the trip to the hall. We arrive to see the ambulance in the driveway. My heart is beating so fast and my breathing becomes erratic.

As I enter the hall there is an eerie feeling. I turn the corner into the foyer and in front of me I see Rev. Perema on the floor with a lot of people sitting around him. A friend of mine, one of the organisers of the event, walks towards me saying "I'm so sorry." I look down at Rev. Perema with disbelief. His shirt is cut due to emergency ministrations and he is covered with a table cloth – not the image of the well-put-together man and church leader I knew.

The next few hours are devastating as the news of his death spreads throughout our church community and the Porirua community at large. People come in shocked with disbelief. I can still hear the sounds of wailing and screaming. I can feel the pain and sorrow ripping into hearts, visibly seen through people's distress as they weep over Rev. Perema's body. His daughters are close by him keeping the physical contact – such a surreal moment. The Session Clerk's wife and some young people bring in a mattress and coverings so he can lie with dignity. The funeral director arrives. We all gather around to say a prayer. Rev. Perema is lifted onto the trolley bed carefully and respectfully. The wailing begins again as he is wheeled out into the hearse.

From that day it was a time of sorrow and pain for our church families and community. It was also a time to be united and work together. The week-long mourning was a special time for the church and Rev. Perema's family. Many people and organisations that Rev. Perema Leasi was involved in came to pay their respects. There were so many people connected with his work as a servant of God.

Rev. Perema was a very busy man who always found time to visit, pray with and for others, pastoral care, visits to our parishioners and people who were not from our church at rest homes, hospitals, in prisons and in their homes. He was a true servant of God who cared for everyone.

I was not an active member of the church when Rev. Perema Leasi and his family first arrived. He had only been in the role less than two months when he was called by our family to visit my newly-born twin nephews who came into this world at less than 24 weeks. Kobe, the eldest, was not going to survive; he passed away 3 days after he was born. Rev. Perema and his late first wife Oliana prayed for him and conducted his funeral. Through this time it brought our family back together and further down the track back to the church. Kobe's funeral was Rev. Perema's first funeral as a minister of Porirua PIPC.

Rev. Perema's first community event was when I asked him to be the officiating minister for the then Prime Minister Helen Clarke whom we were hosting at PIC House. He freaked out a bit and asked if another more experienced church minister could do it. I responded "No," as this community meeting with the Prime Minister was in his church and he was the host. I looked at him and told him I believed in him to welcome the Prime Minister to Cannons Creek and bless the gathering with a clear message from scripture relevant to the occasion. Rev. Perema conducted that community event with clarity in his message and prayer. He went on to be a powerful advocate for social justice and finding ways to address social issues that were impacting on Pacific communities and the most vulnerable.

Rev. Perema for 18 years worked tirelessly giving effect and impact in his church, his family, and community. He never judged anyone, only accepted everyone. His service to the people and his faith in God was the ultimate mantle he held, with a lot of love and generosity of time. He had the biggest and most generous heart. Rev. Perema kept the faith.

• • •

Uili Teó

I have been with the church since the day I was born. The late Reverend Setu Masina baptised me at Lower Hutt Hospital; I was not well when I was born and my parents were told by the doctors I may not survive. My parents always reminded me to Be Thankful for each and every day. I am now a parent and grandparent.

Over the years as a church family we have been through our fair share of grief – different emotions, different reactions. The physical and mental toll can be a heavy burden, but we have stuck together and supported one another during those tough times to remain loyal to our Christian faith.

I was at work the day Reverend Leasi passed away. My younger sister called me. I felt disbelief (Truth be told – whenever my younger sister calls me I suspect something has happened!). I felt sad, sad for the Family and also for our Church. A week earlier as per normal I shook Perema's hand after the service and wished him well for the week. All that happened between then and the following Sunday took time to sink in – a time of asking questions.

I was committed to helping out in any way possible. The day Perema passed away we had a service later on that evening and then that Sunday we had a joint service with other PIC Churches. I was given the privilege of being a pall bearer that day. A week later we had Perema's funeral on the Saturday. The following day my family had lunch together with my siblings and their families after Church. As I addressed the family I broke down in tears talking about Perema.

It has been over 2 years since Perema passed away. We are currently working through the process of finding a new Minister. I see our church family each Sunday – normal pleasantries are exchanged. We continue to fellowship together and give thanks to God for all that he has given us. To this day I still think of him and the kind hearted man that he was.

I was chosen to become an Elder of the Church prior to Perema's passing, and thought he would be the Minister to officiate the proceedings – sadly he was not present. However, for me the drive has continued, to follow my Family's footsteps in being leaders of this Church; and also to be part of the healing process to carry on with God's work and my journey with my church family. There is not a day that goes by that I don't think about my parents who have passed away and also my upbringing with Church of Christ the King. I thank God for my PIPC family and for my own family and all that God has given.

Fakaaue Lahi.

• • •

Mana Fa'ailo Leasi-Paese

Grief is a word for me that brings up mixed emotions and presents in different forms. One thing I do know is that it takes years to absorb. Over time I have discovered that grief is a lifelong process, that begins a new journey of self-healing and peace.

Growing up with both parents immersed in leading within the church ministry, we witnessed many life experiences that involved walking with families in their time of sorrow. Grief was not an unfamiliar part of life. Our mother, a huge anchor in supporting our father in their ministry, passed away in September 2006 from her short battle with cancer. Losing our mother at a young age was a difficult process for our family, however it was made easier in learning how to navigate it together. Losing our father recently was an experience which to this day has been a struggle and at times difficult to talk about. Some days are easier than others, taking each day as it comes through the grieving process. The day he had passed away is a memory I once struggled to speak of. As time goes by it has become easier to share.

I was at work that morning facilitating a team meeting. My phone is on silent but I check it just as my sister is calling. Plus there were about 6 missed calls. I excuse myself out of the meeting room and return the call. My youngest sister answers. What's going on? She starts crying, barely getting a word out. She tells me to hurry to the church hall. I pick up words that she manages to say. "Something has happened to Dad. They tried but ... he didn't make it. Dad's gone."

My heart drops. I'm standing in the reception area looking blankly at the entrance wondering what I just heard. He can't be gone. I just saw him this morning. No, this can't be right. Two of my work colleagues come out. I run into their arms and let out a huge cry. We rush together to Porirua. The ride feels so long. An ambulance passes us.

Inside the foyer some people are having a cup of tea. Well, this looks normal – holding to hope that what I heard wasn't true. But as we enter the hall there are our church family wailing, crying, rushing up to hug me. Our Session Clerk, my father's right hand and an anchor in the church, is in tears and embraces me in a big hug. He cries and leads me to where Dad lies on the floor.

My sisters Brenda and Roseta are one on each side. Dad looks like he is sleeping. I take his hand and hold it. He is still warm. My body feels numb. I break down seeing him lying there, his shirt cut by the paramedics who tried to revive him. The heavy cries and wailing of our church family wrap around us as we hold his hands. The doors swing open as all our church family come as news spreads – all different ages, even the youngest of our church. Each one, the look on their faces and the sound of their cries tugs at my heart.

Although it was such a horrific situation that had taken place, we felt the warmth and comfort of God's love truly embrace us that day. Our church family sat there with us in mourning together. There were moments of silence – a surreal quiet shared amongst all.

During the time following his passing leading to his burial, we were so humbled and so in awe of all the outpouring support from our church family, family and friends. The stories that many shared of him, things we had never heard before, people we hadn't met and those we knew so well, sharing such beautiful memories. Our church family were our pillars of strength. Over those next few days and weeks they gave their all to farewell him. It was such a tough time for everyone. Though it was difficult preparing to farewell Dad after a sudden loss, it was also a beautiful experience coming all together, being in each other's presence, sharing grieving in our own way through the sharing of stories and fellowship.

His loss was truly a painful process to inhale. It helped knowing that he died at the place where the heart of his work brought healing. It was as if he was trying to tell us: it's time to finally rest.

In the months that followed it was difficult for me to accept his absence. I was used to being with Dad for church activities, so attending them without him was painful and felt raw. I know all our church family and many others also experienced this at first – a sense of disbelief that he was not going to walk out of the vestry again.

Our church family held a tribute to Dad in December 2019, a tribute concert where every group of the church shared and came together to honour Dad, everyone from Sunday School right up to our elderly. I could see in their eyes and through their sharing how much they were missing him, just as my family was.

As the years have gone by, grief has its moments. It's been almost 3 years now, and at times the pain still feels raw. I used to find it excruciating when people would tell me: it's time to move on, to let go. You will get over it. It will get easier. Please understand that those things are easier said than done. We must remember that our words and the type of words we use can impact a person, no matter what stage of grief they are in.

There are days I feel it heavier than others. However, I now feel at peace. I remember Dad in how he lived, not just how he passed. I know my father was not a perfect man but he lived his life loving and serving God through every aspect he knew possible. His legacy was to show that God's love is never-ending and continues to strengthen us no matter what season we endure in life. Our parents always reminded my siblings and I that no matter what we faced we were never alone. As my father used to say, never ever think that we walk this world alone when we walk with God.

Through sorrow, joy will come in the morning. Through God's grace, through sharing about Dad's loss, grief has become easier. I grow in strength through each day.

Internally Displaced: a Spouse's Perspective
– *Jenny Flett*

Jenny Flett lives in Prebbleton with her husband Dennis, a Presbyterian minister. In this interview she reflects on the experience of moving from a place where they had been in ministry for many years and had been very settled.

• • •

Silvia: You and Dennis have been through several major transitions. What has been your role in those decisions? Have you been in it together or has it been mainly about God's call on his life?

Jenny: We have been very much all in it together. Very much so. Every decision has involved us and the kids; we involved the whole family in the decision making process. We wouldn't have done any of our moves without us all being on board.

Silvia: Did you feel you had to sacrifice your career for Dennis's ministry?

Jenny: No. I've been able to work wherever I am. I wouldn't call it sacrifice anyway because we do life together. It's not about one or the other. I have always seen myself as being there, not as a traditional minister's wife but definitely being the chief cheerleader and support partner. I get involved where I feel to get involved in church life, not out of obligation. I think the transitions we had with kids were actually really easy. The kids adapted well and made good friends quickly. I'm not saying for one minute it was easy for them, but as a family we tried to make every post a winning post wherever we went.

For me personally it was much easier when I had kids because you got stuck in with your kids' lives. Instant networks, interests, school connections, the 'central railway station' of home with kids coming and going all the time. All that stuff was easy when you had kids. So I don't think any of the transitions before this one I found very difficult at all. In fact I really enjoyed them.

My most recent move was the hardest for me. I put it down mostly to my stage of life. Upping and re-establishing yourself in another town with fresh people, starting again at 60 is much more difficult than at 40 or 30. My peer group are entrenched in their relationships. And this year has been different because we arrived the week before Covid lockdown.

And I lost my father just before I shifted. And I came off four years of an intense travel schedule, out of the country every month. That came to a grinding halt when I shifted. So I was away from my friends and my whole lifestyle changed radically. I felt quite displaced. And then Covid and the world changed. So for a long time I felt – Where do I fit? I have not just jumped in and started running. I floundered around trying to work out where I fit.

Silvia: So did you experience that as grief?

Jenny: Very much so. I had layers of grief going on, because my dad had died, and I had to leave my friends. Of all of our shifts this was the hardest, in terms of what I left behind. My kids have left home long ago. And we had a home that gave us a lot of good soul space up there. So that was quite hard to leave.

I am not by nature a complainer or somebody who goes into great depths of despair. I am by nature a positive and optimistic person. I felt grumpy and displaced; it was kind of "grrr," but not a deep "grrr." Does that make sense? I wrote some quite deep things at a presbytery retreat:

> "Displaced, loss of place, loss of significance, loss of my father, distance from friends and family, distance from God."

I did feel that. I had to really work on that.

Silvia: One of the themes in this book is about exile. Did you feel like you were exiled?

Jenny: No, not exile. I felt probably felt more internally displaced. I felt grumpy that I had to start 'again.' It was like, "Uh! I have to do all this again!"

Silvia: That takes a huge amount of emotional energy.

Jenny: Yes. Having to get to know people, and people having this expectation of you, and trying to filter out the motivations of why people might want to get to know you.

Silvia: Is it the minister's wife they want to get to know or is it Jenny?

Jenny: Indeed. Is this the back door to my husband?

It is also about making connections that are in synergy with myself. It takes quite a long time to do that. I don't have to be friends with everybody. It is nice to make some connections with people, but I don't feel the obligation to be there for everyone. As the minister's wife you are suddenly in this new community where they are expecting – or you feel they're expecting – something of you, and you don't necessarily have the resources within you to give what they expect. It is mostly inside me, how I perceive people's expectations of me, which is not necessarily the reality.

Silvia: Were you aware of doing anything deliberately, in terms of your prayer life or scripture? Or do you just get on with it until it sorted itself out?

Jenny: Oh no, I definitely had to address some things. I had to work through where I felt God was in all of this. Dennis and I have talked a lot this year about being cruciform, allowing the cross to work its way through suffering, and allowing that to happen. I think that is quite important, so that when stuff does happen we allow God to speak, and we work with God through the process.

Silvia: So the fact that it feels uncomfortable doesn't necessarily mean that God is not in it, or that God has abandoned us?

Jenny: That is generally where you find God the strongest, actually. It certainly does not mean you are abandoned. It does mean rebalancing the show a bit. So when it comes around again you have more to offer from being through that process. This transition has been the hardest transition I have done, but that does not mean it was wrong, it just means it was hard.

A Lay Leaders' Perspective
– Alan and Elizabeth Purdie

My husband's parents, Alan and Elizabeth Purdie, have been active members of the Wadestown Presbyterian Church in Wellington for over fifty years. I talked with them about their experience as parish leaders through many ministry transitions.

They described how in the post-war era it was expected that ministers would stay for only a few years in a parish then move on. Where this was part of a "natural progression," as Alan put it, then there was little grief for the parish. I asked them about what helped a ministry to end well. They identified having good relationships as the most important thing. They advocate for ministers having a support group within the parish as a sounding board.

Alan and Elizabeth recalled one situation where the ministry "ended too soon." It felt unfinished. Wadestown had been the minister's first parish, and he was "headhunted" for a national church role in Christian Education. Elizabeth felt this was unfair of the wider church, that they had not considered the needs of the parish or the person. The national role did not go well and he resigned from ministry. This left a lasting sadness, not just for the ministry that could have continued fruitfully at Wadestown but for a potentially life-long ministry that ended before it had hardly begun. "The whole church lost a minister, not just us," said Alan.

The most painful experience in Alan and Elizabeth's parish leadership occurred when a previously strong relationship with a minister soured. What had been a warm and constructive partnership became increasingly conflicted, even hostile. When the ministry ended they were left feeling angry rather than sad, which they found a most uncomfortable grieving process. Alan said, "It took me a long time to get my head around it and to stop feeling cross." This is a form of disenfranchised grief, as anger is rarely socially acceptable in the church: "Not a lot of people in the church knew how I really felt." With a breakdown in relationship there was no opportunity for reconciliation.

Some relationships with ministers ended with the end of the appointment. However, Alan and Elizabeth are highly relational people and forged ongoing friendships with several of their previous ministers. One friendship in particular has continued through many years after a 9-month ministry exchange from the USA. As Alan put it, because "they responded to us too" a friendship grew. They are not people with strict role boundaries. For them hospitality is a central expression of their faith and they have built community and friendships in their own home, at church and around the world.

The Wadestown parish has recently been through a long period of 'vacancy' lasting for over five years. Alan and Elizabeth identified this as a real period of grief for the parish and for them personally: "It's a grief for the people that stay to see other people dropping off," said Elizabeth. They grieved for the church and they struggled with carrying responsibility for parish life without the support of a minister. It was difficult to keep up fresh energy for mission at the same time as dealing with major building issues with earthquake strengthening while also seeking a minister year after year.

Farewells Never Happen – *Hone Te Rire*

Rev. Jonathan (Hone) Te Rire is Tūhoe and Tūwharetoa ki Kawerau, from Onepū and Maungapōhatu. He is ordained both as an Amorangi and as a National Ordained Minister of the Presbyterian Church. He is currently completing a PhD, the recipient of the Ngārimu VC and 28th (Māori) Battalion Memorial Doctoral Scholarship.[15]

• • •

He Amorangi ahau o Te Aka Pūaho, te Hinota Māori. He Nationally Ordained Minita hoki o te Hāhi Perehipitiriana o Aotearoa Niu Tireni. He mea nui tēnei mo taku haerenga whakapono.

Ka whakamahi ahau i te tirohanga a te ao Māori ki te whakaputa i taku ngākau nui mō taku hikoi ki te Ariki. Ka kōrero ahau mō ngā Maunga kārangaranga. Ko te whakatauki o tētahi pepeha, "Whatu ngarongaro te tangata, toitū te whenua." E kī ana te iwi ka haere, ka wehe, engari ka kaha tonu te whenua, ka pūmau tonu. Ko ngā Maunga e kōrerotia nei e au kua kite kua pahemo i tēnei wā i roto hoki i ngā tau. Ka kite rātou i ngā tāngata e haere mai nei. Ko ngā Maunga e whakahuahia ana e au he tangata. Pēnei i ēnei maunga, engari ko ngā tāngata i āwhina ki te hanga kaupapa me te whakatū rauemi ki te whare karakia kia taea ai te haere, haere ake nei.

Kei te mahi ahau i taku Tohu Kairangi PhD ki Te Whare Wānanga o Awanuiārangi. Heoi, kei Te Awamutu ahau me tōku whānau e noho ana. Kei roto ahau i taku tau whakamutunga, a tōna wā, ka tuku au taku Tuhinga roa, Tohu Kairangi hei te mutunga o tēnei tau.

Being an Amorangi of Te Aka Puaho, the Māori Synod,[16] and a Nationally Ordained Minister of the Presbyterian Church of Aotearoa New Zealand has been a valuable part of my faith journey.

I use a Māori worldview approach in sharing my passion about my walk with the Lord. I talk about Mountains talking to and with each other. The Māori proverbial saying, "Whatu ngarongaro te tangata, toitū te whenua," says that people pass by and leave, but the land stays strong and sure. The Mountains I speak of have seen time pass by for aeons. They have seen people come and go. The Mountains I describe are people, as these mountains are, but people who have helped build, shape and resourced the church to be able to continue forever.

I am currently completing a Māori Theology focused PhD thesis at Te Whare Wānanga o Awanuiārangi. I currently live in Te Awamutu, a lovely rural town 20 minutes south of Hamilton city.

Tihei Mauri Ora!

• • •

Farewells never happen in the Māori world. When you change from one tūranga, from one position to another, you will get acknowledged in the farewell ceremony. That is acknowledging who you are, what you have done in the community and with the whānau. You would get a farewell in the context, and Māori do have those, but it is not a farewell as in 'see you later, that's it, no more communication.' That never happens.

A big part of it is because of whakapapa, a person's genealogy. You can never ever cut the whakapapa ties. We are all closely connected; blood whānau relationships. It is mana-enhancing to maintain the relationship. I might have left home but it is for me to keep contact back home. 'Kanohi ki te kanohi' is the main way,[17] but there is also new ways of doing it, there are phones, there is messaging, there is Facebook, whatever it takes. So an Amorangi never leaves home. In fact, an Amorangi never retires. A poroporoaki is only given when we die. That is the only time it is given. The only way out is in a box!

You never sever that relationship. You keep it warm; you maintain it. It is about respecting the mana of the other person or persons that you were with. That is the key thing. Our saying is "Leave with your mana intact." You do not want to leave with a stain on the wall. Kāore (no). You leave with your mana intact, and you leave with their mana intact so that you can maintain the relationships.

Home for me is back in my parish. Home for me is back in the Eastern Bay of Plenty. Home for me is in Te Aka Pūaho. Home for me is in Te Hāhi Perehipitīriana, the Presbyterian church. I never leave home. I am always home, even spiritually. We always get told, "Kaua e wareware, boy – don't forget boy. Hoki mai ki te kāinga – you come home all the time. Kia mahana te ahi – to keep the home fires warm." Ahi kā is very important. For Māori we never leave home. For Māori we never stop the contact.

It is never ever losing sight of respect, aroha, and humility. We are taught a number of things: *Ko te whakapono*, our faith, *Kia ū te whakapono* – be strong in your faith. *Karakia ki te Atua* – pray to the Lord. *Pānui te Paipera Tapu* – read the scriptures, the Word of God. We are taught that. *Whakapono me te tumanako* – we are taught about hope. Through faith you will have hope. There is always hope, never ever give in.

Whakapono, tumanako, aroha – in the Bible, we have faith, hope and love. And in the Māori world: *He aha te mea nui? Ko te aroha.* We are taught that, and it permeates through our lives. The older we get, we never lose sight of that. And we also look at our future, our rangatahi, our tamariki mokopuna. And as role models, we are teaching them the same things: faith, hope, love. How can I show that if I am not a role model to them? And so we never lose sight of it.

A Journey with Endings and New Beginnings
– *Robyn McPhail*

Rev. Dr. Robyn McPhail is a Presbyterian minister who enjoys having time in retirement for family, being an Ambulance Officer around Central Otago, and writing as she feels inspired about eco theology and rural ministry.

• • •

Three endings and three different experiences of grief; simple, complicated, and transformative.

Retirement has brought to a conclusion 32 years in full time ordained ministry. I was just six months into retirement when I read Silvia's work on ministry grief. So much of what she named and reflected on connected directly to my experience. I would like to share some of these connections; much of this has never been put out publicly before but it feels right to do so now. It will surely assist with the current hard labour of transition from recognised stipended ministry. It will enable me to honour people who shared the journey, and all those I have loved and learned from over the years. And perhaps it will help others in their own ministry transitions.

I began in a union parish, which meant an appointment term of five years. By the middle of the fifth year, if the minister wants to continue, a review process takes place. My husband and I and our young family were very happy to stay. I felt I was getting the hang of it, and relationships within the parish seemed really good. There were no sign of issues until the review happened. I was working collegially with another minister, who had always given me support and encouragement. As it turned out, he was concerned there was not enough money to enable both of us to extend our appointments. He had been talking with some people about this but not me, and it had not been part of official parish business. The review committee recommended that my appointment not be renewed. This came as a complete surprise, not just to us, but to the regional powers that be: the Joint Regional Committee and Presbytery.

Things really got in a tangle. I just kept my head down and left the debate to presbytery, who appointed a Commission. This was made up of three gems of the church who came and listened. The Commission's finding was that the process had been unsound, and the review committee offered me a three-year renewal. However, as family we decided that it was best to move on. There was too much brokenness in relationships and in confidence.

There were plenty of positives from my time with the parish and the town and country communities, and from the affirmations of the Commission and the support of the vast majority of parish members during the troubles. All of that could have been built on. However, I just wanted to crawl away into a hole and hide. I felt grief at the loss of what I thought I had: a positive collegial relationship and good prospects for building a durable ministry. The process had been very troubling for the parish, and I felt shame that I had been part of that. Without the loyal and wise support of my husband, my parents and good friends, I probably would have ended ministry then and there.

Fortunately I was able to find a bolt hole and make a new start. With the help of the Begg Scholarship we went to Melbourne for six months and I immersed myself in study as a 'Visiting Scholar' at the Uniting Church in Australia's Theological College. I spent many enjoyable hours with the theology lecturer there. The sister of a parishioner lived in Melbourne and she and her husband were great support to us.

The nature of the ending was such that contacts with the parish were minimal. They were going through their own ongoing turmoil so it seemed best to pull down the blind on that time. It had not been appropriate to have a formal farewell – it just felt too hard – so we gathered for a party at an outdoor community pool and said our farewells by way of chatting among the people. In those days there was no social media, something that is currently very important to me now for maintaining valued connections.

Melbourne was overwhelming for this country kid and her village-raised family. Coping with that became the focus, rather than just my grief. The stimulation of study and new contacts encouraged reflection on pain still raw. I took on helping a PhD student from South Korea with the English language in his thesis. His dictionary threw up English words that I had never heard of, one in particular which related to the crucifixion. He used the word 'cicatrix' to underline that the risen Christ remains also the crucified Christ. Cicatrix means the scar of a healed wound; resurrection heals but the scar remains. This concept became a reference point for me in the years that followed, for assessing how I was faring in terms of recovering from my 'forced exit' ending of my first ministry. Whenever I found myself stirred up by people or problems, I recognised this as scar tissue being disturbed; this helped me keep calm and not lash out. I now notice that the scar tissue no longer flares up in challenging situations.

The second appointment was a Presbyterian parish, so it was a Call and not fixed-term appointment. The ending was the simple kind; after ten years I loved the people and felt they loved me. I was very much part of the local community and it would have been easy to carry on. However I knew that change was valuable not only for a parish but also for me, and especially for my husband who longed for somewhere warm to live. So we tested the waters with a Union parish in the Far North and, praise the Lord, they wanted me.

I faced the task of how to tell my parish about our decision to leave. I chose to do it through a letter to everyone on the pastoral list. The parish was much bigger than those at church of a Sunday morning and a letter gave me the chance to tell the whole community the story of how and why we were making the move. Our family had grown up in this parish and had left for university and work; it was now time for me to do a new thing.

The actual ending was eased further by spending the final weeks on study leave within the parish – doing a research project that was of value to them – during which time the parish council and congregation were free to start talking about a new ministry, without me being in the way. There was a farewell, at which we were able to say things that mattered. That was when I discovered how valuable those occasions are; a time to honour and affirm the people who had taught me so much.

The third ending, the one I am currently processing, was after 15 and a half years. Going beyond ten years in a Union appointment is unusual, although now permitted. It was appropriate because the parish went through a drawn-out building project with a significant community mission. I was willing to stay to see this through, to get the mission underway. What is more, the wider community, Māori and Pākehā, had become my adopted home and I was in no hurry to leave that behind.

Because the ending came with retirement, it was in sight for some time. The grief started in the final year. As Silvia says, "The minister is the one who leaves; the congregation get left behind… how do I support people through the pain of letting go when I am the one causing the pain?" Retirement as the reason certainly helps. They recognised that I had done my dash of over-work and was more than ready to have the time and space for my own life, in our own home. As the time drew closer I found myself responding to their "We don't want to lose you" by saying: "I am losing all of you – you will still have one another."

I was worrying about being disconnected, no longer immediately part of the numerous communities of support that had built up over the years: church, hapū/whanau, local St John, choir, schools. The concept of 'multiple loss' fits this situation. This move was not an exile but a return, coming back to my own maunga, awa, and moana (mountains, river and ocean). But the loss of community continues to tug. Building new relationships and finding people of shared interest is a slow and often lonely process.

There were multiple farewells this time, at community events as the year ended, through to the 'Bit of a Do' at my last service. Plenty of time for tears and for affirmations of the people who all became very dear to me. I was ending in recognised full-time ministry and I knew I had to hear well the comments made about me. They are my resource for the future; for example, the crew at St John gave me a pounamu (greenstone pendant) whose shape represents strength and determination. This definitely fits to sum up the last 32 years!

Ending number three felt like a really good ending, and we had the best kind of departure. With help from the parish's 'gun' packing crew we loaded up our worldly goods into a hired truck and set off down the road on a 1769km adventure into a new future. "Dislocation – Disconnection" is a blog post I wrote soon after the move south. The processing of grief continued with the next post 'Memory and Place.'[18]

The story of 'letting go and letting be' continues. We finally shifted into our new home recently and I was able to show up for worship at the first parish in this story. Yes, we have returned to that same place. Time has passed and the hurt is history. The parish seems also to have recovered. I am assured there is no 'elephant in the room.' I have come back and there is just a huge welcome back. To hear one of them say, "We cried when you left," was very moving. I simply said, "I cried too." That's been the main thing: shedding a tear when that is needed.

And writing. Thank you, Silvia, for the opportunity: for the insights you have given us and the words you have provided for naming significant experiences that, with time, can become transformative experiences.

Rejection and Colonial Mentality – *Joohong Kim*

Rev. Dr. Joohong Kim is a Methodist minister from South Korea, currently at Crossways Community Church in Christchurch.

• • •

The transition to ministry in a different cultural context is challenging, and grief is part of that. In Korea I was in lay ministry, and I did not feel transitional grief because I was part of my culture. After I came to New Zealand I trained for ordained ministry, and it was a very different context to be in English speaking ministry in Western culture. I didn't know much about the Kiwi ministry context. I was learning the community and the people and the history and culture. My first appointment was in a 100% Kiwi parish. I was keen on pastoral visiting; that was important for me to learn about each other and get to know each other, an important step of my parish ministry. However, one pastoral visit has stayed vividly in my mind as a grief experience.

I arranged to visit an elderly member of the church, who had been very active in leadership but was no longer so active. I came on time, knocked on the door, and she invited me to come in. I came in, and she was sitting on the couch, not facing me. She was looking out the window with me on her left side at a distance. She didn't stand up, she just said, "Come in." She didn't invite me to be seated, so I stayed standing by the door. We had a conversation, but it was not exactly a 'heart to heart.' The conversation did not last long; it felt very long to me, but it was in reality less than 10 minutes. I found a way to round up the conversation and left. It was very, very awkward.

Afterwards I had a keen feeling of rejection. I felt put down and not respected. This lady had agreed to my pastoral visit but did not make me feel welcome. I wanted to engage in conversation and develop the relationship, but she did not give me any chance to do that. It was hard for me to comprehend and get my head around it. I kept asking myself: "Why? What did I do wrong? Why should I be treated that way? What happened to me and what happened to her?" I can still remember that sad feeling, the sense of grief and confusion. My sense of rejection continued until she moved to another town.

Through my ministry and post graduate study I have reflected on trans-cultural leadership, which is ministering to people of a different culture. I have wondered about the cross-cultural aspects of that pastoral visit. Was it racism, that this woman was not able to accept me as her minister because of my culture? Or did she respond to other people that way? I have learned to accept that some people do not respond warmly to me or welcome me. That is not necessarily racism. However, feeling rejected and disrespected is a common experience for people of colour in Western culture. When I interviewed other trans-cultural leaders for my doctoral project, there was a commonality. Overall there are aspects of racism in their experience.

There is grief as a trans-cultural leader. The reason for my grief from that pastoral visit is that it would not have happened in the Korean ministry context. If I was in my own cultural context, immediately I can just ask the person, and invite talk about the problem to explore it. Because I was new to this different cultural context I did not know how to deal with it. For me that was a sense of grief as I grappled with: Why? Why should I be rejected? Why should I be put down?

On the other hand, there were many more people who welcomed me and respected me. Eventually that bitter experience did not affect my ministry, because I had a time of healing, through the models of others. This is the grace that we experience as part of ministry. It is helpful to be welcomed at first sight, but relationship development is a process of sharing life together. Building up trust in each other, that genuine sense of being respected, is a mutual response that helps me a lot. If cases of rejection had been repeated over time, I don't know if I could have continued in ministry. Thankfully, the other good examples strengthened me and encouraged me to develop my leadership. So I experienced grief but I am so grateful for others who helped me, through whom God brought healing to me.

Everyone has discouraging experiences as they grow into ministry. For trans-cultural ministers there is an extra layer of discouragement because of the effects of colonialism. It is important to identify the colonial mentality in ourselves. Trans-cultural leaders have to break through. It is not easy; they need help to overcome the colonial assumption that 'other' cultures are inferior. I have worked on this in myself. I need to be bold. I have so much to offer in the name of Christ.

I grew up with images of Jesus as a white man with long blonde hair. How can I as a Korean man represent this Jesus? It has been significant for me to find other images of Jesus, as Asian, as Black. We are each a 'little Jesus.' Anyone should be called by God. Many people are still struggling within the colonial mentality and the challenges of feeling rejected and inferior. As I came into the later part of my life I thank God that I was able to overcome that.

Am I Doing the Right Thing? – *Henry Mbambo*

Rev. Henry Mbambo, from Zambia, is the minister at St David's Union Church in Ashburton.

• • •

In our transition from Zambia to New Zealand, there was grief. The starting point is asking yourself: "Am I doing the right thing?" Firstly, for my family is this the right thing? And secondly, in terms of ministry: "Am I really hearing what God is saying, or this is just me?" There is that tension within yourself, which is a form of grief: "Will I regret this later on?"

Before coming to New Zealand I had been involved in cross cultural contexts for many years. I worked in different cultures within Zambia which has 73 different dialects (tribes) and my wife and I are from different cultures. But that does not insulate from the shock that you get once you come into a culture and settle down, because you are leaving so much. Grief is leaving something behind and not knowing how it will turn out in the new place.

Grief also is brought about by the processes that our churches have to go through. To leave Zambia I had to resign from my parish. By that stage I had already grieved to some extent, because my family and I had been making the decision for some time. But when you announce it to the congregation, to the people that have been very close to you, not only do you grieve again but you grieve more, together with the congregation. In my culture, grief is harder because the people start to ask themselves whether there is something wrong they have done, that you are leaving. It was important for me to assure them, actually: "This is a decision that I am making for me and my family, not because there is anything that has gone wrong here."

They were positives and negatives in how the church showed their grief. One of the positives was when an elder came to me and told me how sad he was that I was going. He talked about a conflict we had had within the Session, a conflict that made life challenging for me as the minister. He told me how sad he had been since that conflict. With me now exiting the parish, he wanted to put things right so that I left in peace.

The negative was manifested through people starting to shut down. They were confused: "What is wrong with us?" Especially for the young ones in the parish, some of them stopped coming to worship. I suppose it was a form of anger; I'm not sure if that was toward me for resigning or toward the system that accepted my resignation. Their grief was expressed by withdrawal.

The other grief for me, as a person coming from a large family, it meant leaving behind all my siblings and my Dad. I was leaving behind my extended family, which is the main support system that I have, and coming here to a place where there was no social support system. And actually this grief has continued even to this day. It is complex, because there are stages that our children have gone through that would normally be witnessed by the extended family. Now they cannot be part of that. So a level of grief is still being experienced.

Still, regularly, I ask myself: "Was it the right thing to do?" This is our 13th year in New Zealand and I still ask this question. Not that there is anything bad happening. Theologically, the question I ask myself is: "Am I in the will of God?" I want to believe that I am in the will of God. And many times there are signs and wonders that show me that I am in the will of God. But at the same time, there's a human element where I wonder whether I am, really.

Jesus, Man of Sorrows

The last word in this discussion of the tasks of grief for ministry must, of course, belong to Jesus. Grief was part of his 'job description' as laid out in prophecy; as the King James Version put it, the Messiah would be "a man of sorrows and acquainted with grief" (Isaiah 53:3). Jesus chose to refer to himself as the Son of Man. This title carries with it suffering with and for the rest of us, all of humanity.[19] Jesus grieved with and for people. Why did Jesus weep at the death of Lazarus? He knew his friend would be OK and that his death would bring glory to God. And yet his grief was real. "You will grieve," he told his disciples, "but your grief will turn to joy" (John 16:20, NIV).

Through the Gospels we can follow Jesus' journey to the end of his earthly ministry and beyond. I am nervous about placing theories and schemas onto scripture, but I would like to explore the 'tasks of grief' in relation to Jesus.

1. **The task of fully deciding to leave.** Mark 8:31 is the beginning of the end: "He then began to teach them that the Son of Man must suffer many things and be rejected" (NIV). Each time Jesus talks about the ending of his ministry his disciples get upset, "filled with grief" (Matthew 17:22), anxiety and even anger (Mark 8:32). Jesus decided to walk toward the cross of his own freewill, out of his complete oneness with the Father.

2. **To end many relationships and renegotiate a few.** When Jesus died, his relationship with many people ended. However, those who loved him found themselves in an extraordinary continuing relationship with him, as expressed in Jesus' words in John 17:23, "I am in them and You are in Me" (HCSB). Others who had not met him in person were able to also enter this relationship, as we are today. The Gospels describe the transition from physical to resurrection relationship through the experience of Mary, Peter, Thomas, the disciples on the road to Emmaus, and the other disciples; each of these stories seem to stretch the limits of language. They saw him but did not recognise him; touched him but could not hold on to him; he was there and yet not in the same way, and then he was not there but present in a different way. Jesus renegotiated his friendships in ways that transformed his friends.

3. **To work through the pain of grief.** The church was so influenced by the idea of God as the 'unmoved mover' that for a long time Jesus was depicted as above suffering.[20] Thankfully these days we can relate to Jesus both as a human being and as the Son of God. Central to this is a full appreciation of Jesus' pain and grief. This is described most poignantly

in the Garden of Gethsemane, where his tears and cries and loneliness were intense. Jesus was real with his friends, but the gospel narratives also point to his need for solitude (when he could find it). Much of his grief Jesus carried alone with his Father.

4. **To tell a grace story of that ministry.** On the face of it, the ministry of Jesus of Nazareth was not very successful, and it ended very badly indeed. He was deserted, rejected, betrayed and assassinated. This was how two disciples trudging broken home to Emmaus after the crucifixion saw it. But Jesus came alongside them and told them a grace-filled, prophecy-inspired story of redemptive suffering. However, the story in itself was not enough to open their eyes to his presence. That happened in the breaking of bread together. Word and worship constitute the grace story of Jesus.

5. **To reinvest in a new ministry.** Resurrection began Jesus' new ministry. It is relevant to our discussion of grief and transition to consider Paul's claim that Jesus 'descended,' in Ephesians 4:9 and Romans 10:8-9.[21] Paul does more than emphasise that Jesus actually died. That Jesus 'descended' into death (or 'hell' as the Apostles Creed states) makes the journey from cross to empty tomb an active journey for Christ, down into the depths from which God 'raised' him to life. It is central to my understanding of the resurrection ministry of Jesus that it connects with every aspect of life, the good, the bad and the ugly. No corner of hell is too dark for the power of Christ. No pain or grief or trauma is beyond the ministry of Jesus. All our transitions, no matter how tough, can become part of Jesus' transition from death to life.

I Cried – *Ana Lisa de Jong*

(Living Tree Poetry)

I cried.

Cried for all that seemed lost.
Cried for all that was not,
all the things hope
had me quietly expecting.

Cried for prayers
that appeared to be circling,
making spirals
in the vast and empty sky.

Cried so that pools collected
as winter rain at my feet,
until submerged
I floundered in their depth.

I cried.

Cried until my present grief
vaguely transformed,
and the future took a shape
I hadn't seen.

Cried until the waters
that consumed
lifted me on currents strong
to draw fresh breath.

Cried for loss still bitter
but which I swallowed as a seed
to see what if given time
it might become.

I cried.

Cried for dreams that
dissolved as morning mist
as painfully I removed
their rose-coloured tints.

And cried for the re-visioning
necessary for grief
to create something new
out of loss.

And I cried for the new,
as I lay not ready yet
to surrender the old.
But prepared to love no matter what.

Endnotes

1 Chapters not attributed to other authors are written by Silvia Purdie.

2 Thomas Attig, *How We Grieve: Relearning the World* (Oxford University Press, 2011), 57-58.

3 William Worden, *Grief Counselling and Grief Therapy: A Handbook for the Mental Health Practitioner, 4th ed.* (London: Routledge, 2010).

4 Steve Moore, "A graceful goodbye: the best way to begin a ministry is by ending well." *Leadership Journal,* vol. 23, Issue 3 (2002): 84.

5 Margaret Holloway, *Negotiating Death in Contemporary Health and Social Care* (Bristol: Policy Press, 2007), 71.

6 Holloway, 72.

7 Stroebe & Schut, 1999, discussed by David G. McNeish, "Grief Is a Circular Staircase: The Uses and Limits of Models of Grief in the Pastoral Care of the Bereaved." *Practical Theology,* vol. 6, issue 2 (2013): 190–203.

8 Worden describes repressed or 'masked' grief in those who "experience symptoms and behaviors that cause them difficulty, but they do not recognize the fact that these symptoms or behaviors are related to the loss." Worden, *Grief Counselling and Grief Therapy,* 144.

9 Marsha Wiggins Frame, "Relocation and Well-Being in United Methodist Clergy and Their Spouses: What Pastoral Counselors Need to Know." *Pastoral Psychology,* vol. 46, issue 6 (Jul 1998): 415-430, 426.

10 David G. McNeish, "Grief Is a Circular Staircase: The Uses and Limits of Models of Grief in the Pastoral Care of the Bereaved." *Practical Theology,* vol. 6, issue 2 (2013):190–203, 192.

11 Nancy J. Moules & Jon K. Amundson, "Grief – an invitation to inertia: A narrative approach to working with grief." *Journal of Family Nursing,* vol. 3, issue 4 (1997): 378-393, 378.

12 "An 'inner representation' of the deceased slowly replaces the external, physical relationship we once shared with the lost person, place, or thing." (32) This can "provide us with a source of continuing strength and insight as we adapt to the loss and reengage life in new ways." (33). Michael K. Girlinghouse, *Embracing God's Future without Forgetting the Past: A Conversation about Loss, Grief, and Nostalgia in Congregational Life,* (Augsburg Fortress, Publishers, 2019).

13 Henry Cloud, *Necessary Endings: The employees, businesses, and relationships that all of us have to give up in order to move forward* (Harper Business, 2011, Kindle Edition).

14 Tokerau Joseph, Masters and PhD theses, University of Otago: https://ourarchive.otago.ac.nz/handle/10523/9335 and https://ourarchive.otago.ac.nz/handle/10523/4591.

15 Jonathan Te Rere's published writings are (all available online): "Hihita me ngā Tamariki o te Kohu", a chapter on Māori Presbyterian origins in Paterson et al., *Mana Māori and Christianity* (2012) "A Bicultural Church – an Amorangi Perspective", in *Bicultural Church, Candour Magazine,* issue 13, July 2014 (PCANZ) "The Dissipation of Indigeneity Through Religion", Master's thesis, University of Otago, 2009.

16 Amorangi is one of the strands of ministry in the PCANZ. Amorangi are ordained local clergy, mostly non-stipendary.

17 'Kanohi ki te kanohi' means face to face, in person.

18 Robyn's writings are on her Chirmac website: 'Dislocation – Disconnection': https://www.chirmac.co.nz/dislocation-disconnection/ 'Memory and Place': https://www.chirmac.co.nz/memory-and-place/.

19 Ezekiel uses the phrase 'Son of Man' for himself, and it is central to his self-understanding as a prophet: "Therefore groan, son of man! Groan before them with broken heart and bitter grief." (Ezekiel 21:6, NIV).

20 In Protestant churches Jesus tends to be portrayed as serene and ever calm, while in Catholic churches Jesus's agonies are portrayed in extreme and often gruesome detail (e.g. in the Stations of the Cross). Both place Christ's emotional experience outside the realm of ordinary human emotion.

21 In both these sections, Paul is exegeting scripture. Romans 10 is a revisioning of Deuteronomy 30's call to choose life or choose death. Ephesians 4:7-10 exegetes Psalm 68 in the light of Pentecost.

Section Two:
Complicated Grief in Ministry Transitions

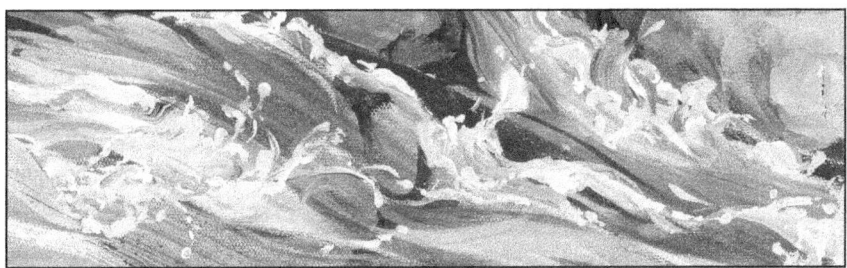

Most people work through the tasks of grief with resilience. They have some bad days but on the whole continue to function OK, and feel joy as well as sorrow.[1] However for other people grief dominates their lives. They get bogged down deep in it and continue for a long time to feel intensely angry or guilty, desperately sad or locked into rituals that remind them of the person who has died. Grief theorists now talk about 'complicated' instead of 'pathological' grief. Some things make the work of grieving more difficult, such as having several deaths to deal with at once, or a lack of social support or acknowledgement. The more traumatic the death, and the more difficult the previous relationship was, the harder grief is. Complicated grief is not just about loss of relationship, it threatens a person's sense of safety and undermines their framework of meaning.

I explore these five aspects of complicated grief in relation to ending a ministry:

a. multiple loss – exile

b. ambivalent attachment – 'the wheat and the weeds'

c. trauma – forced exit

d. disenfranchised grief – grieving alone

e. crisis of meaning – calling

For each aspect I relate the thinking of grief theorists to the ending of a ministry. I connect this with my own personal experience, and draw in narratives from the Bible which inform and potentially transform the experience of grief. And for each aspect there is a personal story and reflection from a minister's own experience.

Exile: Multiple Loss

People who are hit by several deaths over a short space of time find grieving far more difficult than when deaths are spread out. The human heart gets overwhelmed when grief "piles up," as an article on grief for nursing home staff put it.[2] Multiple loss is identified by grief researchers as a major factor in traumatic grief. William Worden notes that when "the sheer volume of people to be grieved was overwhelming … it can seem easier to close down the mourning process altogether." This can be described as bereavement overload, or compound grief.[3]

The ending of a ministry involves losses on many levels simultaneously; the loss of a job, an income, a role with status. Gail Irwin quotes a church leader reflecting on the challenges for retiring ministers: "Clergy want to be loved and needed; that's part of why they go into ministry. Often their identity is wrapped up in their vocation. They have a hard time understanding their role after retirement."[4] When I have left a parish I had to grieve not only for the role I had held but for all my hopes and plans, the mission goals we had not yet accomplished, things that might collapse without me, people who might leave, things left unfinished.

Because housing is often provided by parishes for their ministers, leaving a position can mean losing the family home. Leaving may mean changing towns, new schools for the kids, a raft of challenges for families such as spouse's employment, loss of friendships, sport clubs etc. If the pastor does not move immediately into a new appointment or other job there could be financial stress.

Paramount over all other losses, however, is the loss of community. When a person dies the community mourns the loss of that person. When a pastor leaves, she must mourn the loss of the entire community. Ministers who have retired speak of this ongoing grief. John Buchanan's evocative article "Sunday morning blues" describes how he struggles every Sunday morning with missing his preaching work and how when we walks past his old church "something tugs at my heart." When he and his wife were ill, "we missed the constant, familiar strength of the congregation we love." However, he recognises that in "the painful process of letting go I am learning to let the church continue to be the church, performing a ministry that began before it allowed me to serve and continued after I left."[5]

The pain of grief after a ministry has felt to me like exile, a sudden expulsion from a place of honour at the heart of a community to a place of almost total exclusion. For those whose ministry ends through the disciplinary processes of the church, the banishment is absolute if their names are removed from the list of ministers. Yet even those who held high-profile leadership positions and were greatly loved and admired in the church have spoken to me of feeling cut off when they stepped down from their role, a sense of becoming invisible when they no longer hold the status of their position.

In pre-modern times, belonging in community was literally a matter of life and death. Those who were cast out of community lived a half-life, fraught with danger, with no place and no identity. It is fascinating in the Gospels that so many of the people Jesus spoke with, touched and healed were outcasts, people on or outside the margins of society. He seemed to have a special interest in people whom others did not see.

I'd like to highlight two biblical leaders who experienced exile. First, Miriam, whose exile only lasted a week but was a major crisis for her, her family, and the whole community, in Numbers 12. After challenging Moses on his choice of bride, Miriam and Aaron experience God's anger, which manifests in sudden leprosy over Miriam's body. Aaron and Moses both cry out in fear and beg God to heal her; leprosy was in Aaron's mind like a deformed stillborn baby, a death as though she never lived. Scripture does not tell us how Miriam felt about it, how she survived 7 days shut out of the camp, and how the experience affected her. There is no further record of her speaking or exercising leadership. I feel a real sadness for her, injustice that she was judged so harshly, carrying the punishment for her brothers, and grief that this ended her leadership.

Secondly, John, exiled to the island of Patmos (Revelation 1:9) by Roman persecution. Looking at photos of his cave on the hillside it all looks rather idyllic, but it must have been a harsh experience for him to be removed from the community where he had been in ministry, presumably to die cut off and alone. While he lived, however, he prayed, and he wrote what he saw and what he heard from God. He continued his ministry in a very different way. His suffering and exile broadened his perspective so that he wrote to all the churches, with a vision larger than time and space. John lost everything and everyone he loved, but the presence of Jesus with him in his exile enabled him to find a new calling and purpose.

I Will Sing the Songs of Zion – *Henry Mbambo*

Rev. Henry Mbambo, from Zambia, is the minister at St David's Union Church in Ashburton.

• • •

Leaving my culture and coming to New Zealand, the grief is the ongoing loss of sharing our lives with our extended families. I am both here and in Zambia at the same time. The connections are highlighted when something happens back home or something happens here, and you see how you are missing out.

I sometimes feel like Nehemiah. You hear what has happened in your land, and there is nothing you can do but to pray. At the same time you have a longing to go back and participate in the rebuilding of the wall.

Our children were young when we came here, and one was born here. They adjusted quickly. The life that they know is here. They are more at home here than myself and my wife.

My wife is the first born in her family, and that means a lot culturally. As the eldest, she is the one who needs to step in and makes decisions on behalf of the family. Her parents are retired, and her role would include making decisions about family land and property. But she cannot do that because we are so far away. Her younger brother has taken on some of this role, but sometimes she has to step in. It is a stress and a grief for her.

For me, I am fortunate that I am not the eldest. My brother has that role. But as the only minister in the family I am called the 'Shepherd' of the family and they ask for my opinion before every big decision. The English translation would be: "What does the shepherd of the family say about this?" There have been times when decisions have been changed because I brought in another perspective. But it is difficult for me not being there.

If I could compare myself to the Israelites, I have a continuing sense of being in exile. I don't want to say that God has sent me into exile but I am following God's leading, wherever God is leading me. For as long as God continues to lead me in this place, I will do as much as I can do, God willing, even if I feel that I am in exile.

My sense of exile is literal sometimes. I cannot sing the songs of my motherland, because those songs are strange in this place. I cannot worship the way I worshipped in Zion. Language is very important, especially when it comes to worship. It is communicated in the songs, in the readings. My wife and I have continued to use our language in our home, which is helpful to us. I use the Tumbuka version of the Bible, that is my language. That helps me to be grounded. And I have a hymnbook: *Hymns for Malawi* – Malawi is my mother's country. So not only do I have the Bible from my Zambian context, I have a Malawi hymnbook from my mother's context. These helped me to deal with the grief.

The other thing that helped us, particularly when we were in Dunedin, was meeting up with other Africans. We had quite a strong African community there. I was part of the chaplaincy (unofficially) at the university, attending to international students. Meeting with international students, particularly Africans, helped me to deal with my grief, as I was dealing with their grief. We were grieving together, sharing experiences. I was able to speak and write in African languages, to help the African students feel somewhat at home. During that time two African students died. I liaised with their families and participated in the funerals, mourning in the way Africans mourn.

When you are in grief you can relate to life in exile. Historically we know that where there have been exiles, grief has been present, but there are always elements of hope. Hope is different from optimism. I know many people say they are optimists. While I respect that, I say that I am a person of hope. I am hopeful. Being hopeful does not mean that you ignore the reality on the ground. As in the Psalms of lament, being hopeful means that at the end of the day you are going to say: "Even if I go through this grief, I am still being held by God. I am in God's hands. And at the end of the day I will sing a new song. I don't know when it will happen, but it will happen. I am going to sing the songs of Zion again."

The Wheat and the Weeds:
Ambivalent Attachment

William Worden states that "The type of relationship that most frequently hinders people from adequately grieving is the highly ambivalent one with unexpressed hostility."[6] The more complicated your relationship was with the person who has died, the more complicated your grieving for them will be.

One helpful tool in understanding this is attachment theory. This is best known in relation to babies and toddlers: we form a foundational pattern of inner security through how safe we felt and how predictably we were cared for when we were very young. But all our relationships our whole life long can be looked at in terms of attachment. Some people we feel close to, no matter if we haven't talked for ages. Other relationships we feel ambivalent about, perhaps intimate one minute and conflicted the next; we may feel rejected or rejecting. After a death the quality of our relationship continues to shape our grief journey. A "relationship that was fraught with ambivalence, even hostility, may be more problematic to grieve than one that was generally harmonious."[7] I knew a woman who complained bitterly about her husband for years, but after he died she missed him terribly and became too anxious to go out alone.

I can easily apply this to ministry positions. When I left a church where I had a harmonious mutually supportive ministry I felt sad, and I missed them, but I was OK. When I left a church after some quite difficult experiences it was much harder to 'move on', spiritually and emotionally. I needed time out from ministry, and professional support from counselling and spiritual direction. My grief was complicated because my attachment to the parish was ambivalent, complicated by unmet expectations, conflict and rejection.

Biblically this makes sense through the frame of Jesus' parable of the wheat and the weeds, Matthew 13:24-30. "Let the weeds grow with the wheat," the landowner said. Jesus had plenty of experience of both the good and the bad, the ambivalence of human relationships and the dark side of good intentions. This parable says to me to not get too upset about the broken promises, divided loyalties, hard hearts and refusal to change. "You get that," says Jesus, who sees weeds in me even more than I see them in others. "You can't always tell the wheat from the weeds as they are growing, and trying to uproot the weeds would damage the wheat." By their fruits you will know them (Matthew 7:20), and what is good and true will outlast the rest

(Philippians 4:8). In God's hands the ambivalence and brokenness of human life, including church life, will dissolve away leaving only what endures: faith, hope and love (1 Corinthians 13:13). "Don't stress about it," says Jesus.

A Friend But Not a Friend

(name withheld)

I found Silvia's chapter on ambivalent attachment especially interesting. It resonated with me and took me back to the final couple of months in one of my ministries. I remember feeling deeply hurt, and the conversations I was having at that time highlighted for me an ambivalence in the whole set-up of pastoral relationship between minister and parishioners. I found my journal entries from that time, and I would like to share these excerpts with you.

• • •

I had my last pastoral visit with Eric *(name changed)* today. I have loved visiting Eric, he is so interesting, such a servant heart. Today he talked again about his daughter, who would be my age if she had not been so suddenly taken from him. We talked again about his wife, and the bone-deep demanding process he had been through with her dementia and death, which I had walked alongside him, perhaps filling a little of the hole left by his daughter's absence. And we talked about my time in the parish.

Eric is a staunch advocate of proper process, and values church tradition. As numbers attending worship have declined due to deaths and illness of his friends, Eric felt that if only worship was more traditional, more people would attend. After last year's AGM he wrote a formal letter of complaint to the church council about my informal leadership style of the meeting, and his concerns about worship attendance.

Yet he obviously feels a depth of affection for me personally. Today, on my last visit, he spoke of his gratitude to me. With a tear in his eye he presented me with a small family heirloom, a little vase, which he wanted me to have as a parting gift. I accepted it, reluctantly. I decided that to refuse it would be unnecessarily hurtful.

We went on to talk about the ending of my ministry. Then Eric said that if it had come to a congregational vote, he would have voted for me to go. I did not know how to respond to this, and left his home feeling hurt and confused. I put his vase in a box. What will I do with it now?

This mix of affection and rejection is a strange thing to process. I feel affection for him, and admiration for his long legacy of leadership and service. I am aware of the transference of his attachment to his daughter onto me, and my own counter transference from my deceased father. His long grief that

I shared through 5 years of close pastoral ministry created a unique bond. However, I believe that he has struggled to attribute to me as a woman minister the authority that he would be have given to a male minister; of his long years I was the first woman minister he has had. He struggled to release his commitment to a particular way of being church, and began to see me as a threat to that. He blamed me for the absence of his peers from church, at an emotional level, despite knowing that their deaths were not my fault. Church was not what it used to be, and that deeply affected him. His own declining health also played a role. Perhaps he feels let down by God, and this got transferred onto me.

Finishing is hard. All these 'ending' pastoral conversations are leaving me confused. What am I as a minister in relationship? I am a friend, and not a friend. I am a blank slate onto which people project their hopes and loves and hurts. And then I leave and it is over. I am a paid professional, in a role, but I am also being me. I am paid for a service which is friendship, but it is not a real friendship, for it is essentially one-way. These people for whom I care do not have to care for me. They do not have to ask about me, or listen to my truth. I am there as the minister, I am there for them. But at what cost? Am I willing to enter again into the fundamental non-honesty of the pastoral relationship?

I know these people so well. I understand what drove them to push me away. I have compassion for them; I can honestly say "Forgive them, Father, for they know not what they do." The issues they thought we were arguing about were not the real issues at all. But they were so committed to their position that I had to leave.

There's a voice in me of righteous indignation. I achieved so much! How could they not see that? How could they not value me? How could they pull the rug out from under me? It feels unfair. I feel it catching under my ribs as physical pain. I feel weight pushing on the back of my neck.

What hurts the most is not that some in the church struggled to work with me (though that hurts my pride), or that they disagreed with me about my role (though I believe their views were patriarchal). They could have raised those issues and we could have found a process for how to work together. But some in the parish leadership consistently communicated to me that my opinions did not count. My approval was not required. There was no commitment to agreement. My voice was discounted. I was simply overruled. The powerlessness of this deeply affected me. It undermined my sense of being safe at work. I could not trust that my views or wellbeing were seen as important.

Eric's ultimate rejection of my ministry, despite the richness of our pastoral relationship, hurts in a way I did not expect and cannot quite describe. Teasing out this complex web of relational and spiritual and institutional facets is not easy. I need to acknowledge both the reality of the love that existed in my pastoral relationship with this man, as well as the pain. When I am in 'pastoral' mode my empathy for the person I am with tends to speak louder than my own emotions. So empathising with the motivations which led him to ultimately reject my ministry has the potentially to be doubly traumatising for me. My task is to disengage from this pastoral empathy, to the extent where I might disagree with him, even feel angry with him. A cognitive understanding of the dynamics of patriarchy and the patterns of homeostasis and the functioning of power within the church are helpful to me in that. As a patriarch in a conservative system, Eric wielded considerable power. He did not ask me to leave but he had ways of making his concerns known which had real influence on parish leadership, and functioned to diminish my authority and capability for leadership and ministry in that context. So grieving for my relationship with him is complicated for me.

Pastoral ministry is not a straightforward role or employment. The boundaries are blurred. We talk about being family, the body of Christ. We offer friendship, and the minister leads in offering herself in warmth and affection. I do, anyway. But I have discovered this year that this is only sustainable when I feel well supported by parish leadership. I can't do this alone, or in opposition with core leadership. It just doesn't work. The ambivalence between friendship and professional role stretches too far and I fall in-between.

Forced Exit: Trauma

Grief researchers tell us that the more traumatic the death of a loved one, the more difficult grief will be. In ministry terms this means that the more stressful things were, and the more stressful the ending of the ministry, the more time and energy is needed for recovery.

Feeling unsafe in ministry is a traumatic experience. This can involve a range of experiences that damage relationships and undermine a minister's authority and confidence. Bullying is an ongoing pattern of personal attack, exclusion from decision making, or subtle threats and intimidation. Sadly this is not an uncommon experience for women in ministry, despite my denomination's acceptance of women in ordained roles for many decades.[8]

Perhaps the most traumatic experience in ministry is being forced to leave. There are various ways this happens. Some parishes can no longer afford a stipend. Some parishes close down, putting the minister out of a job. Ministers can violate ethical standards and the church cuts the pastoral tie. Some ministers resign due to ill health (often termed 'early retirement'). And some pastors end up feeling as though they have no choice but to resign. 'Forced exit' is described by researchers as deeply traumatic and damaging for ministers and their families. "Pastors who had left ministry under circumstances not of their own choosing, or who felt that they had in some way been mistreated, mourned the loss of pastoral ministry most intensely."[9] A study of clergy whose parish closed (or 'died') found them to be vulnerable to a sense of failure and shame which threatened their identity.[10]

Of these possible scenarios, forced resignation is particularly damaging. It is also illegal; or it would be if ministers were employed, which we are not. Constructive Dismissal is a violation of New Zealand employment law and is grounds for a personal grievance claim against the employer, where a 'dismissal' is 'constructed' out of events that led up to, and ended with, an employee's resignation. For ministers, "Forced termination is both the process and result of psychological, emotional, social, and spiritual abuse directed toward ministry leaders by members of a congregation or denominational leaders, such that there is no other option for the minister but to leave the post."[11] Research in the USA found that 25% of ministers experienced this during their careers.[12] It can be very damaging; Donald Hicks cites a nation-wide research in 1999 which found that a massive 45% of pastors who had experienced forced termination did not return to church related vocations.[13]

The biblical word that resonates the most for me in terms of dealing with trauma is 'crushed.' In the Old Testament 'crushed' means total defeat, as in David's song of victory in 2 Samuel 22:38; either Israel is celebrating the crushing of their enemies or they are themselves feeling defeated, crushed by God. Crushing is also the process by which wheat becomes bread, olives become oil, and grain is offered as a sacrifice on God's altar (Leviticus 2:14). It is important in Isaiah's prophesies of the coming Messiah, who will be "crushed for our iniquities" (Isaiah 53:5) but "will not be crushed until he has established justice in the earth" (Isaiah 43:4, NRSV). In 2 Corinthians Paul describes himself and his friends as being crushed to the point of despair by attack (2 Corinthians 1:8) and yet he goes on to declare that "We are afflicted in every way, but not crushed" (2 Corinthians 4:8, NRSV).

This paradox of being crushed and yet not crushed is central to the Christian experience of trauma. The metaphor of crushing reveals God's process of transforming people, like grains of wheat become flour which becomes bread which becomes the body of Christ which was broken for us in the greatest act of love. This is a circularity in which human pain is matched and held within Christ's suffering. The work of grieving in the aftermath of trauma, informed by the Christian faith, is a work of willing sacrifice to unwelcome suffering, surrendered into a power made perfect in weakness.

Faamagaloga: Forgiveness
– *Mua and Linda Strickson-Pua*

Reverend Mua and Linda Strickson-Pua describe themselves as Pasifika Urban Archivists (PUA), Poet Healers Educators Ministers Workers, and Pasifika Urban Street Historians (PUSH). Their inter-generational community development encompasses diverse contexts, including broadcasting and media. They are leading in the contemporary arts, especially poetry and spoken word with Māori and Pasifika young people, based in Auckland.[14]

Mua's Gafa Whakapapa genealogy is Ngāti Hāmoa, Cantonese Saina, Irish and French, born here in Aotearoa Niu Sila. Aiga Pua from nu'u village PapaSataua Savaii in Samoa and Laiman Canton in China. Aiga Purcell from nu'u village Malaela Aleipata Upolu in Samoa also Ireland and France.

Linda's whakapapa to dad Fred Strickson Peterborough Fulham to London England; and mum Ann Hull from Southampton England – hence Engari English Ngāti Pākehā descent. We are both children of the migration.

• • •

Faamagaloga [Samoan] – forgiveness,
Kuo fakamolemole'i [Tongan] – forgiven,
Te murunga hara [Māori] – forgiveness

"So'o le fau i le fau"
Join hibiscus fibre to hibiscus fibre: unity is strength.

[Fa'asamoa Alaga'upu – Samoan Proverb]

"Ehara taku toa i te toa takitahi,
engari kē he toa takitini."

I come not with my own strengths, but bring with me the gifts, talents and strengths of my family, tribe and ancestors.

[Whakatauki – Māori Proverb]

"Papa Mua, when you are in a dark room, turn on the light!"

[Pasifika urban Whakatauki Alaga'upu , Proverb from our Mokos]

Kangaroo Court

By Rev. Mua and Linda Strickson-Pua

> *Verse 1*
>
> We
> Linda and Mua Strickson-Pua
> Ngāti Pākehā Ngāti Hāmoa
> England Samoa
> Tangata Whenua Tangata Pākehā Tagata Hamoa
> Aotearoa New Zealand Niu Sila
> Faletua Minister's wife Faifeau Minister
> Anglican Presbyterian
> Kerisiano Kalisitiane
> Kavaitiano Christian
> Ngāti human tribe
> our family of humanity
> Atua fa'afoaga Fakatupu Otua God's creation
>
> *Verse 2*
>
> We
> were called
> to Tautua serve
> our Pacific Churches
> Autalavou Rangatahi
> young people Youth Ministry
> their families, communities
> and nations
> of Cook Islands, Niue,
> Samoa, Tokelau, Tuvalu,
> Afakasi mixed heritage
> inter-cultural inter-generational
> New Zealand born
> throughout Aotearoa Niu Sila
> Atua Otua Ariki of Alofa Aroha Agape
>
> *Verse 3*
>
> We
> instigated
> Miti Fa'aliga
> dreams and visions
> Misi Visone
> dreams and visions

Moemoea Matakite
dreams and visions
continuing the pioneering
Pacific urban Ministry
faith traditions of migrant parents
Fa'atuatuaga Hope Ministry
three glorious years
Atua's creation our shared Ministry

Verse 4

We
were summoned
by Mātua Kaumātua
esteemed Ministers and Elders
informed a review
would take place
they were not happy
when I requested
Linda's presence
for ours
was a shared Ministry
together with
Creator and Creation
praise Atua

Verse 5

We
arrived
to be informed
we were not permitted
to speak to respond
or engage
we
were to sit
be quiet and listen
Linda and I
sat by ourselves
facing thirty to fifty
Pacific leaders
mindful of Atua's presence

Verse 6

We
endured
a morning session
of rebuke reproof
recrimination
I cried silently publicly
Linda was stoic
a deep sense
of disappointment
washed over us
a realisation
how much more
change was required
we were being removed
Atua answered our Lotu

Verse 7

We
were invited
to share in lunch
on my way
I stopped at the toilet
silent ones passed
on their words of encouragement
while critics freely shared
their views supposedly privately
I would name this experience
Toilet Theology
meanwhile in the hall
Linda sat alone
on a table
reserved for us
away from the main table
conspicuously
down the other end
next to the Exit sign
Atua heard our Karakia

Verse 8

We
a week later
would meet
with Rev. Papa Leute Sio
and Rev. Papa Ned Ripley
beloved faith fathers Toe'ina
excellent servant leaders
role models of our Ekalesia,
Falelotu Hāhi Church
lovingly walked us through the
Spiritual Cultural Political
Pacific Fa'avae Tikanga Pasifika
world views come understanding
protocol, process, praxis practice
sharing their experiences, insights,
Poto wisdom and reflections of their
deep love for Autalavou Rangatahi
the future of our Church
our Tagata Pasifika
our family of humanity
our loving Atua
appealing inspiring
nurturing challenging
to uplifting Linda and I
not to walk away from our Ministry
but to work to Tautua serve
outside of the Church
with Creator amongst Creation
today over 30 years
of Ordained Ministry
today over 40 years
of community work
all honour and glory to a loving God
Fa'atuatuaga Hope Art praxis community Ministry
Miti Fa'aaliga Misi Visone
Moemoea Matakite

Poementary:

- A painful spiritual emotional and intellectual experience grieving for one's Ministry and one's Fa'atuatua/faith. For me personally it took five years before I could laugh at this – which Samoans will understand

- These Luke Gospel readings came flooding as we experienced our nightmare moments: Luke 9:57-62 the cost of following Jesus, Luke 22:7-30 the last supper, Luke 22:66-71 Jesus before the council, and Luke 23:1-25 Jesus' trial before Pilate.

- Praise Atua for Linda Strickson-Pua's deep faith courage and never doubting our shared Ministry response of Fa'atuatuaga/Hope Poto/Wisdom and Filemu/Peace [Proverbs 31: 28-31 A wife of noble character]

- "I wish I could speak Samoan now, and I'm sure all the rest of my family do too." (Joe Stanley)[15]

Fa'anoanoa, Ngaru, Feau, Grieving

Fa'anoanoa
Ngaru
Feau
grief
grieving
Exit of Ministry
faith journey
feeling rejected
by God's people
God's Church
possibly by Atua God

Asking Atua
those hard questions
drowning in human emotions
spiritual yearnings
cultural rejections
political praxis
biblical beatings
theological commiserations
crucified Atua Otua Akua
Iesu Sisu Jesus on a cross

This theme of grief
loss māmae forgiveness

loss called into Ministry
loss experiences off and on
loss on a Ministry journey
we hide our true emotions
we hide our raw anger
we hide our disappointments
we hide our vulnerability
not wanting the Church uncomfortable
whilst denying our own pain

Miti

New Zealand Born Dream

By Aiga Strickson-Pua three generations

TUPULAGA TOLU Generation 3

Fast flying shooting star
changes through the past
goes on to the future
never stops forever, Alofa

*[Cheden Sofi Ah Yek Strickson-Pua 6yrs
Atali'i grandson]*

TUPULAGA LUA Generation 2

With these eyes I have seen the past
with this mind I see the future
with these feet I create stability
with these hands I create change

*[Feleti Sofi Strickson-Pua 27yrs
Atali'i son tama]*

TUPULAGA TASI Generation 1

Dreams open the door
freeing our searching spirit
allowing us to fulfil
a life of Alofa

*[Muamua Sofi Strickson-Pua 54yrs
Tamamatua grandfather]*

Poementary:

- First Aiga Tupulaga family 3 generations poem to be published in Aotearoa Niu Sila. Aiga Tupulaga inter-generational has been a strong theme in our Ministry currently doing inter-generational poementary with our children and grandchildren. Blessed to do inter-generational community Ministry with students, families, communities and nations.

- One of our tags is *Art Of Aiga* (family) hence part of our shared family Ministry is our Aiga Strickson-Pua art exhibitions, storytelling, comedy, Siva dance, hip hop, poetry, performances for community gigs to corporate gigs. Guest lecturing at universities, teaching sessions at schools and community presentations sharing our Fa'atuatuaga message of Hope.

- We were blessed with our Aiga Tupulaga Tolu 3 Generations of being a Broadcasting Ministry family on the airwaves. My father Sofi Pua was the first Samoan broadcaster with New Zealand Broadcasting Corporation. Fofoga Samoa *Calling Samoa* programme 1959-80s with my brother Sofi Ulugia-Pua we produced and presented *New Zealand Born Crew* on NZBC. Our radio name was a homage to our father on Reo Atamotu 1593 AM Pacific Youth Ministry Auckland. Previous to this Linda with our children Ejay and Feleti we did the Pacific one-hour weekly show at Otago Student FM radio station late 1980s. Feleti at 11 years old was the youngest Radio DJ in Niu Sila Aotearoa with his own one hourly show the *Youngstas* – a hip hop word play on Young Stars – mid to late 1990s. Linda, Sofi and I were his producers. There is a lovely *School Journal* (part four number one 1998) cover photo of Triple F and radio partner in crime *Supa Fly* article 'Mikes Up' by Cynthia Todd Maguire pages 6 to 9. Even our Presbyterian newspaper did a story. Blessed Ministry memories.

Fa'atuatuaga Hope

We offer this poementary commentary of Spiritual Cultural Political reflections of grieving Exit and Transition of one's Ministry.

Linda and I instigated the Dreams and Visions programme to address New Zealand Born issues of the day 1990 to 1992. Radically we went into Pacific parishes around Aotearoa Niu Sila doing poetry workshops to explore express and empower our Rangatahi and Autalavou for their Malaga Ola life journey. This was an honour a privilege and yes a blessing to contribute to an exciting dynamic Pacific urban Ministry of social justice and social change.

30 years later *Miti* (the Samoan word for dreams) and *Fa'aaliga* for visions – also linked with revelation how appropriate. *Fa'atuatuaga* hope has been a

major theme of our Ministry. Now the *Gagana Samoa* the Samoan language aspect begins to open old doors reclaimed reconnected and redeemed – especially when making that linguistical and political link with Te Reo Māori – hence our Pasifika Tuakana role to *Gafa* to *Whakapapa* to Tangata Whenua Māori – in our historical Christian covenant relationship Te Tiriti o Waitangi partnership.

For Linda and myself, we acknowledging Creator is not only in the Church. We truly believe in Atua being in Creation means outside reconnected reclaimed redeemed. We the members of Christ body are no longer in denial or in hiding but with Atua's Holy Spirit we are prepared to face the challenges of life's struggles in a secular post-modernist technological neoliberalism context. We need to be outside to be the salt the light amongst creation. Jesus Christ is our bridge with Atua and redemption, allowing us to transcend the Va the space through Wairuatanga the Holy Spirit the graciousness of Atua. We hope to assist the current and on-going discussions of what it means to be the Church the body of Christ in communion as we attempt to understand decolonisation and the Gospel for social justice and change in Aotearoa Niu Sila New Zealand.

Fa'afetai lava thanks to the Pasifika Ekalesia for sending us out to engage traditional gangs to street gangs, teen sex workers abuse survivors, drug addicts to P labs, clubs pubs weddings and funerals, mental health and wellbeing suicide intervention, violence prevention, education to healing, poverty, unions, high performance sports Chaplains, Fa'afafine Gay and Lesbian communities, broadcasting documentaries TV and films, Pasifika urban street history projects, Pasifika artists communities. And ten years being interim moderator and resource Minister for St. Pauls Presbyterian Waiheke island – again praise Atua.

Fa'afetai lava thank you Silvia for the invitation to participate in your research for Exit and Transition in Ministry. This has allowed Linda and I to share our experience of exit allowing closure and healing and then to celebrate our many years of ministry. Thirty years on I am now able to laugh at the learnings but in a positive way. As NZ-born Samoan we also address our Samoan parents' cultural world views and practices and navigate how we get through together Fa'atasi – unity united – in Māori kotahitanga. Amongst our Pacific traditional conservative side of the Presbyterian Aiga/Whanau there is a Spiritual Cultural wall of silence to overt reactions of Shame. Since graduation we have talked to Pasifika and Pākehā ordinands who have not been appointed or chosen, or rejected after a placement. We honour the deep hurt, sometimes loss of Faith and the anger that has been shared with Linda and myself. The Pasifikans could not speak out because the conservative theology stated – you were not chosen because Atua did not choose you. This became a Fakama/embarrassment for the Ministry family and extended Aiga/Whanau. This amazing Taonga of Grieving, Exit and Transition begins another new level of awareness, education and Christian Best Practice phase for our Church and wider dialogues, discourse and discussions – praise Atua.

We acknowledge two Cultural advisers Maori Kaumatua Dr Leland Ruwhiu and Samoan Toeinia Rev. Elama Maea. We never tire of thanking Rev. Roger [Faife'au] and Carole Wiig [Faletua] of St. Andrews Palmerston North Manawatu Presbytery and national Church for testing our calling and funding our training back in the 1980s – praise Atua.

I also want to especially thank my best friend partner patron and sponsor Linda Strickson-Pua. Linda has sacrificed financed and blessed our shared Non-Stipendiary Ministry to allow me to do the Tautua serving our people outside of the Church amongst creation with the Creator. All honour and glory to Atua.

> "God saved you by his grace when you believed. And you can't take credit for this; it is a gift from God."
>
> *[Ephesian 2:8, NLT]*

> "And let the peace that comes from Christ rule in your hearts.
> For as a member of one body you are called to live in peace.
> And always be thankful."
>
> *[Colossians 3:15, NLT]*

> "Ia outou faamalosi, ma outou loto telele,
> aua tou te fefefe, aua foi nei matatau, i o
> Iatou luma, aua Ieova lou Atua, lua te o
> faatasi ma ia. Na te le tuna oe,
> na te le lafoai ia te oa.
>
> *[Teuteronome 31:6, Samoan Bible, 1884][16]*

> So be strong and courageous!
> Do not be afraid and do not panic before them.
> For the Lord our God will personally go ahead of you.
> He will neither fail you nor abandon you.
>
> *[Deuteronomy 31:6, NLT]*

Grieving Alone: Disenfranchised Grief

"Grief is really a social process and is best dealt with in a social setting in which people can support and reinforce each other in their reactions to the loss," writes William Worden.[17] Where there is a lack of social support this is called 'disenfranchised' grief, where grief "remains hidden, unrecognized, or unhealed;"[18] others do not acknowledge or validate the loss and people grieve alone. After a miscarriage, for instance, a father's grief is often not acknowledged as much as the mother's.

A study of the impact of grief on hospital chaplains highlights the effects of disenfranchised grief. "When chaplains are overwhelmed by personal and professional losses and do not utilize adaptive behaviors, their grief tends to become hidden, poorly expressed, and unprocessed." Steven Spidell and colleagues researched what happens to chaplains when "grief begins to pile up in the workplace." They found that fatigue was the main symptom, but identified other 'red flags' as a sense of 'going through the motions,' or chaplains withdrawing into themselves.

One key question the researchers found helpful as an indicator of unresolved grief was asking chaplains what topics they avoided in their pastoral care. For parish ministers this is also a good question: what do we avoid? What do we find triggering? What do we find difficult to hear about? Spindell *et al.* were concerned for chaplains whose own grief is avoided, diminished, or unprocessed: "Chaplains may become at risk for burnout, or, at worst, vicarious traumatization."

Grieving the end of a ministry may be a form of disenfranchised grief. The church expects ministers to move immediately from one ministry position to the next. This disenfranchises their grief. I have personally found that people expected me to quickly 'let go' and 'move on' from each parish I left and immediately begin something new. There is a sudden ending of support systems such as supervision and ministers' groups. I found myself having to totally take responsibility for my own recovery, a rapid lesson in self-reliance which would have been made easier by more recognition from my denomination of the challenges of post-ministry grief. There is little curiosity about the experience of ending. Ministers forced to resign are typically required to keep silent about their experience and not given the opportunity to inform the congregation of the reasons for their resignation.[19]

It is difficult to speak about painful experiences in parish ministry. This is disenfranchised grief. I was reluctant to tell my family, especially my sons, because I do not want them to lose faith in the church. It hurt when my sons were relieved when I resigned, and I was afraid that my journey damaged their relationship with God. However, as I get older I find myself less compliant with the rules of politeness that govern church life, and the 'don't air the dirty laundry' cultural norm. I am more critical of 'passive aggressive' communication in the church, and less willing to choose silence in the face of bullying. As God the potter roughly handles his clay (e.g. Jeremiah 18), so these painful experiences form us, release us from our need to please everyone and keep everyone happy all the time, and find more courage in speaking up against injustice. This is how we recover from imposed silence and solitude in grief.

The story of Hagar in the desert in Genesis 16 is a moving one. Hagar has run away (a 'forced resignation'!), a victim of Sarai's unresolved grief around her own fertility. She finds herself lost, desperate and alone. And God meets her, speaks to her, blesses her with promise and a future. In return, she gives God a whole new name, El-Roi, God Sees. And her son's God-given name is Ishma-El, God Hears. When we grieve alone we sit in the rocks with Hagar and are found in the wilderness by the only One who can truly see and hear us.

That Sense of Being Alone – *Don Hall*

Rev. Don Hall is a retired Army Chaplain and Presbyterian Minister

• • •

When leaving the New Zealand Defence Force (NZDF) I was not fully prepared for the major shift in the focus and exercise of my ministry. In the military I worked in a collaborative environment, involving people in and out of uniform and covering many different branches. In this environment the chaplain's role is clearly established by 'law' and by lore. Those gone before have left a legacy which makes the chaplain's role readily accepted by people of varying faith and none. The chaplain is part of a team and contributes to that team. Chaplains minister to the whole person, which includes work, leisure and family life, and have some influence in bringing about change for service people and their families. Chaplains work mostly among those younger than them, and also minister to those in command.

Life in a suburban Presbyterian parish in Auckland was somewhat different. I used to say that I now ministered to the 'tired and retired.' I no longer had access to the 'whole person' and had little if any influence in shaping any change in the community. From having an influence in a wide community as I did in the NZDF, my ministry was now with individuals and within the church. I missed the collegial manner of working. I used to say that I walked down the stairs into the study, sat at my desk, the dog at my feet and the cat in the other chair, turned on the computer and I was at work. Nothing prepared me for the deep sense of 'being alone' in my ministry.

Now that I am retired, I have found many areas of interest: Rotary, RSA, being a board member of a community house, my garden, etc. I kept a connection with military chaplaincy, and was on the chaplaincy Advisory Council for a number of years. But there is still that sense of being alone.

I have not felt very involved with presbytery since I retired. I have been used for a couple of roles, but it seemed to me that presbytery cuts off those who are retired unless there is a job for them to do.

Crisis of Calling: Meaning and Purpose

For 63 years Jacob Dirk Epping was a pastor and author for the Christian Reformed Church. Back in 1963 he preaching a stirring message to a pastors conference: "Is there anyone here thinking of quitting the church? Granted that you can find reasons. They are not hard to find. But I can think of a better thing to do: stay! Christ does. And further — improve it, and do that by beginning with yourself." He referred to the apostle Paul who had been discouraged but what "loomed largest in his mind was the truth that he was called by the Holy One ... he was called; therefore he could do no other."[20]

This same attitude was woven through my training for ministry, and reaffirmed each time I was inducted into a parish. I am called by God, and I am called here and now to this place and this people. I was determined to be resilient, to stay the course, for I "could do no other." To come to a point of resigning from a ministry confronts this foundational life directive head-on. It is not just a readjustment of personal identity but of the foundations of faith, our convictions of a God who saves, who empowers, who protects. Feeling unsafe, undermined and struggling with physical and mental health is an faith crisis.

Grief theory describes this as an 'existential' component to grieving. "These spiritual adjustments can challenge the core of who we are and can be the most difficult to make. ... After a loss, our basic sense of trust can be shattered."[21] Psychologist Ronnie Janoff-Bulman highlights the deep assumptions that can be challenged by trauma and lass, especially those that make us feel safe in the world, that the world is meaningful or fair. She pointed out that, "It is those with the most positive pre-existing assumptions whose core schema are most deeply violated. Extreme negative events produce tremendous psychological upheaval and anxiety, for their inner worlds are shattered."[22] The church claims to be a safe place, of belonging, family, meaning and justice. When our experience contradicts that it is a profound grief.

This grief work is also theological work. As a minister of the Gospel my primary frame of reference is the Bible, which thankfully just so happens to be full of marvellous material for dealing with injustice, attack and grief. In scripture the goodness of God is always in tension with the brokenness of humanity. If we have idealistic expectations of the church, we did not get these from the pages of scripture! Betrayal, exile, imprisonment, and (heaven forbid!) even crucifixion are the stuff of faithful ministry. We just don't think it will happen to us.

The hardest part of this theological grief work is that for the most part it must be done alone. On the whole, I have not found my colleagues in active ministry to be keen for these conversations. Others who feel in exile from the church may be too wrapped in their own grief, or too sucked into bitterness, to be much help to me. My family got bored with the whole thing, 'over it' long before I was. Excellent spiritual direction has been, in my experience, an absolute necessity. Calling and overload, ambivalence and trauma and loneliness, these are all part of the story but they do not have the last word. God made us to be resilient, and gives us his Spirit "to strengthen and to guide, to warn and to revive."[23] We can, and do, recover from grief.

I Thought I Was Called – *Jill Kayser*

Jill Kayser was for 13 years the Kids Friendly Coach for the Presbyterian Church. She lives in Glendowie, Auckland, and is currently the Community Centre Manager & Transitional Ministry Leader at St Helier's Presbyterian Church.

I talked with Jill about the process of finishing as the national director of children and family ministry, and her transition into a challenging year of inner city chaplaincy, then chaplaincy in a retirement village. She talks about feeling diminished by loss while continuing to trust God and grow in faith. She describes her process of rethinking her understanding of calling.

• • •

Silvia: When you finished up with Kids Friendly you were farewelled, you were honoured by so many people. People were sad that you were leaving, and they expressed so much respect and love for you. And then – boom! Suddenly all those relationships ended, and it was almost like Jill Kayser just ceased to exist.

Jill: That's it. It was almost like attending my own funeral. But then I woke up and I wasn't dead! I thought that by taking six months to leave I could have more control of the grief and the transition and the inevitable changes. I read books and thought I was well versed in what was going to happen and how I was going to feel.

Silvia: You had done some anticipatory grief in the process of handing over?

Jill: It was huge to have to pack up the office and cull resources. I had hoped be able to mentor someone and show them the ropes and go through the files together, coach them. But none of that happened because the church did not reappoint straight away. That was really hard because then I couldn't go through that final process of handing over 'my baby.'

And then there was a major change of moving out of our house, my home of 29 years, because my new role was calling me to move home as well, into the inner city. I suppose that was a bit like a minister moving parish. So I packed down the Kids Friendly office, boxed up everything and threw out. And then I went home and packed down and threw out. It was a huge thing. It should have been cleansing but actually it was quite traumatic.

So then I moved into a new house and into a new job. And I sensed within two weeks that this new job was not going to be what I hoped it would be. I knew right from the beginning that this is going to be really, really hard: "Have I made a big mistake?" The whole sense of adventure and hopefulness and positivity was already threatened. I had a huge expectation of myself. And everyone was watching: "Let's see how she re-creates herself and what she's going to do now."

The whole year of that ministry was a year of grief. There was little joy in it. There was struggle and challenge and confrontation. I remember walking down to top-up my bus card and walking past a Glendowie bus and bursting into tears. I just wanted to go home and be embraced into the spirit of that place and be out of the strangeness. It was really being in exile, that ministry in the city.

I can't lay blame for my grief. I can't say: "This wasn't done right" or "That wasn't done right." It just 'is what it is.' I don't even blame my choices. I did feel called to leave Kids Friendly and I did feel called to take on the inner city chaplaincy,

Silvia: But you did end up questioning that. And you had multiple loss: not only did you lose this huge community, nationally and internationally, but also your local community and sense of home.

Jill: And my local church, I left that. But I chose it. None of it was imposed.

Silvia: That doesn't necessarily make it easier.

Jill: I had a sense of: "I can't grieve because I chose this."

Silvia: So you almost disenfranchised yourself?

Jill: I couldn't blame a parish or the national leadership. I couldn't blame anyone. I could only blame me, because I chose to do it. I didn't really have regrets because – it sounds so weird but I heard that voice, when I stood in my office one day, saying: "It's time to pack up your goods and go." And I followed that voice. I had come to the end of my time.

But through that year there were all these doubts about my calling: "What does it mean to be called?" and "Why did I think I was called?" and "Why is this so awful?" and "Why am I not rising to it?" and "Why is it all going wrong?" There was lots of angst and grief.

Silvia: The meaning questions and the why questions can be hard. Particularly for us in Christian ministry, it gets a divine edge to it, because it's not just us deciding for ourselves what matters to us but it is a conversation with God. So if it doesn't work out, or if it feels like it is dying – then what?

Jill: Your whole faith comes to question. Because then you say: "Well, who is God?" and "Am I deluded to think that I can hear God?" and "What does it mean to be called?" "I thought I was called!" I would say to myself.

Once a month I preached in an inner city congregation. That was very healing, being part of that little faith community. They held me and loved me and I needed that. I was able to work through a lot of my own questions in that preaching. I chose topics that helped me process, like 'Who am I?' and 'Who is God to me?' and 'What is calling?'

I came to the realisation that of course I am 'called.' But I am not called over and above anyone else. My calling is not superior to my child's calling or my friend's calling. I think that as Christians we are all called, every second of the day, to remember the path we are on, and to respond to the invitation to be agents of compassion and peace and love. That is our calling. Our calling actually isn't to be the Moderator or to be the Kids Friendly Coach or to be the inner city Chaplain. Our calling is to **be love** wherever we find ourselves and however we find ourselves. And so for me now that is my constant challenge – how to be that called person.

I still have doubts and questions and I second-guess. My current role *[at time of interview, as a retirement village chaplain]* is much less visible. I find it hard to be in a role that's not visible. And I have to keep saying, "Yes, but I am called to this for now." Whether you are on a stage or whether you are sitting next to someone's deathbed, you are called in the same way.

Silvia: You have been thrown into a small and humble place.

Jill: I am humbled in what I'm doing now. What I do now is just a daily thing. It's not a legacy I'm building. It's not a new thing. I'm not creating something, which I find hard in a way. It brings me back down to the basics. I'm just dealing with people in life and in death.

Silvia: So what have you learned about the experience of grief? You also have very much walked through grief with losing your best friend to cancer. Is grief at its core the same? Or have you experienced it differently in different situations?

Jill: I think it's the same. Grief is a sense of loss. To me it is a hole that enters into your life. And the hole doesn't ever cover up again. The hole doesn't go away. You just learn to walk around it. Every now and then you'll fall into it, because it so happens that you just do. And other times you circumnavigate it. But those holes become part of who you are. Of course the holes have different sizes; not all grief has the same intensity. The grief over my best friend's death has immense intensity and it endures. It pops up just about every day, the sense of loss. But the grief around Kids Friendly doesn't pop up every day, just when something reminds me or when I miss something. There are smaller holes and bigger holes. You have to learn to live with them. The real challenge that I've been thinking about lately is, "How do I live with them in a hopeful way?"

Sometimes I feel very sad and I feel diminished by that sadness. At the moment I am grappling with: "How do I work with that? How do I live with those holes so that they don't diminish me and take away my sense of hope?"

Silvia: Does your life expand around them? Or is the sadness a feeling of becoming less than we used to be?

Jill: There are moments where I have an experience and think: "Wow! I've got a sense of that: that joy, that living in the moment." But I don't think I have yet honed the art of living to my best with these holes. I have more learning to do, and I am open to that. These things are all part of my journey. They are not given to me to diminish me. They are given to me to expand me, but I haven't quite worked out how yet. I sense this holey-ness is inviting me to more holiness. It reminds me of Leonard Cohen's 'Anthem' (1992):

> Ring the bells that still can ring
> Forget your perfect offering
> There is a crack in everything
> That's how the light gets in.

Holiness indeed! My concept of God, and who God is and where God is, just increases and increases and increases, even though I feel diminished. This whole thing I've been through, although it has been a challenging journey for the last two or three years, it is not all bad. It has been like sharpening the iron. I am in this learning. Even though it is hard to be diminished by grief it's not bad.

Long Shadows – *Ana Lisa de Long*

(Living Tree Poetry)

Some sorrows cast long shadows,
some hurts hold us in their grasp
as long familiar friends.
Some crosses do not bear removal
but etch marks upon our skin.

Some things do not change.
Some matters never reach resolution
but ever circle the injured parts.
Some things cast long shadows
to sit with us in the dark.

Some things are not removed,
or repaired.
Some choices are to our detriment.
Some hurts are never fully healed
but reappear to haunt.

Some things cast long shadows.
Some sorrows evade the searching light.
Some pains we carry in black boxes
to replay in snatches
in our minds.

Some injuries result in limps.
Some sicknesses in long suffering.
Some burdens prove too much
and we yield with them
to the ground.

But...

But for the shadow we might
not recognise the light.
But for the hurts we might not hold
happiness as complete in itself
when it comes.

But for the frustrations
and the limits of our human interactions,
we might seek in each other
the fulfilment that only
God's wholeness can bring.

But for the injuries and the sicknesses
that this earth cannot heal
we might mistake this place
for heaven and now for
eternity.

But for the limps we cannot fix,
and the dark shadows we cannot remove,
we might not look out for each other
and walk on alone,
instead of arm in arm.

But for pains that revisit
and ego's wasted gains,
we might glorify ourselves
rather than recognise the
one who lifts us up.

Yes, some things cast long shadows.
And some of us reflect the light more
for the backdrop of the night.
And some of us see in the shadows
the shape of his wings.

Endnotes

1 George Bonanno's research shows that the majority of people who have experienced bereavement or major loss "maintain relatively stable, healthy levels of psychological and physical functioning," i.e. resilience. Their grief may cause "perturbations in normal functioning" but they "exhibit a stable trajectory of healthy functioning across time, as well as the capacity for generative experiences and positive emotions." George A. Bonanno, "Loss, Trauma and Human Resilience." *American Psychologist*, vol. 59, issue 1 (2004): 20–28, 21.

2 Steven Spidell, AnneMarie Wallace, Cindy L. Carmack, Graciela Nogueras-González, Crystal L. Parker, & Scott B. Cantor, "Grief in Healthcare Chaplains: An Investigation of the Presence of Disenfranchised Grief." *Journal of Health Care Chaplaincy*, vol. 17 (2011): 75–86.

3 Worden, *Grief Counselling and Grief Therapy*, 130.

4 Gail Irwin, "Blurring the lines." *Christian Century*, vol. 134, issue 3 (Feb 2017): 20-23, 21.

5 John M Buchanan, Sunday morning blues." *Christian Century*, vol. 130, issue 17 (Aug 2013): 3.

6 Worden, *Grief Counselling*, 127.

7 Holloway, *Negotiating Death*, 67.

8 Recent research with women ministers in the Presbyterian Church of Aotearoa New Zealand reported that "unsafe practices are occurring within the church for some women. Any form of bullying or inequality within the PCANZ is unacceptable – we would seek increased awareness of the issue and tools with which to recognise and prevent such behaviour." Vivienne Adair, *Women of the burning bush: still burning 25 years on*, PCANZ, 2018. https://www.presbyterian.org.nz/about-us/research-resources/research-papers/women-of-the-burning-bush-still-burning-25-years-on.

9 David Wood, "Exit Interview." *Christian Century*, vol. 122, issue 25 (Dec 2005): 33-35, 34.

10 Gail Cafferata, "Respect, Challenges, and Stress among Protestant Pastors Closing a Church: Structural and Identity Theory Perspectives." *Pastoral Psychology*, vol. 66 (Jan 2017): 311–333. She found that one of the most powerful resilience factors for clergy who had to close a church was feeling respected by their denomination, rather than blamed.

11 Marcus N. Tanner, "The Process of Forced Termination: Couples in Ministry Share Their Experiences." *Pastoral Psychology*, vol. 64, issue 6 (Dec 2015): 861–873, 862.

12 Donald Q. Hicks, "A study of the conflicts within churches that lead to the termination of pastors within the southern baptist convention, accompanied by a proposal of preventive and interventional solutions," Doctor of Ministry

thesis, Liberty Baptist Theological Seminary (ProQuest Dissertations Publishing, 2010): 85. Hicks also reports on a survey of over 1000 pastors which found that a shocking 78% had been forced to resign at least once.

13 Hicks, A study of the conflicts, 80.

14 *Matua/Parents* by Rev. Mua Strickson-Pua, published by Pohutukawa Press 2006. Mua writes: "This has been a blessing seeing ones poementary published. Again celebrating and honouring our Pacific migrant parents' generation of their Fa'atuatua Faith, Taulaga sacrifice and Alofa love."

15 *Smokin Joe* by Phil Gifford (Rugby Press, 1990), 31. Joe Stanley is also P.I.C. Newton our Aiga of the faith, highlighting another form of grieving for Gagana Samoa our Samoan language.

16 O Le Tusi Paia O le Feagaiga Tuai ma le Feagaiga Fou Lea ua Faasamoaina. *Holy Bible in Samoan* Reprinted edition 1884, published by the Bible Society in the South Pacific. Blessed to have our Father Sofi Pua's copy with all his footnotes and Poto wisdom.

17 Worden, *Grief Counselling and Grief Therapy*, 132.

18 Spidell et al., "Grief in Healthcare Chaplains", 76. This can happen when (a) the relationship is not recognised, (b) the loss is not acknowledged, (c) the griever is excluded, and (d) the circumstances around family members' deaths are deemed socially unacceptable, for example, suicide, AIDS, or the death of children.

19 Hicks, 85.

20 Jacob Dirk Eppinga, "Why quit the ministry?" *Reformed Journal*, vol. 13, no. 1 (Jan 1963): 18-20, 19.

21 Girlinghouse, *Embracing God's Future*, 29.

22 Ronnie Janoff-Bulman, quoted in Henry Krystal, "Shattered Assumptions: Towards a New Psychology of Trauma." *Journal of Nervous & Mental Disease*, vol. 181, issue 3 (1993): 208-209, 209.

23 The Church of the Province of New Zealand, *A New Zealand Prayer Book* (Auckland: Collins, 1989), 486.

Section Three: Recovery

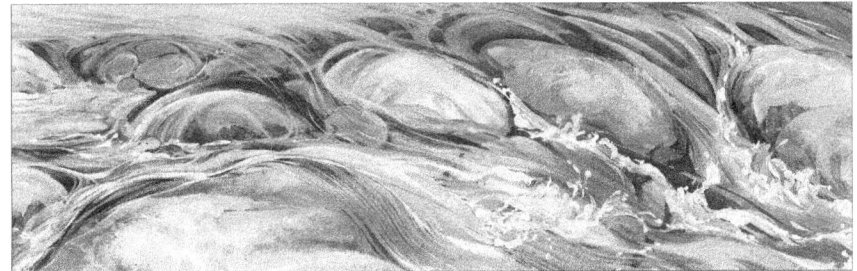

The Only Way Out is Through

Grief becomes more and more simple.
Initially, loss is so complex,
so many aspects to the changed relationship,
so many things said and unsaid, done or undone.
The work of grief attends gradually to these entanglements
until only pain remains,
like a great rock, wordless and heavy,
which we carry around for ages
until we try putting it down for a while
and maybe it finds a place to rest
where we can visit it occasionally.

The only way out is through. Grief for the end of a ministry will take whatever it takes. For those of us immersed in the Christian story, the process of recovery will lead us through crucifixion before we see the light of resurrection dawn. I would like to highlight five key ideas, some of them in a paradoxical relationship with each other, that have, for me, formed my recovery.

1. Rest

My first call to those dealing with the grief of a ministry is to rest. Rest is not an optional extra of grief. The brain and the body must have space to uncurl. The soul must breathe if it is to heal. Those of us in ministry know that rest is God-ordained, even commanded, and we encourage others to rest, but resting ourselves is another matter. Why is it so hard for us to give ourselves permission to rest? I have set myself to the task of learning to rest, to let a whole day go by without achieving anything, to read purely for the joy of it, to watch trash TV, to blob about in my pyjamas till lunchtime, to amble slowly instead of 'going for a walk.' Don't rush in to new things. Let yourself grieve.

2. Own it

Secondly the challenge is to fully accept responsibility for yourself. No one else can get you through this. Some people can help, but most people won't know how. All my emotions and reactions are mine. I am not a victim, I do not need rescuing. I can hold my own pain and endure it. I can forgive, when I'm ready.

3. Surrender

Once we hold our grief fully, we can give it away to the only One who wants it: Christ. If only this was quick or easy. The grieving process is a gentle relinquishing, bit by bit, finding my way into each aspect of loss, entering it and turning it over to God. The spiky bits are hardest, things we find unacceptable, a sharp thread of bitterness wound around a remembered conversation, a reaction I am ashamed of. Nothing is unacceptable to God. He'll have it all, and make of it something beautiful, in time, through surrender.

4. Get in the Flow

Spirit wounds require Spirit healing. Betrayal, disappointment, abuse or rejection in the Body of Christ cause grief that only Jesus himself can heal. But spiritual grief, especially for those who minister in the name of Christ, inserts pain into the very things that should bring peace. This requires new ways to connect with God; it needs ancient traditions, soul friends and wise counsel. Go out of your way to place yourself in the flow of God. Ask for prayer from people you trust. Enter worship as a nobody, treasured by God alone.

5. Work it Out

A vital component to resolving grief is finding a way to drag it out into the light, finding a form of memorial. Communities build statues, churches write names on a board, families plant a tree. Me, I write and find safe ways to tell my story. I printed some photos from my previous ministry in order to celebrate wonderful moments. How might you honour in a tangible way what you had and what you have lost? Name your experience. Tell your story.

These exist in paradox. Grief is work and it is rest, it is holding and it is letting go. Psychologists talk about 'dual process' to describe how we turn back toward loss and turn forward away from it. Christians talk about it as the cruciform path, sharing the cross of Christ in order to share in his resurrection. Ultimately it is not 'recovery' at all, as though the purpose was to regain what we have lost – certainly not. The purpose is formation, maturity, growing up into our full stature in Christ, knowing him that we might 'gain Christ.' For this everything is gladly lost (Philippians 3:8).

Grief and Gratitude in Two Hands – *Lynne Baab*

Rev. Dr. Lynne Baab taught pastoral theology at the University of Otago from 2007 to 2017, and she also served as adjunct tutor at the Knox Centre for Ministry and Leadership in Dunedin. She is the author of numerous books. She now lives in Seattle and continues to teach and write. Her blog and books can be found at: www.lynnebaab.com.[1]

• • •

I have been thinking about grief in leaving ministry. I would like to share my experience of leaving a pastoral position many years ago, and the sources of grief in that.

I was an associate pastor at a wonderful church in Seattle from 1997 to 2004. At the beginning of 2004 our son told us he is gay. Up till then I had kept silent about my views on gay marriage and gay people in church leadership. I figured it was not my issue, and I didn't want to get into conflicts with people about it. But within a minute of him telling us, I knew I would have to leave that church. I was not devastated about him, in fact it was an answer to prayer that he felt the confidence in his parents to tell us. But I knew I could not stay in my ministry, because that congregation promoted the view that heterosexual marriage alone pleases God, and that is not my view.

I waited and prayed. About a month later God gave me a very clear call to pursue a PhD so I could go into teaching. I resigned from the parish. In print and in my sermons I didn't say, "I'm leaving because of this congregation's policy about gays and lesbians," but I was not secretive about it.

The first source of grief I want to mention is that several people said to me, "That's an interesting decision you have made, but we take the Bible seriously." I felt (and still feel) such grief that Christians can look at other Christians and say, "We take the Bible seriously, and you don't." It happens over and over and over on all sorts of topics. I have experienced this numerous times related to the ordination of women. People in more conservative churches say, "We take the Bible seriously, and we don't allow women in positions of leadership." As an ordained woman, I had been grieving that viewpoint for many years. My reason for leaving the church precipitated more grief in this area, and I felt really sad.

My second source of grief was a horrible thing that caused a whole lot of trouble in my final year at that church. Two staff members got into a big conflict. They both misinterpreted what the other said and the conflict grew.

I was there, listening in on the original conflict, and it seemed to me to be a fairly simple misunderstanding. I had no idea it would blow up into such a big, personality-driven conflict.

After they had bad-mouthed each other in many settings, I wanted to say to them, "Come on, you two! Stop fighting!" but neither of them was willing to disengage. An elder on the personnel committee waded in to this conflict and tried to help, and she ended up losing her faith over it. She walked away from the church. It deeply grieved me that the conflict between these two Christian leaders had ruined the faith of a third person. Why do leaders in the church do this?!

I wanted to protect the elders and the congregation members, so I chose not to talk to people within the congregation about this situation. I had a great spiritual director at that time, and also a clergy women's support group. Both were hugely helpful. I feel very strongly about the importance of clergy support groups. So many things are helpful to talk about with peers.

My third source of grief relates to being an introvert in a pastoral role. I loved my job as an associate pastor for those seven years. I got to preach just the right amount for me, about once every two months. I taught a constant stream of Christian education classes for adults. I taught on every possible subject, and I loved it. I was assigned to work with the administration committee and the missions programme. I invested myself in caring for individuals, to love them and draw near to them. People would come up and ask to meet with me, and I enjoyed one-on-one appointments where we talked about the person's spiritual life.

I did fine emotionally, relationally, and spiritually for the first few years, but by my fourth year I would walk into the sanctuary on a Sunday morning and I would look around at all the people and feel overwhelmed. That woman over there doesn't like having sex with her husband and she asked me to pray for that. That person she is chatting to has a teenage son who is using drugs and they are thinking about sending him to military school. And that man – oh! He is the husband of the wife who came to see me because she found on her credit card bill that her husband was paying for lap dances when he travels! And then the next person …

I felt overloaded with others' pain. I would walk into church and feel crushed by the personal needs of these people I knew too much about. As an introvert I only have so much brain and heart space for other people's problems. When I left, I grieved that I was so happy to be leaving! On the one hand I grieved all the things I loved in the job. I loved teaching classes for adults, I loved missions, I loved the people, I loved the church. It was a good church in so many ways. But I was so crushed by the personal needs. After I left I grieved that the only thing I missed was the photocopy machine! Where do you make photocopies when you don't have a church office?

My mother is a super strong extrovert. I was raised that extraversion is 'the' way to be, and being an introvert is inferior. I felt inadequate because I was really glad to be away from all those personal stories. I grieved that these needs were too big and I didn't measure up. I grieved that I wasn't 'enough' for the job.

I went on to teach ministry interns, and when I talked to them about pastoral care I said, "The biggest mistake I made as a pastor was I thought I was supposed to solve all those problems that people had." I grieved that I had taken all those problems on my own shoulders. I was sorry I couldn't see that those people and I could together bring their problems into God's presence. These problems are God's responsibility, not mine. All I am is a person walking alongside another person, bringing these things into God's presence for God to heal and God to deal with. So as the years went by I grieved that I had not had the right attitude to pastoral care – I had just dived in and felt responsible.

I recently read that a mark of maturity is to hold gratitude in one hand and grief in the other. We have to hold them both. That was what I couldn't do as I left that church. I was grateful for so much in those years, but I was grieving. I loved my job but I didn't know how to handle all the grief. I had the idea that if there are things we can be thankful for then we should not be sad about anything – an 'all or nothing' view of life. I felt guilty for loving my PhD studies so much. I felt ashamed: "I shouldn't be this happy to be away from that congregation." I wish I had been able to hold grief and gratitude in two hands.[2]

So I had three sources of grief. The first was for my idealistic belief that Christians should all agree about how to interpret the Bible, especially in relation to homosexuality and women in ministry. Second was for the pain of an unresolved conflict and the cost of that conflict on the wider community. My third grief was my attachment to the idea that ministers should be extroverts, and my sense of hyper-responsibility for the challenging issues people face. So much of the grief that I have experienced in ministry transitions relates to me telling myself how I 'should' feel – all these 'shoulds!' The advantage of getting older is you don't have to beat yourself up as much.

Silvia: How did you stop beating yourself up?

Lynne: A combination of therapy, inner healing prayer and spiritual direction. Learning to not beat myself up has been a big part of my personal and spiritual journey.

Silvia: What do you do instead of beating yourself up?

Lynne: I try to be present to the gifts of each moment. I look out the window at trees, the sky, and our tiny slice of a view of water. I read poetry. I play the piano. I get regular exercise. I try to relish every precious moment with friends and family members. I also try to be honest about the things I feel sad about. I pray the Psalms, I use breath prayer to quiet myself in God's presence, and I imagine myself holding Jesus' hand as I talk with him about my concerns. I confess my sins to God, and I try to receive the deep joy of being forgiven. I continue to talk with a spiritual director each month. Recently, understanding my Enneagram type (One) has been helpful in understanding the ways I grieve when I cannot do a really good job at something.

Silvia: Joy and gratitude. Are these the fruit of the work of grief?

Lynne: Gratitude is not necessarily the fruit of grief, because people do all kinds of things with their grief that are not healthy. And given the way life is, there is no gratitude without some grief going on at the same time. Life is so complicated and painful.

Silvia: So you have to hold them both together; it's not like 'you do this' and then 'you get that'?

Lynne: Gratitude can be the fruit of lament, of bringing grief into God's presence, but often grief also continues to be present on some level even when we choose to thank God for the gifts God has given us. The Psalms demonstrate a pattern of back and forth between grief and thanks/praise. Sometimes we move between grief and thanks, and other times both are present and we have to grow in holding both in two hands at the same time.

Silvia: Complicated grief feels like fighting your way through; it is tangled, like a thicket.

Lynne: Is it ever!

Silvia: Once you have worked it through it feels more simple, not so much like hard work.

Lynne: I hope so. Grief is exhausting, no doubt about that. Our call is to bring our grief into God's presence and rest there as much as possible. Maybe later on we figure it out. Here I am, telling you about leaving a church almost twenty years ago. I can now see that the grief I felt was complicated by my own negative self-talk, but I didn't know that at the time. I really wish I had known that I can hold onto grief and gratitude at the same time.

Is Your Concept of Ministry Restricting?
– *Elsa McInnes*

Elsa McInnes is a spiritual director and author in Feilding.[3] She was widowed at 41, suddenly no longer a minister's wife but a widow, single parent of four, and beneficiary. "In time, God reaffirmed my basic identity as God's child and reshaped my ministry to include writing on grief and working for Open Home foundation supporting foster families. Further training led to offering retreats, spiritual direction and supervision. Life is rich and satisfying."

Elsa offers this reflection on times of endings, and assumptions about ministry.

• • •

Your ministry is over!? Whatever the reason, is it really all washed up? As a living breathing Christian this is not possible. From the moment of adoption into the family of God, every Christian's calling is to ministry. But sadly that word 'ministry' has been hijacked to apply only to those ordained to lead a church or who hold positions of governance within the institution. This runs counter to Jesus' teaching where **all** who own him as Lord are invited to live **all** of life reflecting the love of God and the fullness of God's character, wherever and whenever. Ministry is the calling of **every** Christian. It is living **all** of life in relationship with God, initiated by Jesus life death and resurrection and empowered by the Holy Spirit.

Paul says in Ephesians 4:11-12: "The gifts he gave were that some would be apostles, some prophets, some evangelists, some pastors and teachers," yet the reason for this was "to **equip the saints for the work of ministry** for building up the body of Christ until **all of us** come to a unity in the faith and of the knowledge of the Son of God, to maturity, to the measure of the full stature of Christ."[4] Not some of God's people or a few special ones but **all** the saints.

There are no boundaries or limitations. The shape of each one's calling may differ but the concept remains. It's time to break out of the limited concept and tight boundaries, the preciousness around the word 'ministry.' Just as the concept of 'teaching' is not limited to the idea of students in a classroom but may be fulfilled in many ways and in a whole range of situations (many times with no words spoken at all, but learning takes place), so the concept of what defines ministry needs to be broken open and expanded. The foundational calling to 'ministry' remains whether you retire, resign or are removed.

When the role as minister is gone, grief is the normal and natural reaction. Deep grief is especially felt if ministry was seen as only being fulfilled in the role of church leader, and as being the only expression of your God inspired calling. Then these questions are bound to arise: What is my purpose? Have I a role? How now do I fulfil the calling I felt so certain of? God's call remains. The key is to break out of the restricted concept and discover the new shape of 'ministry' God is drawing you into.

We Want to Hear Your Voice – *Hone Te Rire*

In this chapter Rev. Hone Te Rire reflects on culture shock in his training for ministry.

• • •

I grew up in Te Ao Māori, 'a Māori world view'. I was raised in the Māori Synod, called Te Aka Pūaho. In Te Aka Pūaho.I grew up around the old people, my grandparents, and both my Mum and Dad. These people were staunch in the church. Dad, with the Presbyterian Church, Te Hinota (Synod) Māori, as it was called back then, and my mother, with the Catholic Church. My Koro, my grandfather, was also an Amorangi in the Hinota Māori. I am fourth generation in the Hāhi (church), it is in my blood. I grew up on the marae, learning how to manaaki tangata, literally loving your neighbour. The Bible is immersed with it, aroha ki te tangata. 1 John 3 explains it clearly. We grew up around those Christian values, alongside and mixed with Te Ao Māori. The Christian and Māori worlds joined together, not a problem at all.

After my teen years I joined the army, and church was far from my mind. My Dad became a minister. It was not until my father passed away that I became involved in the Hāhi. My aunties said to me: "We are missing your father. Can you come to church? You will remind us of him, and we won't be so sad." Very clever, those old biddies! So I went along to church, I engaged in church activities. I was a kanohi (a face) for my father. Then one day Auntie Millie (former Te Aka Pūaho Moderator, Millie Te Kaawa) said to me "Johnny, come here. I want you to sign this paper. We want you to go to Amorangi training." So my life as an Amorangi began. I did not have any say in the matter! I thoroughly enjoyed it. I loved the journey. The Amorangi training was all together in the meeting house, Te Maungārongo at Ōhope. Everyone slept together, ate and prayed together. The whole experience was a together thing; it was about whanaungatanga.

Then I was invited to transition to National Ordained Ministry. That was an overwhelming experience. You can count on one hand the Māori who have gone through to NOM. I was humbled by knowing that I had these big giants standing on my shoulders, those people who had walked the path before me. I was joining a small rank of Nationally Ordained Māori ministers. I was humbled by that. The old people would say to me: "Me whakaiti i a koe." Be humble and walk that journey.

In between all that I was lecturing at Te Wānanga o Raukawa, and Te Wānanga o Aotearoa, immersed in Te Ao Māori. I had written some books and provided material for some articles. I had joined with my whanaunga, Rev. Dr Wayne Te Kaawa, at a Symposium on Māori Theology. These two little humble lads from Onepū! From that a book called *Mana Māori and Christianity* was written.[5] I wrote about Sister Annie Henry, 'Hihita me ngā tamariki o Te Kohu.' What a wonderful journey that was.

I remember my first day at the ministry training centre in Dunedin, starting my internship. Talk about a transition, from the Māori world where I was around my whānau, my people, in Te Reo Māori, in my comfort zone. Until then the only world I knew in the church was Te Aka Puaho. To step out of the nurturing comforting manaaki, to come away from their embrace, te korowai aroha, was a tough thing, even for this seasoned Amorangi.

In Dunedin were 14 of us and it was a noisy classroom. I remember feeling "It is so noisy in here I cannot hear myself think!" The lecturer picked up on it and said, "We want to hear your voice, Hone." I was frightened and I felt alone. Being in that classroom took me right back to my own schooling. The whakamā, those feelings of shame, started to well up inside of me. As a boy, I had to fight my way through education. You sat very quiet, hidden at the back of the class. You did not open your mouth. Do not talk unless you are asked a question. So when I first started my internship I reverted to that. I thought, "I am just going to be quiet."

I found my new environment overwhelming and intimidating, with all the knowledge around me. I could engage with it, but I was reverting back to being a good little Māori boy. I would only speak if someone asked me a question, asking for a Māori perspective. If I had a question I put my hand up and waited for my turn. But the people around me were jumping in, even before another person had stopped talking. It was going around and around, I could not think!

That was day one. By day two I had had enough. I got on the phone to the Te Aka Pūaho Moderator, and I said: "Me hoki ki te kāinga. I want to come home." And he replied: "Hey! Kia tau. Me noho. Whakarongo. (Stay, listen.) That is all you've got to do." That was the cultural norm.

I was able to put on my academic hat, analyse the situation and go through it stage by stage. And I had to speak up and say, "Could you try it this way?" Then I could see it, hear it, and the lights came on: "Yes, I've got it!" It was frustrating and I felt I was losing it at times – a hard road to go through.

I found the preaching course one heck of a challenge. In our Amorangi training we were taught that a sermon came from our heart. At Knox Centre for Ministry and Leadership we were being taught a structure, and I just could not get my head around it. Until one day I said: "In my world, if you are going to teach me how to do a sermon, you get up and give me an example. You do it, then I can learn from you. Titiro, whakarongo; I will listen and I will watch you. If you only explain it on a blackboard you are losing me." So they started to do that. And I got it. When I went back to my congregation they noticed a difference in my sermons and they said, "Wow, beautiful!" But it took that transition in approach.

What was good about that was I found I could contribute and add to the group. In Māori wānanga, in a Māori context, learning is done by everybody. Everybody is part of the learning, and everybody is a teacher. From the elderly to the youngsters to the young parents, everybody contributes to the learning because everybody has something to say, something to add to the continuum of learning. Whereas in a Pākehā world you are listening to the lecturer and that person is expected to know everything. I found those things a bit, well, amusing.

I found that to get anywhere I had to engage. I had to make my voice heard. As time went on in the block courses I started noticing that if I motioned that I wanted to say something, it suddenly went quiet. A friend of mine, an Islander on the course, said: "E hoa. He rangatira koe." (Friend, you are a chief!) I said, "Why is that?" He said, "Every time you say something, everybody goes quiet and listens."

But then I would go home and I had to revert back to listening. There you have got the kuia saying, "Hey boy!" and waving a tea towel at me: "You might go down there and be clever, get a Tiwhikete (a Certificate) and all that, but here's the tiwhikete back home, the tea towel!" I call it 'tea-towel-tanga.' That is the manaaki tangata, helping tangata, helping manuhiri, helping your visitors and also hūmārie, being humble, being whakaiti (small).

As a minister, you are something, he tino tohu (an important symbol) for the people, so I have been given a lot of respect. Having said that, I was humbled with it, I was not arrogant, I was not whakahīhī. We always get told, "Me whakaiti, be humble, don't be whakahīhī." To be whakahīhī is to be disrespectful and arrogant, to be a whakaputa mōhio, a know-it-all. We are taught to always be respectful.

As a NOM I went to that level, and everyone was: "Woah, he tino tohunga koe. You're a NOM." I go home now and there are my uncles who have been Amorangi for many years and they will make way for me. They will say: "Boy, haere mai. Kei a koe te karakia" (you lead the worship). I do have that status, but I am still the 'boy.' You have to wait to be invited. The elders, both the men and the women, they hold the responsibility to give that authority and the role. It has to be conferred on you. It would be whakahīhī and disrespectful of me to assume that right. That is their nice gentle way of reminding me, "Hey, I'm the elder. You're still the rangatahi." 'Boy' is used as a term of endearment, in a nice way, not a belittling way. And I like that.

When I get up and talk, I am not speaking for myself, I am speaking for the people. An individual way of doing things is strange to Māori. I can adapt to it when I need to, but that is not often. I am always yearning, pining to go home. When I do go home the biggest thing for me I see is Pūtauaki. And whenever I see that I get a nice warm feeling in my puku, the seat of emotions: "Ah, my Maunga is calling out for me. Home is calling out."

For All That Has Been – *Alister Hendery*

Rev. Alister Hendery is an Anglican priest in the Hawkes Bay. He has written on grief, including *The Grief Walk* and *Earthed in Hope*.[6]

• • •

Over the course of four decades of ordained ministry I have experienced more leavings than most, because for half that time I have served as a transitional priest. This means that a ministry may last between six and twenty-four months – permeating my life with hellos and goodbyes.

How I respond to these goodbyes has been influenced by an ending that occurred over thirty years ago. Within eighteen months of taking up my second sole-charge ministry, I was on sick leave suffering acute burn out. When I left the parish, my departure was not facilitated in the most life-giving manner. There was no recognition, either by myself or church leadership, of the deep and multiple losses I was experiencing. It was a classic case of disenfranchised grief – including self-disenfranchisement.

The farewell, which followed my final service, was a restrained occasion. I recall acknowledging mistakes I had made, though there was no recognition of the emotional pain and grief that I and my family were experiencing. A small group of my colleagues picked up on this and insisted on spending an evening with us as a family. I shall always be grateful for their all-important act of caring solidarity.

Following that experience I carried for some years a deep sense of failure and shame, accompanied by feelings of anger and resentment. It took me time to acknowledge the depth of the loss and grief, but when I finally did, I was able to recognise the gift that this experience of loss has become. Looking in the rear vision mirror I see the gradual process of transformation. I relate to Silvia's reflection on the word 'crushed.' Yes, it is a paradox. As a result of that experience several things changed in my life, including my theology and spirituality, and the shape of my ministry.

Because I have held so many ecclesiastical appointments, I ask myself if I have 'denied' or 'minimised' some of my experiences of loss and grief. Many experiences of loss and grief do not challenge our sense of meaning, as did the one I have described. Yet they are real, and I do not always accommodate them. It seems to me that the important thing is to acknowledge the grief that accompanies any significant experience of change.

Over the years I have welcomed each new appointment, embracing the challenges and opportunities it presents. I know that with each there will be grief, though it will be different each time. This has been described as the grief of new gains – a grief that embraces excitement and sorrow, anticipation and loss. Nevertheless, it still means the loss of what I have come to know and care for. I must farewell what has become familiar. I must say goodbye to a developed routine, a familiar environment, and significant relationships. Ministering with a faith community in a time of change and transition leads to the formation of deep pastoral relationships which I must let go of. And so, the loss and grief of change has become a 'normal' part of my ministry.

I do not always acknowledge significant changes in my own life, whether imposed or freely chosen. I think of my experiences of moving from parishes but also of the ending of relationships, the death of long-held hopes and dreams, crises of faith, and failures in ministry. When I fail to honour these changes, when I do not allow myself to grieve, these losses come back, perhaps many years later, and tap me on the shoulder, inviting me to heed their presence in my life.

My learning is that I must enter the darkness of my grief. Pain, disorientation, even discomfort, has a way of breaking us open. It invites us to ask questions more deeply and explore options we might have not otherwise considered. Reflecting on the many changes in my life, I must admit (rather reluctantly) that in the end they usually turn out to be doorways to new creativity. Even though I may at first resist them, these times of change become seasons of awakening. I begin to walk a new path and sing a new song.

Soon I will end another ministry. To embrace the grief that I know will come, I will take time with my supervisor to intentionally reflect on the ministry that is ending. I will name what I celebrate. I will identify learnings and seek to recognise my regrets and sorrows. I will spend time with parishioners for whom my leaving may be particularly significant. I will also visit places in the parish that may have become special to me. Most importantly, I shall give myself the permission and space to grieve what I am losing.

The ministry always ends with a liturgy of farewell and release – releasing both the faith community and me to enter a new season. I have learned to hear and accept words of gratitude and blessing that are spoken at these occasions. Not infrequently I am taken aback by the emotion I feel, even when my sojourn with the community has been brief. And yes, I've learned to beat back the cultural dictum I grew up with, that big boys don't cry, and allow myself to shed a few discreet tears.

Transitional ministry is about change. How I leave can model how an ending can be the beginning of something new. As former UN Secretary General Dag Hammarskjöld wrote, "For all that has been: Thanks. For all that shall be: Yes." Leaving each faith community, I am no longer a part of their daily life; I become a part of their ongoing story, as they become a part of mine. I retain them in the community of my heart.

To live creatively with so many beginnings and endings I have learned to recognise the seeds I have sown and the hope I have modelled, in the belief that a loss can be the beginning of something new. I wonder if this is what Jesus means when he talks about a grain of wheat having to fall into the earth and die, otherwise it remains just a single grain; but if it dies, it bears much fruit.

After many years I revisited the parish from which I had left in much pain. As I wandered around the site, I knew peace. I knew that the story of loss, of shame, and failure, had been transformed. I was able to embrace that experience as a gift – a gift of resurrection.

Unravelling and Re-ravelling – *Steve Taylor*

Rev. Dr. Steve Taylor is a ministry educator and mission innovator. His books include *First Expressions: Innovation and the Mission of God*, *Built for Change: A Practical Theology of Innovation and Collaboration in Leadership* and *Out of Bounds Church? Learning to Create a Community of Faith in a Culture of Change*.[7] His website 'Emergent Kiwi' includes regular blog posts on films, mission, culture and worship.[8]

• • •

Unravelling

How does it feel? What helps in the unravelling?

Video reflection: View a video (by Lou Baker) at: https://twitter.com/i/status/1351837069920907265. Watch the first minute.

I offer the chapter from my book *First Expressions* as a way of thinking about communal unravelling, the times when a project we are part of dies.

There is also personal unravelling. For me personally, the last 3 years have been this experience in ministry. My church council agreed to a strategic plan, and then spent 3 years undermining that plan. The result was an unravelling: of the plan, and of energy, dreams and hopes.

Recently I sat with my partner, knitting. As we knitted we talked about *'What helps in the unravelling?'* I identify three practices:

Attend to your body

For me, it was essential to keep doing exercise and eating well. I had to watch my intake of alcohol. I had to deliberately keep connecting with other humans, particularly in normal relationships, outside of work.

Add season-specific practices

As a minister, I have regular spiritual patterns, including of reading Scripture and journaling. In the unravelling, I had to keep them but I needed to add more, to spend more time in self-care. For me, this was greater time in nature and solitude. For you it could well be different. But it was important to seek extra input as I experienced extra drain.

Attend to big picture

I had to keep returning to my foundational sense of call in order to not be consumed by what was happening. I did this in two ways. First, I used colour (I explain this more in *Built for Change*, 142-146). I needed to reflect on how I spent my time using a number of colours, to which I attached meaning: Grey = clarity; blue = wonder; yellow = explore; green = create. The use of colour helped me see a bigger picture in what I was doing and to work with my experiences.

Another way was through key words. A friend gave me three words: Create, Persist and Rest. Each day I would seek to do one thing that enabled me to embody these words. This gave me a sense of agency and was empowering for me.

Re-ravelling

Watch the video to the end.

How does it feel? What helps in the re-ravelling?

In the grace of time, after unravelling comes the potential to "re-ravel," to let God re-knit that garment that is our ministry. Again, three practices helped:

Practice gratitude

It was easy for me to get angry with 'a council.' I still am and that emotion is valid and real. But that is only one reality. That 'council' has individuals. One day, I found myself making a list of people who had blessed me and individual actions that were grace. After I resigned, I wrote a specific thankyou card each day. This helped me reflect on grace, alongside my anger.

Rituals of transition

On the day I left, I asked a ministry colleague to work with me on a personal transition ritual. After the door was locked, I plunged my hands into a bowl of water they held. I heard words of forgiveness. Then we shared a bottle of 'bubbles.' We toasted to forgiveness. This was important in helping me 're-ravel.'

New practices

I started a new journal. In the months of unravelling I had been writing in an A5 journal. My writing had got smaller and smaller, tighter and tighter. In order to 're-ravel' I purchased an A4 journal with no lines. I turned it 90 degrees, to write in another direction. I used paint to provide new 'prompts' for reflection. This helped my spiritual practice of journaling enter a new space.

You will have your own approach to spiritual formation. I offer these as examples. We will all face unravelling. We are part of world and a church that is experiencing enormous unravelling. But God is a weaver and God uses spiritual practices as knitting needles. Our ministry is not to avoid unravelling, but to experience God in all the feelings.

Heart Song – *Ana Lisa de Jong*

(Living Tree Poetry)

(Psalm 137)

> I had hung up my harp
> but my God still demands a song.
> How can I draw a note
> I asked my heart within grown cold.
> I have weighed justice and mercy
> until mercy has hardly registered,
> and bitterness become a weight
> that kept me counting my losses.
> But we are asked to hold all things lightly.
> Despair and hope can both draw notes in hands
> that recognise the qualities
> of height and depth,
> light and dark needed to make music.
> Have you hung up your harp?
> Will you take it up again with me?
> Together we can extract the gold
> we can yet mine from sorrow.
> And hope can rise from the ashes of today
> to make a brand new song.
> Together we can draw meaning from all
> that befalls us, good or ill.
> We have stilled our hearts,
> but God can thaw the fingers which refuse to bend.
> Until they move again
> as dancers on the strings,
> of harps, which because of hope we have taken down.
> Because hope, unlike anything else we encounter
> springs eternal in our souls –
> that we might each, always have a song.

The Remains of the Day – *Ana Lisa de Jong*

(Living Tree Poetry)

You have resurrected me.
You, who rose once and for all,
lean down each new day,
restore me with your loving hand
replace me where I stand.
You who have resurrected me,
have taught me how to rise,
to undo all the ropes,
and the remains of the day
which keep me tied.
You my resurrection,
are my high and holy place
from which I can see
from a different vantage,
and renew my perspective.
You who are resurrected,
teach me how to follow.
Show me where my eyes
and heart must rest,
lead me to living waters.
You, my resurrection,
restore me to your side
and cleanse me
from the ashes
of the days left behind.

Being Well: Mission, Trauma and Healing
– *Sarah Beisly*

Sarah Beisly and her husband Paul founded The Loyal Workshop[9] in Kolkata, India as a social enterprise for women escaping human trafficking. Now living back in Aotearoa, Sarah still works for Loyal, guiding the business into a more sustainable model of being locally owned, led and governed.

Sarah is a Pākehā Kiwi, originally from Auckland, with a bachelor in business studies and a bachelor of applied theology.[10]

In this chapter, Sarah identifies the impacts of childhood trauma on how people experience ministry transitions and other forms of challenge and loss. She shares insights from her own therapy and healing journey, and gives fascinating glimpses into cross-cultural mission and the experience of women in the sex trade in India.

• • •

Paradoxically, my transition back to New Zealand from our work in India has been made easier because three years ago I became sick with post-traumatic stress (PTSD). The long process of healing and therapy after my illness means that I am now well. In the process I have learned a great deal about God, and myself, and the long-term impacts of trauma.

In 2010 (after some years of research and preparation) my husband Paul and I, together with our two young children, moved to India to start a leather-working business to offer alternative employment to women trapped in the sex trade. Our children Mikayla and Malachi have lived most of their lives in Asia – they are now 12 and 14 – so it's a big change for them to come back to New Zealand.

I took a year out for treatment and rest in 2019, and we were just heading back to India in 2020 when COVID hit. We supported Loyal Workshop from New Zealand, but for the first time there were no foreigners in the workshop. It became a real gift. The team was forced to run without us and they did an absolutely brilliant job. It created a natural time for us to begin to transition out. So we went back to India in 2021 in order to hand over. We created a succession team to help the business transition through this huge change of losing their founders and moving towards local leadership, local ownership and local governance. Paul and I are still working for the Loyal Workshop, but now as 'transitional directors.' The leadership team in

India is going through this change journey. They believe in it and they are helping the rest of the team to positively engage with the change.

The move has come at a good time; our daughter has just started high school, a bunch of things came together for us.

Silvia: How have you known God through this transition?

Sarah: I have felt so held by God. God has given me the confidence that nothing will be too much for me. In the past I was afraid of being overwhelmed by loss. My childhood trauma created in me the deep fear that the pain would kill me. I used to feel that it would be impossible for me to leave the woman in Kolkata. How could I endure that? God helped me to understand my place in their journey. He showed me that we had done what he wanted us to do and that it was OK to come home; it was not failure. God had to help me re-define success and failure. I can hardly believe that I have been able to come home so well, so healthy, with such a sense of his peace, knowing that this is the right thing for them and the right thing for Paul and I and the kids. To see the way that God has weaved God's best for everyone in that story – it is very beautiful and I am so thankful. I couldn't have planned it, but somehow God can do these things!

My time of therapy enabled me to begin to envisage leaving and to process my grief. I knew there would be a huge amount of loss for me in leaving India, but I started to feel ready to let go. This took a lot of ego work; previously my ego was all wrapped up in the work we were doing.

Silvia: What is the grief for you in leaving India?

Sarah: I am definitely grieving the loss of my primary place of belonging. I still feel like that is where I belong, with those ladies. Being far from them is hard. I am in an in-between space, losing that place of belonging and finding my new primary place of belonging. It helps that I have a few really good friends here, they feel like home. I can be myself with them and talk about the big important stuff. They are a holding space for me in the in-between place.

Part of my grieving is that most people don't ask me about the last decade of my life. People say, "Oh, you're back. How did India go? OK, that's good" – just close the chapter and move on. That feels isolating, and sad to me. India is a big part of who I am, and when others don't know how to engage with it they just get a part of me. They seem happy with that, but it's a grief for me. I want to be all of myself with those I love.

It helps that it has not been a total separation or a harsh ending; we're not cut off, we are still involved in supporting the Loyal Workshop, part-time. And we have a sense of meaning and purpose that we're helping the business to stand on its own two feet.

Silvia: Missionaries navigate between very different worlds. How is this transition a challenge for you?

Sarah: India and New Zealand could not be more different! Especially the subculture we work with in Kolkata, going there is like traveling back in time. It is hard to reconcile that people are living, struggling and thriving in that context, while I'm over here in modern New Zealand. And when I am there, New Zealand seems almost impossible. It's hard for them to both coexist in my brain!

Silvia: How does that affect your faith? Is God more real for you in one or the other place?

Sarah: It is much easier for me to connect with Jesus in Kolkata. When I sit and read scripture alongside our artisans it is just so alive and so easily applied. You read a Gospel story and the setting is happening then and there. People instantly understand: "Oh, yeah, a blind beggar on the road – yeah, yeah, there's one just outside the workshop." You don't need to explain the context, they just get it!

The Bible scriptures that talk about judgment read very differently. When I read judgment texts in New Zealand it's deeply uncomfortable, unsettling or harsh. But when I read it there with them it is so full of hope and meaning! It is so redemptive, and it gives them handles to hold on to. It's just such a different perspective on the scripture.

So I struggle in New Zealand, in this very self-sufficient land of Aotearoa, where it is easier to convince yourself that you don't need God.

Yes, here we are a lot further away from the context of scripture. You have to work a lot harder to see the relevance in your daily life. Every time I have come back to New Zealand I felt this very strong cultural pull towards independence and self sufficiency; living like you don't need God. I get pulled into it! So it is definitely more challenging to live out my faith here.

Silvia: What helps you deal with transition?

Sarah: I am still very much in transition; we are in the thick of it, a lot that is still uncertain. Friends have graciously allowed us to stay on their land, and we are living in a caravan, a cabin and a train carriage – we call it our '3Cs'! We are in the process of trying to buy land and hope to build a new home. It's huge – an excellent practical opportunity to trust God!

Things that are good for dealing with depression are also good for transitions: having routine, doing something life-giving every day. I try to do lots of basic self-care: relaxing, sleeping, eating good food. I try to lower my expectations of myself. I have always been my own harshest critic, so it is a big thing for me to learn to be kind to myself.

I am a runner. I've realised how helpful running has been, all my life, as a way that I process emotion. So I decided to train for a half marathon: it works for me, it helps my mental health immensely, and it's good to have something to work towards. So I did the training and ran my half marathon on the weekend. And it was awesome! So hard, and very challenging mentally, but so good for me. It puts me in a good head space for the day to have that routine, something familiar to do.

Being in a transition is uncomfortable. I want to get everything organised so I can get to the next stage. But being uncomfortable is an excellent place to be, for God to work in our lives. So I am trying to accept the season I am in; to accept this is where I am right now. If I rush to the next stage, I won't receive the gold from now. And the next thing might not be all it's cracked up to be either. I keep thinking "It will be great to have a house and settle down and have roots" but I stop myself: "No. Look for the gifts in this season." Change is hard and uncomfortable, but I am OK and I am safe and there is gold in this too. I am trying to slow down and appreciate the gifts of being in transition.

It is so much easier because of my healing journey. This is still going on, but I feel like a very different person to who I was. I very aware of the grace of God that has lead me through and out the other side. I am more who God created me to be. This has involved changes at every level of my being – a huge process for me.

I have learned a great deal about the way that trauma, in my case early childhood trauma, shapes the way we handle transitions.

Silvia: How did you experience that physically?

Sarah: Trauma is held in the body. I would often have a flash of heat: a wave from the toes right through my body to the tip of my head of a fear response. I would often have this wave of feeling of immediate danger. I had a friend in Kolkata who'd had a similar childhood as me, and we had a similar sensation when we got stressed: a clutching gripping feeling would rise in our throat. I also remember tension in my shoulders, cloudy thinking, shallow breathing, holding stress in my hips. I have had a digestion problems my whole life. I've always been intolerant to wheat, and as I got progressively unwell my body was unable to process more and more food. I had a very unhappy gut. I am now the best have ever been, able to eat most foods, which is lovely.

Silvia: How does trauma affect the way we handle change, loss and challenges?

Sarah:

Change

Trauma 'ups the stakes' on everything. Until the age of five when my abusive father left, I feared for my life. Early trauma has affected absolutely everything for me. It became the glasses through which I saw the world. Change feels life-threatening. When a big change is on the horizon I don't know if I will survive it. My brain can't imagine getting through the change and out the other side. Before I received trauma treatment, every change came with existential dread: this might be the one that kills me.

It was all subconscious. I would not have described it like that back then. Only by working through my trauma can I now see how it affected me. At the time, I just used all my coping strategies: 'I will just try really hard and cope!' Looking back I recognise constant anxiety, but I masked it pretty well. I had a lot of practice.

Change is still daunting for me. I don't know what counts as normal because everyone struggles with change. But I still struggle to imagine what life could be like on the other side of change. It is heading into the unknown. So I make a deliberate practice of looking back: "OK, God was faithful to me in all these other big changes where I couldn't see a way through. So I can trust that God will get us through this one." It requires a blind leap of faith; it is all on trust. God has not let me down. My attitude with decision-making is: "We think this is the right thing to do, even though I can't see a way through. It feels big and scary but God is with us. Let's remember all the ways he's been with us. Let's do it!"

I rely on the peace of God. I move towards where I feel a sense of peace. For example, I needed to find another part-time job, and I had a real peace that I didn't have to find my calling as soon as we got back. It was OK to do a job that seemed interesting, maybe even fun. I have taken the pressure off myself, and God helped me to do that. It's great!

Loss

Loss used to be an unbearable feeling that I had to avoid at all costs! My overwhelming fear was losing my kids in India. In my mind, if I lost my kids, somehow I would cease to exist. So if I controlled everything, and did all the right things, then I would not experience loss, and I would survive. That showed in hyper vigilance in my parenting, which was exhausting. High anxiety and high need for control is absolutely exhausting. It was a waste of energy, because of course you can't control loss. I have come to accept that loss is a part of life. Losses will come and I will live through them; I believe that now. This healing has brought me into a very different posture towards loss, and life is a lot less tiring.

Challenge

How a traumatised person manages challenges depends on the coping strategies that they develop. I find the thinking around Internal Family Systems very helpful for understanding this.[11] At a young age, I developed a very 'adult' part of myself in order to protect 'less-than-five-years-old Sarah,' who was in danger for her life. At age six or seven I developed a part of myself that I call Manager Sarah. Her job was to protect Little Sarah and keep her safe. There was no adult there to do that for me so I had to create that within myself. An adult should have done it, and no adult did.

Manager Sarah did the very best she could. She believed that in order to keep Little Sarah safe she had to do everything right, so there could be no mistakes and she couldn't show any emotion or express any needs. So that's how I approached challenges: "I can't fail. Failure is not an option. I have to dig deep, work overtime, wrack my brain to spot anything I'm missing." I put impossibly high expectations on myself.

Basically what happened when I crashed in 2018 was that Manager Sarah had a breakdown. That driving part of me stopped working. I find it helpful to see this in terms of different people in a car. Manager Sarah has been at the driving wheel almost all my life, out of necessity. She is an important part of me, she did a good job and got me to 38 years old. I needed to encourage her to stay, but ask her politely to sit in the back seat so that another part of me can have a turn at driving. And I needed to welcome Little Sarah back into the car. Manager Sarah didn't like Little Sarah because she had too many needs, was too emotional and vulnerable. I gained the assurance that Adult Sarah, recovered Sarah, was now in the driver's seat. This transforms the way that I take on challenges. I have a lot more room for mistakes, and lower expectations on myself.

I am learning to be curious and explore and try new things. I am learning to play the ukulele. That's huge, because previously I wouldn't learn new things in case I failed. It is a radical new idea for me that I can be bad at something and that's fine! It doesn't threaten my existence anymore. That's quite wonderful.

Silvia: So you would recommend therapy?

Sarah: My gosh yes! I totally recommend therapy.

I was raised to believe that psychology was dangerous to faith. I considered studying it but my mother said: "No. People who study psychology get led away from Jesus. And it's hocus pocus!" – that was her understanding. And there is still a lot of distrust of psychology within the church. People say you should only go to a Christian therapist, assuming that God could only work through a Christian therapist and you'd be unsafe if you weren't with a Christian therapist. I disagree with those assumptions. I think that God can work through anyone.

God is at work in science and psychology, especially in the things that they are finding out about trauma recovery. My treatment included EMDR, Eye Movement Desensitization and Reprocessing.[12] I highly recommend it for anyone who has had trauma in the past; it is such a powerful tool for recovery. It is really helpful especially for pre-verbal experience because you don't have to find words. You don't have to even know where the trauma is; your subconscious just brings it up. You replay the trauma story in your head like a movie. It's not as scary as it sounds. If the therapist is good they have created an very safe space within their therapy room, so you feel safe the entire time. You have the choice whether to verbalise the movie or not. I chose to verbalise it, because that helped me to process the memories. A friend of mine was dead keen on not having to talk about it, so she didn't talk about it with her therapist, and that was helpful for her; it was still enormously effective treatment.

Silvia: How does therapy change your relationship with traumatic memories?

Sarah: Trauma is stored in your body in a way that other memories are not. Normal memories are put in a wonderful filing cabinet in your brain and they keep their proper place. Trauma is held in your body and can intrude in a nonlinear fashion at any moment. What EMDR does is reprocess traumatic memories into a filing cabinet of normal memories. So the trauma no longer has any power over you. It cannot intrude; you no longer re-experience it as if it's happening right now.

I am a big fan of therapy. I used to be afraid of what was in my body: I feared that if I opened the can of worms it would be too much and overwhelm me. But God has designed us in an amazing way. I now trust that my trauma comes up when I am ready to process it, and it will never be more than I can handle. The trauma was held in my body all those years, and my Manager kept me safe. Then when I was ready, it came up and it came out and it was OK. It was hard work to do the treatment, but absolutely worth it.

Silvia: How has therapy improved your ability to minister and to work in your calling?

Sarah: Hugely. Before my therapy, so much energy went into my own survival – without me realising it. I have so much more energy now to serve others. I still need to meet my own needs, but that does not take nearly so much effort. I have learned self compassion. I used to be very hard on myself, and now I can see how counter-productive that was. As I learn to show compassion to myself it is a natural outflow, I am able to show more compassion to others. It's not either-or!

In the church we have made a virtue out of being hard on ourselves. I once did a short course on biblical counselling. We memorised lots of scripture, including "Love your neighbor as you love yourself." I distinctly remember the person teaching it saying, "We already love ourselves, we're selfish, we always look out for number one." She painted that as a bad thing. Her teaching was: "We all know how to love ourselves. The challenge is learning how to put the other person first."

I look back on that now and think: 'No way!' We love others **as** we love ourself. Lots of us are **not** good at loving ourselves, and that actually makes us bad neighbors, because then we are harsh judges on ourselves and our neighbours. People can feel our judgment, through our Christian veneer. This weird kind of martyrdom, 'beating ourselves up' thing that I grew up with, has taken me a long time to work out of. Learning how to be kind to myself and non-judgmental of myself enables me to not judge others, which is much nicer for the person that I'm engaging with.

Where did we get the idea that loving ourselves was bad? Maybe it was a reaction to the indulgent self-love of 'do whatever you want, whatever feels good.' But it is so unhealthy.

Silvia: Is there a gender aspect to that? In a patriarchal society, perhaps men need to hear the 'put others first' message more than women.

Sarah: I totally agree. There is a gender dynamic. That still is a challenge for me in learning how to communicate my needs. My needs and wants are important too, not just my kids' and my husband's. And when I communicate those I can get interesting responses from others who expect me to be in a gender role.

Silvia: How does trauma affect the woman you work with in Kolkata?

Sarah: All of our women have complex trauma. For all of them trauma started in their childhoods, and it comes out in a myriad of ways depending on their coping strategies. It creates challenges in learning new skills – any work in the prefrontal cortex – and processing emotion. They very quickly go to 'fight-mode.' Their amygdala fires easily. A lot of them grew up in red light areas or were trafficked, and they had to fight for their lives. Even in our workshop for the first few years they fought with each other; physical fights that we had to get in the middle of, to prevent bloodshed. But they are getting better. As they find healing in an accepting community, in a place of belonging, they fight less and they are triggered less quickly. They are learning how to emotionally regulate.

When women are new to our work they go into their childhood trauma very quickly. I would engage with them and find they were in a childhood state, feeling loss or fear or being rejected by their parents. Trauma is intrusive. And in a community this looks like chaos!

Thankfully I had done enough reading on trauma that I knew what was going on. We made a huge effort to create a safe, non-judgmental accepting space where they could work through that and experience healing. We have not had professional counselors, we haven't been able to give them the trauma treatment that they richly deserve. But the one component of a loving accepting community has enabled so much of their healing.

They are now different woman than when they first started with Loyal. Now they can look you in the eye. If you come and visit the workshop they will welcome you, ask if you want a cup of tea. They used to be hunched over; it was difficult to engage with them. Some of these women I talked to maybe 30 times while they were standing in line waiting for customers in the red light area. At the beginning they could not look me in the eye or talk to me, even about the weather. Now they have this calm confidence and sense of worth. It is so beautiful. It has made everything we have done totally worth it to see that transformation in their lives. Their trauma story has come a long way, though they still carry a lot of pain in their bodies. I would love to help them get access to trauma therapy. But they are doing great; they are incredible, incredible women.

Silvia: How does God work to bring that transformation?

Sarah: It is the Holy Spirit; it is a miracle to witness. We read scripture a lot. We focus on the Gospels, we read the stories about how Jesus interacted with women, the respect he gave people on the margins. And we see the

Holy Spirit slowly convincing them that it is true. They go from thinking: 'I'm worthless, because that's what my community has told me my whole life: I'm just a commodity to be used and I don't have any worth as a human being.' They go from that to: 'Oh, these people are treating me with respect and dignity. And Jesus treated women like me with respect and dignity. And maybe, maybe I am worthy of respect and dignity!' You can see in their bodies when they start to believe it. That can only be God, re-writing their story. It has been absolutely incredible.

We have scriptures and mantras that we say regularly, to put the building blocks of truth in place for the Spirit to use. Once a week we affirm together: "Your life has a lot of value. My life has a lot of value"; "Jesus loves you, Jesus loves me"; "What are we? We are family. What what we do? We make beautiful things. Why do we make beautiful things? Because God made us beautiful." We say these things regularly because the lies about their lack of value are so deeply engrained. Those old neurological pathways have been walked along thousands of times, so to make new pathways needs practice and routine and the Holy Spirit.

Silvia: Do you use English or Hindi?

Sarah: No, all Bengali. The main language in West Bengal is Bengali. Wealthy people speak Hindi more often, but our woman speak Bengali.

"Your life has a lot of value." *"Tomar jibone onek mullo ache."*
"My life has a lot of value." *"Amar jibone onek mullo ache."*
"Jesus loves you." *"Jishu tomake bhalo bashe."*
"Jesus loves me." *"Jishu amake bhalo bashe."*

Going back to India last year and spending nine months as a well person was just amazing. I experienced the whole thing so differently. I was able to truly enjoy the woman we worked with, rather than being triggered by them. I was finally able to enjoy the vibrance and street life of India that previously had made me feel quite unsafe. It was a profoundly redemptive experience for me.

God has been shaping me through the process of healing. I love the whole concept of wounded healers: it is precisely out of our wounds that God's glory and grace shines brightest. Our God has beautiful ways of being present in this world. I choose vulnerability because God shines out of us when we don't hide our wounds.

143

On the Mat: Grief and Ministry
in the Samoan Church – *Fele Nokise*

Rev. Prof. Dr. Feleterika Nokise is the Minister at Pacific Islanders' Presbyterian Church in Newtown, Wellington. Born in Samoa, he moved to Wellington at the end of 1960 to live with his step-parents, the Rev. Pepe and Lili'a Nokise who were ministers at the Newtown PIC Parish. Fele brings 45 years of ministry in diverse cultural contexts; 23 of these in New Zealand in parishes, social services, chaplaincy, university, before moving to Suva. He spent 20 years at the Pacific Theological College (PTC), as Lecturer and Vice Principal (3 years) before serving as Principal for 17 years (the longest serving principal in the history of PTC). As well as his parish work he is currently an Adjunct Professor in the School of Social and Cultural Studies at Victoria University of Wellington and an Honorary Fellow in the Theology Programme at the University of Otago.

In this section Fele explores 'meanings within meanings' of culture, tradition and theology in order to share insights about ministry in the presence of grief. Rev. Fele is deeply grounded in the Samoan church, and also able to see a 'birds eye view' of the wider church in Aotearoa and the Pacific. From this unique perspective, Fele critiques his own context from within, challenging the ties of culture and tradition, speaking with a distinctive leadership voice.

Fele shares at a deeply personal level, and readers are also encouraged to reflect on their own experiences. At the conclusion of each section there are questions designed to stimulate personal engagement with the issues that Fele raises. Learning about a culture different to one's own is not just an interesting intellectual exercise. It can throw our own cultural assumptions into sharp relief. Nowhere is this more important than as we address human pain in the name of Jesus Christ.

• • •

Encountering grief is part of the drama of life, experienced at different levels and contexts during one's lifetime. Understanding grief in cultural contexts reveals meanings within meanings. This can challenge our thinking, even our theology, as we follow our Lord Jesus Christ even through 'the valley of the shadow of death.' Grieving can lead us beyond the expected.

Knowledge and understanding of grief gained from first-hand experience in the context of Pacific Island parishes is the major strand that shapes the pattern and framework of this contribution. It is offered to lie alongside other contributions in *Moving On*, in the hope that what emerges will inform each other and enhance the spiritual co-existence of what creates life. Five questions are examined, covering cultural, practical and theological aspects of ministry and grief. My presentation offers insights into the intriguing complex world of how grief is understood and experienced in a Pacific Island parish context, specifically those in the Presbyterian Church of Aotearoa New Zealand.

Pacific Island Presbyterian parishes are multi-ethnic in composition. The main groups are Samoans, Cook Islanders, Niueans, and Tokelauans, plus there are Tongans, Fijians, Kiribati and Tuvaluans as well as others from different parts of the globe. Because they constitute a large majority of the overall membership, and because I myself am a Samoan minister, Samoan culture is the focus of my reflections

Ministry and Authority

In a Pacific Islanders church context, how do Samoan cultural expectations shape the relationship between a minister and a congregation?

Samoan cultural expectations play a prominent role in defining and shaping the relationship between the minister and a congregation. This was one of the essential strands of their life pattern that they brought with them when they migrated to New Zealand in significant numbers during the late 1950s and 1960s.[13] Its purpose was clear: a determination that their cultural understandings and interpretation of life needed to survive, in their quest to rebuild their lives in a foreign land.

Samoan ministers who served in the Pacific Islanders Congregational Church (PICC) continued as ministers within the Presbyterian Church of New Zealand (PCANZ) from 1969 until now. Their ministries have been shaped by the unique expectations of their people concerning the nature of their relationship. On the surface, the minister is invested with much authority, but in reality, he[14] is controlled by a subtle system of checks and balances that rests with the people. This is not a juggling act on the minister's part. The expectations are a clear set of 'do-s and don't-s,' a compulsory ethical code of proper behaviour and attitudes as defined by the culture. To appreciate how this drama is acted out in real life it is important to understand two things.

First, the relationship is perceived and presented in a cultural framework. Thus it is a cultural model that is communal in both context and emphasis. It is a drama of 'Homage in Motion.'

Second, it is a model imported from the island world. Its roots were planted there. Having a clear understanding of these roots is crucial in order to appreciate the complex web of expectations that entangles both parties as the drama is in motion.[15]

The relationship between a Samoan minister and his congregation is understood by both parties as shrouded in elusive strands of sacredness. Samoans regard such a relationship as simply 'sacred.' It is a perception that originated from the Samoans' traditional religious belief that those designated to act as a medium between the people and the gods perform very special 'spiritual' functions. This belief is accentuated by the understanding that all matters relating to the spiritual world are, in essence, sacred. The spiritual world and the physical world are not separate entities. They are parts of the total reality wherein Samoans live out their lives.

Before Christianity was introduced to the Samoan people by missionaries in 1830, the leading matai (chief) of the aiga (family) performed the functions of an intermediary on behalf of the gods in relation to the lives of the people and what they wanted the gods to do for them. It was a position and a role that enhanced the status of the matai to the extent that he was treated with much respect and decorum.[16]

After the peaceful transition of religious allegiance by the Samoans, once Christianity was adopted as the official religion during the 1830s, the religious role and functions that were once the prerogative of the matai were transferred initially to the European missionaries in charge of the Samoan Mission, and then in time to the faife'au (the Samoan pastor/minister) once he received a 'call' by a nu'u (village) to be their pastor.[17]

The fact that the pastor was not appointed but 'called' had a significant bearing on how the relationship between the pastor and the people was perceived by all concerned. The sacredness of the relationship embodied in the personhood of the faife'au was cemented with the acknowledgement of the faife'au by the nu'u as their feagaiga (covenant). As such, the faife'au was treated with the utmost respect, as reflected in the honorific salutations given to him. He was the feagaiga, the sui vaaia ole Atua (physical manifestation of God), Tamā fa'a-leagaga (spiritual father). He and his wife were referred to as Mātua fa'a-leagaga (spiritual parents). Samoan culture went further and offered a rare accolade: 'Ao o fa'alupega' (the pastor is accorded the foremost greeting in any religious-cultural context).

These salutations define the official parameters of the relationship. The apex position that the minister occupies is safeguarded by distinct attitudinal, linguistic and behavioural patterns. Formality is the general rule. Generally speaking, only people of status can speak to the minister. For example, if there is an important pastoral issue in a family which necessitates the attention of the minister, only a matai from the family can go to the minister's house and request him to visit the aiga. The language used in the ensuing dialogue belongs to the upper echelon of Samoan oratory, where the use of metaphors is the norm. There is therefore the expectation by the people that the minister should be well versed in the formal usage of the language, as this is the expected norm when conversing with representatives of the people.

There are many other forms of expressing homage and respect used by the villagers to acknowledge the importance of their minister. They would provide him not only with the best house in the village, but also all the necessary household chattels. There are instances when such acts of generosity and support become quite overwhelming. For example, a minister and his wife discovered to their amazement on their arrival at the manse that the parish had supplied quadruple amounts of everything. Instead of two bath towels, there were eight, and likewise with bedsheets and other household essentials. Utensils, crockery and cutlery in the kitchen were enough to cater for dozens of people. In addition to these physical manifestations of their love and generosity, a constant supply of food and financial gifts were freely offered on numerous occasions.

This spirit of giving is genuine and much appreciated by the minister and his family. But it is also a subtle reminder from the people to the faife'au that, as far as they are concerned, he is accountable to them. Acts of generosity bind the faife'au to the people. In a way, the people are saying to the faife'au: 'You serve God and you serve us.'

People have very high expectations of their minister. They expect him to be available to attend to their spiritual needs at any time of the day and night. The scope of what is understood by the people as 'spiritual' goes far beyond some other cultures' understanding of what is spiritual.

Life to the Samoans is within a relational spiritual world, where the main drama is the acting out of the relationship between God and humans, and vice versa.[18] God is regarded as the centre of all things. This means that God has to be acknowledged first and foremost in the celebration of any life-giving event. Apart from his pastoral and liturgical responsibilities, as God's representative in this drama, the minister is thus expected to lead devotions of the aiga to honour God who has blessed the aiga: by the success of its sons or daughters in their studies in schools and universities; sports achievements; those to be bestowed with matai titles; those departing or returning from overseas travels; birthdays of all ages; blessings of a new house; and numerous evening devotions with the aiga during and after the death of a family member. The minister's presence in all of these kinds of gatherings gives such occasions not only a spiritual ambiance but a mark of approval, that both cultural and religious protocols have been properly performed.

Almost all facets of the minister's life in the public sphere come under the scrutiny of the people. The emphasis on being 'proper' at all times is an unwritten rule which a minister cannot afford to treat lightly. The expectation to be seen with formal or semi-formal attire, to use formal language and display formal body language, puts immense pressure on the minister to conform. 'Status' imposes enormous strains and pressures on the minster. Conformity can erode one's sense of self-confidence and a genuine appreciation of who one is as a person.

Some ministers – including myself – have attempted to re-arrange the status hierarchy. This effort emphasises 'equity' and seeks to recognise that all parties are of equal importance.[19] What is highlighted is the importance of integrity, honesty and justice in the relationship. In this the minister takes the responsibility of portraying his true self to the congregation. It is a huge risk because there may be aspects of his true self that may not resonate with what the people expect of a minister.

The Samoan minister is aware of the people's expectations from growing up in the Pacific Islands church. Those raised in such a context are in a good position to successfully navigate the hazards embedded in congregations' expectations. There must, however, be a strong determination to examine all these expectations in a healthy critical manner. Failure to do so will make the minister a puppet of the people.

If the minister really cares about the parish, he needs to understand that the issue is not about who is in control but about what constitutes a healthy, honest relationship. He must have the faith to not allow the engrained expectations to control and determine who he is in the relationship. Instead, he must take an enormous risk in revealing who he really is to the people. The risk lies in what could happen to the relationship if he does so. In other words, the minister takes the risk to redefine the relationship for the wellbeing of everyone.

There are also risks for the congregation. If they really care for their minister, then they need to be honest with him. This is not easy for them because they have been brought up to respect the minister, which means being polite at all times and avoiding any confrontation or expressing differences of opinion. Traditionally it is a relationship that is rigid in structure and how it operates: whatever the minister says goes. Therefore, to be open and honest takes a lot of courage and faith on everyone's part.

Samoan ministers, as by-products of Pacific Island parishes, are themselves part of the socio-religious cultural milieu that keeps such conservative expectations of the minister alive. Many are aware of the psychological effects that contribute to the strain and pressure on both parties in the relationship. Some enter the ministry determined to introduce much needed changes in the dynamics of the relationship so that it is healthier and, in theological terms, just and righteous. But such a dream can die once they leave theological training and succumb to the pressures of parish life. The benefits of holding a high-status position may be too inviting to ignore, especially as they are trying to make a name for themselves.

Cultural norms can lock the relationship between minister and congregation into a familiar pattern of conformity, with both parties as willing participants. This is portrayed in phrases such as: "We are here to serve God and you the family of God." There is a general assumption that both the minister and the congregation benefit from such an arrangement. But if the truth be known, no one benefits, not even God!

The burden of these expectations can significantly impact the physical and mental wellbeing of ministers. One of my colleagues was greatly admired as a leader both within his parish and through his wide community involvement. He responded to the many requests and invitations he received: to conduct devotions, to open community meetings, to be a member of countless committees, as well as to fulfil his pastoral responsibilities for his parishioners. It is deeply tragic and ironic to me that he collapsed and suddenly died in his church hall just as he was opening a workshop organised by a community organisation promoting the wellbeing of Pacific people.

For Reflection …

In this chapter, Fele digs deep into his cultural history to draw out the roots of how ministry is understood in his cultural context.

- How does your culture shape ministry in your church?
- What would you name as the often unconscious assumptions that make up your church culture?
- What is its history?
- How is your cultural context changing?
- What changes do you notice happening in your church?

In particular, Fele points to power imbalances in the church, as ministers are given authority.

- How do you see power dynamics in your church context?
- Who holds authority and how is this expressed?
- Do you find any of these dynamics unhelpful or unbiblical?
- What would you want to challenge?

Fele's challenge is to grow authentic honest relationships in ministry.

- How do the roles you carry enable or prevent open relating with others?

When a minister dies

How would you describe the grieving process that a congregation goes through after they lose their minister, especially if that loss is unexpected?

Our cultural framework shapes how the grieving process plays out when death severs the relationship between a minister and a congregation. In this section I discuss the events after my colleague's death, to highlight Samoan cultural values around communal grieving, and the particular challenges facing a parish in this situation.

The sudden tragic way in which the minister died meant that the parish faced a highly charged situation. This was a high-profile, well known and loved minister. This meant that the context wherein this death was to be handled went far beyond the boundaries of the parish: across the city and across churches, nationally and internationally. The parish was not alone in its claim on their minister; parishioners were only part of a much wider circle of mourners. This also meant that factors beyond the control of the parish shaped the funeral organisation.

Hosting the grief of an entire community is a huge undertaking. The church was suddenly required to accommodate the grieving of the many people who came to pay their respects, and attend family devotions, parish devotions, the family service and the funeral service. The parish organised the grieving process for all visitors. My concern is that this came at the expense of their own grieving.

The Samoan emphasis is to grieve in a culturally appropriate manner. This means the presentations of carefully worded speeches by orators, the exchange of 'ie toga (fine mats), food and monetary gifts. It means continuous catering to ensure all visitors throughout the whole process are provided with refreshments, leading up to a full feast in true Pacific style after the burial. All this entails significant financial cost for both the family and the parish.

So when does the parish grieve for their minister? The answer is simple: afterwards. The cultural demands on the parish propel them to focus primarily on the welfare of the many visitors, rather than on their own wounded spirits. A good example can be seen in who attended my colleague's funeral service. Most of those inside the church were visitors. The only parishioners to be seated inside were office bearers and a few elderly members. Young people entered the funeral to present a song and then leave. Most of the women were in the hall preparing cultural presentations and the after-burial meal. Parishioners, whose lives were intimately connected to the life of the minister, were serving in the background. After the funeral an elderly parishioner confided in me: "Now we can start mourning for our minister."

A major issue for the wider church is the importance of pastoral care for parishioners who lose their minister. Who can the parish ask for pastoral support and guidance? There should be a process in place to guide presbytery in offering pastoral support in grief situations. It is vital for any support person appointed to have the mana, cultural understanding and wisdom to help a parish navigate the uncharted territory of sudden grief. Cultural awareness and sensitivity are of the utmost importance when assisting a congregation to express their grief in ways that affirm their integrity.

There is no doubt that all parishioners share a deep sense of loss. But in a Samoan context this is carefully monitored and controlled. Expressing grief openly is not regarded as appropriate behaviour; to do so would be frowned upon as improper. What is important is to make sure that all preparations are made and enacted to welcome and ensure the comfort of all the visitors who come to pay their last respects, and that they are accorded culturally appropriate decorum. This is the parish's ultimate responsibility. There is little room for grieving as a parish – that comes later, when all others have gone. Then the parish can begin to come to terms with the truth that their minister is dead, buried and gone.

In summary, the grieving process that a congregation goes through after they lose their minister, especially if that loss is unexpected, can involve a delayed reaction, and take a long time.

For Reflection ...
In this case study Fele describes a situation in which a church community experiences a significant loss, yet there is little space to process their grief due to the immediate demands of providing opportunities for others to grieve.

- How have you seen congregations grieve the loss of significant leaders or core members?

- What does a congregation need in order to honour and recover from a major loss?
- What plans does your denomination have in place ready to assist a church in a time of sudden crisis, such as the death of a minister?
- Have you ever delayed your grieving in order to care for others?
- Does your ministry role require you to put aside your own emotions for a time?
- What effect does that have on you?
- How do you make space for your own grief?
- What support would you appreciate from the wider church?

Pain and Faith

How has grief formed your own relationship with God and with ministry?

Grief has been an unavoidable part of my life journey. Initially I felt it as an irritation and an unavoidable itch. In time I learnt to embrace it as a life-giving aspect of my life and theology. In a very radical way, grief has played an important part in re-defining and re-shaping aspects of my relationship with God and with ministry.

Because I was born outside of marriage, I had the misfortune of being branded as an 'illegitimate' human being, before I even entered this world. Being an illegitimate child was a constant reminder to my immediate and extended families of the shame that I brought to the name and honour of the family. In Samoan traditional ethos, death is better than shame. That I survived and lived meant a life of hardship and constant abuse. From an early age I knew what it was to be rejected. I was reminded every day of the shame I had brought to the family. So accompanying the abuse was a rationale that I deserved such treatment.

My parameters for existence were determined. Survival was paramount. I always knew that the stigma was a burden that I would have to carry. This heavy burden became a life-long companion. It meant accepting grief as part and parcel of daily experience. To be ridiculed and beaten caused so much deep pain and sorrow for me. Worse was not knowing what to do about these agonising experiences. Every day there were moments of despair and suffering. How does one survive such an onslaught?

Despite my young age I was very aware that I needed to develop some life-giving alternatives, not just to survive but perhaps more importantly, to try to understand what was happening in my life. I had to find ways to affirm my own self-esteem, my own sense of being an important person, to believe that there were good things about me as a person. In other words, grief helped me to become more positive and proactive in finding alternative ways of coping and understanding life. This urge to find meanings became a catalyst to seek out God.

My awareness of God was grounded in our daily evening family devotions led by my grandfather. I enjoyed devotions because it was one of the few situations where I was not being scolded or beaten. I felt safe and relaxed. There was no hitting or verbal abuse. I felt a sense of peace. Listening to my grandfather's brief talk about the passage that he read, as well as the emphasis of the prayers on God and his Fatherly Love and Mercy, convinced me that God was someone who loves and looks after people. This understanding was reinforced by what I was taught in Sunday School: we must ask God to forgive us and to help us in what we need in life through prayers. At last, I found an opening that I could explore without having to ask permission or risk being reprimanded for doing so.

My prayer life started then, mostly in silence. They were simple and unstructured petitions asking God to take away the sadness and the pain. Maybe God answered, because although the abuse did not go away, it became less frequent and severe. As I got older my focus in connecting with God shifted to coping with the grief and using it in a positive way to help me grow as a person. This quest was aided by the fact that most of the time I was left on my own. It gave me time to think, especially about God.

I began to verbalise how I felt. I talked to myself and created another character so I could have a two-way conversation. This imaginary character was God; I would talk to God and God talked back to me. I created a distinct old-person voice for him. My prayers evolved into a two-way conversation whereby I asked questions and God gave the answer. I would ask: "God, do you love me?" One of my favourite questions was, "God, are you my Father?" because I never had a father; my biological father ran off after he got my mother pregnant. Because I created the script all the questions and the answers were in my favour, but it helped me form a very positive picture of God as someone who really cares. The play-acting kept my hopes alive. This model of relating to God eased off when I was at university, where exposure to other ideas and beliefs contributed to reshaping my rather simplistic views of God.

19th century missionary theology had dominated the teaching and preaching of my home church. The image of God we were supposed to grasp was as presented in the Old Testament: far away, majestic, almighty, everlasting, powerful, far removed from the reality of what was happening to our lives. To approach such a God was not straightforward. One must express full repentance of one's sinfulness. The emphasis on 'sin' and 'guilt' were pre-requisites one must first confess and own before you can have a relationship with God.

The theology we received had important bearings on our understanding of the Triune God, the Bible and the Church, and this theology was packaged in culture. Without proper exegesis, scripture is at the mercy of cultural perceptions, and teaching can be unrelated to the original intended meaning of the text. By adopting culture as the defining principle in interpreting scripture, our church (perhaps unintentionally) diluted the original meaning of Gospel values.

My development during university and Theological Hall studies was more asking questions than finding answers. What emerged was a clearer and more pastoral understanding of grief and where God was in painful situations. I re-read scripture with an open mind, in order to re-enter and highlight the theological meaning of pastoral concerns. A focal question of my enquiry was, "Where is God when grief happens to a person?" From re-reading parables and connecting understanding gained from personal experience in my life and in the ministry, I came to the conclusion that God was in the grief itself.

This new insight has brought the peace that I have been looking for all my life. I used to believe that God was there only to offer a solution, to give help and directions in one's life. But I discovered it is much deeper than that. I was drawn into the God question: "Who is God?" This opened up other crucial issues: "What is a human being?", "What is Life?" Wrestling with these offered a new radical way (for me anyway), a more meaningful and humane understanding of the connection between God and grief.

Grief is not an isolated emotion. It is a strand that contributes to the overall pattern of life. This is accentuated by circumstances beyond our control. Things happen to us and in us; a combination of external and internal factors cause us to be in grief. The pain at such times is real. These are difficult moments in our lives.

In response we tend to activate defensive mechanisms developed through life experience as attempts to lessen the pain. And we try to bring God into the picture: we pray, we seek help from the Church, we ask for healing. But this is where my understanding has changed: I am no longer **trying** to bring God into the picture. God is already there. God is in the grief. God knows and understands and cares about what is happening to me. I now consider grief as another dimension of God's presence in our lives. Perhaps God **is** the grief. This is not mere speculation or an exercise in semantics. It is affirming the core of our faith: God.

Theologically, God can be and do whatever God wills. To treat God as someone who turns up only to rescue us from grief is to treat grief as a problem. If grief is only a problem, then all we want is a solution. As far as I am concerned, God is not interested in solutions. God is concerned for our whole personhood, about us as whole human beings. We are not a problem. We are a part of who God is. What happens to us is happening to God. When we are in grief, God immerses God's self in our situation. In essence, God grieves with us.

With this new insight I understand that what is required of me is to be completely honest and open to the possibility of new meanings. I am growing into an understanding that emphasises life and God's presence in life. It is not an open-and-shut case. Old patterns of dealing with grief have a tendency to put God in a box of already-thought-out solutions. But dealing with grief is an evolving and fluid reality. God's caring spirit moves within the open walls of our lives. God massages our whole being with love and care in his own way and in his own time; not just parts that are hurting, sad or in pain.

In our Pacific Island context, grief is understood in a communal framework. One's grief (whatever the cause) becomes the concern for the whole family, and so there is no shortage of 'solutions.' There is a felt need to solve the problem so that the harmony of the family is restored. The down-side of this approach is that grief is seen as the problem. A grieving individual is perceived as the cause of the problem, indeed, as the problem itself.

However, as for dealing with the actual grieving emotions of the individual, that is for the individual to handle. The steady increase in suicide cases among Pacific Island youths in recent years is a clear indication of the enormous tension young people go through in their efforts to have their voice heard in a pastorally caring and dignified way.[20]

Pacific Island parishes need to own and accept that this situation exists. The need is urgent because the drama that is being played out in the family context also happens on the bigger stage of parish life.

To conclude, grief has re-defined in a radical way my own relationship with God and with ministry. God is with me as God all the time. God knows and understands everything about my past, my life at present and whatever will happen in the future. This truth has altered my understanding of prayer. My prayers are shorter, simpler and mostly in silence. They focus on one thing: to be the agent of God's will. That is my hope in life, in what I do, think and speak. Grief affirms that such hope is not a lost cause.

For Reflection …

Fele's personal story includes early experiences of shame and abuse, and significant theological insights about the person and presence of God. He describes how these have enabled him to relate to grief in new ways.

- How do you recognise grief in your own childhood story?
- How did these early foundations shape your ministry and relationship with God?
- How would you explain your current 'theology of grief'? For instance, if a teenager experiencing significant loss asked you "Where is God in my pain?" what might you say?

Fele critiques approaches to teaching from the Bible that reinforce cultural norms with inadequate exegesis.

- What would you identify as core biblical teaching about loss and grief?

Practical Suggestions

What principles of healthy grieving do you encourage for congregations and ministers?

I firmly believe that there are healthy ways of grieving and recovery from loss that congregations and ministers would do well to cultivate. I offer insights gained from 45 years in the ordained ministry at different places and in different contexts. I bring these to lie beside the insights you have already. I offer these suggestions in the hope that they might enhance understanding and appreciation of grieving processes across the diverse cultural contexts of the Church.

First, simplicity

Keep the process simple. Use less words and have more time for silence. In other words, cultivate a meditative approach. Silence is not an easy state to feel comfortable in, but it is an essential avenue to calm one's troubled spirit. Words are not always the best means of comforting the wounded heart.

Such an approach creates an even playing field for all participants. It is important that all are at ease with the process. Social status should not interfere with the grieving process. I am aware of the value we Pacific Islanders place on the spoken word, but only a selected few are given this privilege. Healthy grieving demands that all should be treated as equals.

Liturgies of funeral rites also need to use less words and more symbolism. The arts can make a useful contribution in enabling the liturgy to be more creative and healing. The usage of meditative contemporary music and symbols can provide creative openings for a life-giving grieving process. A participatory approach seems to be more conducive to healing than a one-person approach. Children, young people and women should be part of the team that delivers the liturgy. The merit of this lies in cultivating a wholistic approach that encompasses all members of the grieving aiga and the parish as a whole.

Secondly, good planning

Family services and funeral services are important parts of the grieving process in our Pacific parishes. Many people wish to speak on these occasions, but this is getting out of hand. Family services can go for as long as three to five hours, with most of the time taken up by 'off the cuff' eulogies. Ministers tend to allow all who wish to speak to do so. However, a prominent characteristic of these personal testimonies is the repetitiveness of what is offered. There is the lack of a proper prepared script; as a result, what started off as a testimony about the dead person turns into a testimony about one's self and what he/she did for the dead person.

Five minutes at the most should be the duration of such eulogies for everyone. Often people abuse this aspect of the privilege to speak. When no time limit is given, eulogies tend to become ill prepared sermons. I recommend careful leadership, to keep the number of eulogies to a few and allocate specific time slots for such presentations.

Ministers need to have an honest discussion about this with the bereaved family. There are important and sensitive questions to be raised:

- What would be the basis for anyone in the family to speak?
- Should all the children and grandchildren speak?
- How many in the immediate family should speak?

There should be a mechanism in place concerning friends and acquaintances who wish to speak. The family should exercise control on how many and on what basis they are permitted to speak. Failure to control this properly can create a 'free for all' situation. With proper guidance in consultation with the bereaved family, the minister has clear basis for wise decisions.

Thirdly, role clarity

There are expectations on the minister by the family that should be revisited to assess their merits from a pastoral viewpoint as well as their theological relevance and integrity. I am aware that it is not easy to advocate for changes that may upset the comfortableness of familiar procedures and habits. But the necessity for change cannot be ignored when what has become normal practice becomes a heavy burden.

Let me preface what I am about to say by pointing out that the relationship between parishioners and their minister is one governed by a deep respect for the minister. The possibility of any change that may affect the structure and harmony of this relationship can therefore only come from the minister. The minister needs to take the initiative. It is too daunting for parishioners to contemplate such a possibility. The challenge for the minister therefore is twofold: to assess the pros and cons of a changing relationship, and to be willing to act on the changes needed to make the relationship beneficial for both parties

A central practice after a death is the daily evening devotions. The family invites the minister to come each evening and preside over the family devotion. Afterwards gifts are given to the minister as a way of showing gratitude and respect. The family would never regard what they give as a burden, but it is, especially when such evening devotions go on for several days prior to the funeral.

I would like to suggest a possible change: for the minister to discuss with the family that perhaps his presence is only needed on the first and last evening. In between, the family could take responsibility, by having one of their leaders preside. The merit of this lies in the opportunity for family members to share in leading devotions. It may encourage dialogue among the family. The role of the minister as the minister of the family is intact, by opening and closing of this part of the grieving process in the family home. But theologically, it moves away from the belief that unless the minister is present the devotion will not be meaningful or acceptable to God. Make the family members active participants of the grieving process.

There can be tensions between what is culturally appropriate and what is theologically appropriate. Often, in my experience, cultural etiquette and values dominate the content and expression of what is happening. There is a latent assumption that what is offered culturally also conveys biblical values. In other words, culture become the primary avenue to transmit theological meaning. When the emphasis is on the contextualization of values, cultural considerations will always dominate. The theological meaning is merely taken for granted.

My final suggestion is that ministers and congregations should put aside time to reflect upon the grieving process. This could include discussion or a workshop on the theological basis of grief, and the roles of different people and involvement in healthy grieving. Navigating new roles requires open dialogue.

For Reflection …

- How are the principles of simplicity, good planning and role clarity relevant in your context, as you lead processes of grieving?
- How do you cultivate healthy silence?
- What are the planning challenges in your context?
- When do you want to re-define your own role?

In the examples given, Fele highlights potential tension between our theology and our cultural assumptions, especially as these are expressed in the roles we are expected to play.

- If you were asked to speak at a workshop on healthy grieving processes, what convictions would you share about God and about grief?

Mat Theology

What is your emerging theology of grief in ministry?

My emerging Theology of Grief is based on the belief that God is in the Grief. This defines the meaning of grief, that God is inter-related with it. My personal experience has informed this theology.

Pacific traditional religious beliefs portrayed a reciprocal relationship between the gods and the people. In essence it was a practical arrangement to satisfy the spiritual needs of the people. The people did things that they believed would please the gods; and in return the gods would bless them by granting whatever they asked for. When the people carried out tasks such as building a house or launching a fishing expedition, rituals would be performed to appease the gods so that success would follow. Rituals were offered to the gods of the forest, for example, to ask for permission and forgiveness in cutting down a tree for building a canoe. The principle of reciprocity governed the inter-dependent nature of the relationship.

When the people suffered, rituals would be performed asking the gods for forgiveness, comfort and healing. People perceived grief in negative terms. They assumed that they were the cause of any misfortune that resulted in grief. So they asked the gods to forgive them and their actions. Rituals acknowledged that the wrong they had done could only be put right by the gods.

This world-view from the pre-Christian spiritual life of Pacific people has heavily influenced the way we understand God in the church today. Traditional Pacific theology sees God as existing in a faraway place called heaven, far removed from the happenings of everyday life. It is a convenient arrangement that benefits the people. God is regarded as the core of faith; everything centres on God. God is the primary cause of all blessings in life. However, anything to do with God projects a different reality from that of ordinary life. God is treated as a kind of absentee landlord who occasionally visits us. So when pain or grief occurs, God is expected to turn up with a solution from another world to solve the grief in this world.

The problem with this understanding of God is that it not only limits the capacity of what God can or cannot do, but it also suggests that God can be controlled by human beings. History reminds us of the many attempts man has made to try to control God, only to discover the absurdity of such efforts! What is projected as a relationship is not a relationship at all. It is a one-dimensional scenario.

A catch-cry prevalent in Pacific parishes is, "God is good," with the response, "All the time!" This makes God nothing more than a 'do good all the time' figure. In other words, we have moralised the existence and nature of God in dualistic terms: good and bad. The relationship between a person and God is perceived in this way as well; God is good and the person is bad. But these moralistic categories and divisions are unhelpful, in that it makes God out to be merely a problem solver. God exists only to solve our grief. Theologically this is unsound and untenable.

Our tendency to treat sensitive issues as problems creates a vacuum in our available pool of solutions. When we have exhausted other options, God is called on to conveniently fill the gap. If God is just our problem-solver, then we are abusing our relationship with God.

God, as God of Life, is in all life. As such, God is a part of the complexity that we experience in what happens to us. To appreciate this perspective, we need to think outside the box, to reconfigure our perceptions of meanings and understandings in a more open and vulnerable framework.

God is in the grief. In this way, God's presence is already available and assured. Our strength reaches a low point when we experience grief. Our minds are not able to function properly. Many strands of our being are disorientated. For many, trying to pray and connect with God can be quite agonising. But God is already with the grieving person through the caring and love offered by those surrounding the grieving person. In this way, we become messengers of God's grace and healing. We become bearers of good news, of new life, that gives strength and lifts the spirits of those in pain.

Don't under-estimate the value of our just being there. For Pacific people, it is not OK to visit a grieving family without an offering of some kind, so it's not an option to 'just go and be.' This is a missed opportunity for those grieving and those visiting to experience the presence of God in the grief.

One of the joys in perceiving God in the grief is to picture God being with us by sitting on the mat with us. This removes the idea that God is sitting on an armchair and we are on the floor. Our grief binds us together with God. It removes the separation that we have been brought up with. God and us are on a level playing field. We sit on the mat together.

This should be the basis of everyone being treated in the same way. This is the challenge to reconfigure our thinking outside the box and accept vulnerability. God shares with us our discomfort, pain, sorrow and wounded hearts. The mat portrays openness and vulnerability. We see one another.

On the mat we no longer structure our grieving according to who is more or less important. There is no merit in differentiating levels of grief as though some people's grief matters more than others; that serves no purpose except to perpetuate status and rank.

In acknowledging the presence of God in our grief experience, we re-affirm the connection of God's Spirit with our spirits. The divine in our humanity is a life-giving relationship that breaks down human-made boundaries and barriers. A new awareness is required from us.

Grief is an opportunity to encounter and embrace the presence and the voice of silence. Listen to the silence. Hear God's small voice. Feel its pulse and rhythm. It is in the wind, in the forest, in the flowers and plants. It is on the sand and the waves, the hills and the mountain tops. It is in Life, where God dwells.

To conclude, the image of sitting together with God on the mat when we grieve is a powerful metaphor. It suggests to the church that there is a real need to re-evaluate our understandings of the theological basis of the grieving process. Where is God in our grief? I advocate that God is in the grief. God is on the mat with us.

Manuia,
Fele Nokise

For Reflection …

Fele challenges our assumption that God is there to solve our problems and ease our pain.

- What is your own 'theology of grief'?
- In the presence of suffering and loss, where is God?
- What do we ask of God?

Throughout his contribution, Fele highlights the connections between theology and ecclesiology.

How we understand God shapes what we expect of ministers, and our experiences of ministry shape our relationship with God.

- What images of God are often used in your church?
- How would you describe the central theological understandings of who God is, in your context?
- How do these affect the way leadership and ministry is understood in your church?
- And how does the way leadership is exercised inform people's relationship with God?

How Good – *Ana Lisa de Jong*

(Living Tree Poetry)

God I would tell you how good you are
but I can't.
Good things come in small packages,
gifts of generosity and sacrifice
or through great acts made by
surrender to the self.
This goodness
is what you stand for,
and you are all that.
God I would tell you how good you are
but I can't.
Good things are made of sweet offerings
that melt as liquid delights on the tongue,
and would have us bowing
in grateful thanks.
This goodness
is what you would give to us,
your heart is that large.
But God I would tell you how good you are
but I can't.
Good things are how we measure
the favour bestowed upon us
by your smiling countenance,
the reward for our endeavours.
This affirmation you would impart
tells us in part that we've arrived,
plateaued on some higher plane.
Yes God I would tell you how good you are
but I can't.
The God who is all good is also the author of travail
and the pain that turns us inside out,
breaks us into smithereens
to shine like broken glass.
This goodness
which comes with a holy veil
keeps us yet from complete understanding.
So that we might tell him how good he is
but can't.

At least not until we can say thank you
for everything that comes,
good or ill,
whether meant for benefit or harm.
For God, more than our measurements
could ever gauge,
is great.
So that we might tell him how good he is
but can't.
For the Sovereign God is all that
we might call him, and more,
more good and more great
than any mere words could convey.
And it's not until we lie prostrate on
the ground,
in our Gethsemane,
that we can say with any truth
"Your will prevail."

Endnotes

1 Lynne Baab's books include *Nurturing Hope: Christian Pastoral Care for the Twenty-First Century* (Fortress Press, 2018), and *Sabbath-Keeping: Finding Freedom in the Rhythms of Rest* (IVP Books, 2005).

2 Lynne Baab's most recent book is *Two Hands: Grief and Gratitude in the Christian Life*, available in paperback, kindle and audiobook.

3 Elsa McInnes, *Shattered and Restored* (Castle, 1990, reprinted 2003), and *A Grip on Grief: Youth face to face with loss* (Castle, 2001).

4 NRSV, emphasis added.

5 Lachy Paterson, Murray Rae, Hugh Morrison and Brett Knowles (eds.), *Mana Māori and Christianity* (Wellington: Huia Press, 2013).

6 Alister Hendery, *The Grief Walk: Losing, Grieving and Journeying on to Something New* (Wellington: Philip Garside Publishing, 2020) *Earthed in Hope: Dying, Death and Funerals – A Pakeha Anglican Perspective* (Philip Garside, 2014).

7 Books by Steve Taylor: *First Expressions: Innovation in the Mission of God* (SCM Press, 2019), *Built for Change: A Practical Theology of Innovation and Collaboration* (MediaCom, 2016), *Out of Bounds Church? Learning to Create a Community of Faith in a Culture of Change* (Zondervan, 2010).

8 Emergent Kiwi: www.emergentkiwi.org.nz.

9 The Loyal Workshop: www.theloyalworkshop.com.

10 Sarah is profiled on 200 Women: www.twohundredwomen.com/sarahbeisly.

11 Internal Family Systems Institute: https://ifs-institute.com.

12 Eye Movement Desensitization and Reprocessing: www.emdr.com.

13 For an excellent study on Pacific Island Migration to NZ: Isabelle Sin and Judd Ormsby: 'The settlement experience of Pacific migrants in New Zealand: Insights from LISNZ and the IDI', Motu Working Paper, December 2018, 18-17, Motu Economic and Public Policy Research.

14 I (Fele) acknowledge that there are some Pacific Islander women who are ordained ministers in the PCANZ. However, they do not typically serve in Pacific Island parishes, which is why the male pronoun 'he' is used to describe the work of Pacific Islander ministers in this contribution. The ministries of Pacific Islander women in the PCANZ merits its own separate discussion. Recent research by one of these female ministers, Rev. Marie Ropeti-Apisaloma, provides the following information on Samoan women ministers in the PCANZ: "Eleven Samoan women have served in different ordained ministries in the PCANZ in the last four decades… The dates of their ordinations range between 1980 and 2015. Of the eleven, one has passed away, one is now retired, four are ministers in *palagi* (white) parishes, one is a minister in a union parish, two are working as chaplains in the education and health sectors, one is serving two Samoan

parishes, and one is serving a Congregational Christian Church (CCCS) parish in Hawaii." See Marie Ropeti-Apisaloma, "Nafanua Theology: A Samoan-Christian Argument for Women in Ministry in Samoa," PhD thesis, Pacific Theological College, 2021, 123.

15 John Fraser, 'The Samoan Story of Creation,' *Journal of the Polynesian Society* volume 1, 1892, pages 164-189. The early record claims to "tell the tale in its fulness and purity" of the foundational cosmology of the Samoan people, who the Polynesian Society suggests are "a nobler people than most of the other islanders" (!?!). It is available online at www.jps.auckland.ac.nz.

16 Tui Atua Tupua Tamasese Tupuola Tufuga Efi, 'In Search of Harmony: Peace in the Samoan Indigenous Religion,' *Suʻesuʻe Manogi: In Search of Fragrance*, Tamasailau M. Suaalii-Sauni, et al. editors (Huia Publishers, 2008).

17 Ronald Crawford did a PhD thesis (University of Otago, 2013) on 'The Lotu and the Faʻasāmoa: church and society in Samoa, 1830-1880.'

18 A couple of general works that offer excellent accounts on Samoan spirituality as well as intriguing relationship between Culture and the Gospel: Sr. Emanuela Betham, 'Aspects of Samoan Indigenous Spirituality and Christian Spirituality and Spiritual Direction' (SGM, 2008, available online) Lolomilo Kamu, *The Samoan Culture and The Christian Gospel* (Methodist Printing Press, Apia, 1996).

19 Marie Ropeti's PhD Thesis as mentioned in footnote 2 is an excellent example of this long overdue essential research on reconfiguring male dominated existing paradigms in the ministry.

20 The number of Pacific Islanders who took their own lives increased from 7.77 per 100,000 to 11.49. "The increase in the last year is just devastating," said Monique Faleafa, chief executive of Pasifika support service Le Va. 'Māori and Pacific Islanders young people lead 'horrendous' suicide increase.' 1News, 26 August 2019.

Section Four: Praying Goodbye

Liturgies for Grieving

This section follows an approach to liturgy for grieving developed by Joyce Rupp, together with other prayers, songs and poems, including a chapter by Malcolm Gordon on the theology and practice of lament.

A Process of Healing: *Joyce Rupp*

Joyce Rupp is a Catholic sister, writer and retreat director in Iowa. Now well into her 70s, she has been globally appreciated for her simple way of expressing deep things and inviting people into relationship with God. Her book *Praying Our Goodbyes* is a beautiful and powerful encouragement to allow the Spirit of God to facilitate healing from grief, across a wide range of human situations. I have followed the general pattern and philosophy of these pastoral liturgies in writing prayers for ministry endings.

Rupp's understanding of the role of prayer in healing is that ongoing prayer is needed "to sustain us and heal us day by day."[1] She identifies four aspects of 'praying our goodbyes' as part of a process of prayer. This process begins with recognition; identifying and naming the loss that has been experienced. The recognition of hurt and pain, and the sources of these, is "a moment of honesty" between the person and God. The next movement in Rupp's prayer process is reflection, the challenge of giving our pain "full attention" by "slowing down, with stillness, with solitude and aloneness, with not being afraid to look inward or to go deeper."[2] The goal of reflection is to face inner emotions and through this "to reconnect our lives with God."[3]

These tasks of facing loss and honouring uncomfortable emotions are not unique to Joyce Rupp's approach. What is distinctive to her prayers is her third aspect, of 'ritualization.' She claims that physical actions and tangible symbols are very helpful, especially when these connect, for Christians, with Biblical narratives and metaphors that "speak to us deep down at the centre of ourselves." She encourages people to "act out some of the pain in us" by incorporating the image or symbol into a "gesture of expression, some significant movement, out of which comes a connection with God, our self, and our life."[4] The prayer process moves towards reorientation, in which the praying person is invited to see their pain and situation differently out of a lived experience of relationship with God. Knowing that our loss is part of God's story brings "a renewed direction and energy." Through liturgy "we are drawn into healing in a quiet sort of way" which gives "courage to go on."[5]

I have chosen Rupp's approach because it fits with my understanding of the nature and action of God in dealing with human suffering. She assumes that God meets with people when we take the time to be still and listen. This empowers us to take responsibility for our own experience rather than be dependent on others. Her pastoral theology of the importance of metaphor and physical movement aligns with the person (as embodied God) and teaching (often using metaphor) of Jesus Christ who reveals the heart of God through the presence of the Holy Spirit.

The liturgies below use Joyce Rupp's process of recognition of loss, reflecting on the experience and emotions, relating with a biblical text, a physical action, and prayer which invites God to speak into the lived experience. Biblical and theological resources connect us into the Gospel story. This is important because loss, especially traumatic loss, threatens to tear us out of God's story. The ending of a ministry can be an experience of gratitude, release and blessing. However, it can involve multiple loss for ministers and their families, particularly a loss of community. Where the minister has experienced a betrayal of trust, bullying or rejection, this is a form of spiritual abuse which requires spiritual healing. Prayer and support for ministers and their families is an important gift in ensuring their wellbeing through ministry transitions. These pastoral prayer liturgies can be done alone or in a small group, facilitated or self-led, with no set time frame.

Prayer of One Going with Gratitude

Ministry is loving others in the name of Jesus. When a ministry comes to an end, the love must be offered back to God with gratitude. Every gift given and received, together with every hurt or disappointment, becomes a sacrifice of thanksgiving.

Prayer action

- Cut long paper strips, preferably of various colours.
- On each strip write something you are grateful for, different aspects of the ministry that has been. Jot down moments, roles, people, events, words and feelings.
- Then weave the paper strips together.

Song

Choose a song expressing gratitude to God, such as 'Thank You Lord' by Hillsong.[6] Listen to a recording.

For all that you have done, I will thank you,
For all that you're going to do.
For all that you've promised, and all that you are
Is all that has carried me through –
Jesus I thank you.
Thank you Lord.

Read

The New Testament is packed with gratitude. Jesus often gives thanks to God, and most of the epistles include prayers of thanks and encouragement to say 'thank you' no matter what comes (1 Thessalonians 5:18). Things are transformed by our choice to receive them with gratitude (1 Timothy 4:4).

Pray

Choose a scripture of thanks, and expand on it with your own prayer of gratitude.

Prayer of One Forced to Leave

Sometimes we feel that we have no choice but to leave a community where we felt we belonged. Being forced to leave is a painful experience which can include feeling betrayed, disillusioned, rejected or abused. It can leave us feeling alone, and uncertain for our future.

This prayer is an invitation to join Hagar who meets God as she is forced to leave her home.

Image: An almost empty water bottle

Read: Genesis 16 and Genesis 21: 8-21.

As you read the story of Hagar, reflect on:

1. Her changes of role, status and place, from Sarah's tent, to Abraham's tent, to wilderness and back again.

2. Her complex changing relationships with Abraham and Sarah, from being trusted servant, to lover, to honoured mother of the heir, to victim of abuse and exile. How might she have felt toward Sarah? Toward Abraham?

3. How do you evaluate the actions of Sarah and Abraham toward Hagar?

4. Sarah abuses Hagar. How have you felt abused by the words and actions of others?

5. Abraham betrays Hagar and Ishmael. He fails in his responsibility to care for them. Despite his feelings for them he rejects them in favour of Sarah and Isaac. How have you felt betrayed or rejected?

Action and reflection

Drink the last of the water in your water bottle. Remember Hagar, exiled with her son, desperately thirsty after she had drunk all her water. What is it that you are thirsty for?

Prayer

> Lord, have mercy, I am thirsty.
> Hear my prayer.
> Kyrie eleison.
> Christ, have mercy, I am lost and alone.
> Hear my prayer.
> Christe eleison.

The first time Hagar leaves, she runs away and God sends her back. The second time, Abraham sends her away and God creates a new life for her, a new home and community in the wilderness. Both times, God meets her and cares for her, and both times the presence of water is the gift of life and hope.

- Re-fill your water bottle, and take some time looking at the water.
- You might like to get a bowl and enjoy the feeling of the water on your hands and face.
- If you can, go to a river or a spring to refill your bottle from a natural source.

God Sees, God Hears

In Genesis 16, hurt and alone, Hagar meets God for herself for the first time. She knows herself to be seen and heard by God, and blessed by God. She names God with a new name: 'El-Roi,' God Sees. Her unborn son is named by God: 'Isma-El,' God Hears.

- On a blank piece of paper write the words 'God Sees' and 'God Hears.'
- Write or draw what you are feeling and experiencing as you grieve for being forced to leave. What does only God see and hear?

Closing prayer

> All-seeing, all-hearing, all-knowing God,
> all that I am is known to you.
> I bring you my cry today …
>
> *(Read aloud the words you have written of your feelings and experiences)*
>
> In your loving gaze I am safe
> in your arms I may rest.
>
> Keep me as the apple of your eye; hide me in the shadow of your wings.
> *Psalm 17:8*
>
> Amen.

Prayer of One in Exile

Sometimes we are cut off from those we love, and unable to continue with a role we enjoyed. Dealing with loss can be a lonely experience. Others are not always able to be there for us or offer the support we need. This can feel like exile.

This prayer is an invitation to join John in exile on Patmos.

Image: a cut-off place

Read: Revelation 1

John had been a leader in the church before being arrested by the Romans, charged with being a magician because of his gift of prophecy, and banished to the island of Patmos. He lived in a cave on a hillside until he died, cut off from the Christian community. He was able to continue his ministry through prayer and through his writing. Despite his isolation and suffering he continued to worship. The book of Revelation is a record of his visions which express his keen awareness of both eternal spiritual realities and the political realities of his day. His passion for Christ shines through every word.

Prayer action

Find a place to sit which is cut off from your home and church. Take a picnic chair and sit beside a high fence, or out in the middle of an exposed field. Make this your 'island of Patmos.' Let it be a place where you feel quite alone and isolated, unable to go home.

Prayer verse: Revelation 1:9

> I, *(insert your name)*, your sister/brother and companion in the suffering and the kingdom and the patient endurance that are ours in Jesus, was on the island of Patmos because of God's word and testimony about Jesus.

'Sisters and brothers'
God of love, you have made us to be family.
At the moment I feel cut off from my family. I cannot be with them.
I'm not even sure who my family is any more.
But I am still connected in your family through Jesus.
I am still a sister/brother in Christ. Thank you, brother Jesus.

'Companion in suffering'
God of power, you know my pain, you are closer than my struggle.
Be my companion in suffering.
Make me, in time, a companion to others in pain.

'Partner in the Kingdom'
God of glory, you have shown me, in part,
the wonders of your ways
and the beauty of your Kingdom.
Thank you for the place I had in your Kingdom fellowship.
Even as I feel cut off from that place, I ask for your blessing on your people there.

'Patient endurance'
Faithful God, your mercy is everlasting.
Right now I feel that my pain will also last forever.
Give me the grace to endure.
Give me hope that joy will return.

'Because of God's word and testimony about Jesus'
God, your word is my passion.
I confess that I have not always spoken your word right,
not always given good testimony about Jesus.
Forgive me.
Lord, your word is not always welcome.
I have not always been welcome.
Lord, forgive those who have rejected your word.
Forgive those who have rejected me.

'and the voice said "Write"' (v10)
Lord, I need a new calling.
I treasured my old calling but now I give it freely into your hands.
Tell me who I am in you.
Give me new work to do in your Kingdom.

'I turned to see' (v12)
Lord, I turn again to you.
Turn me away from my loneliness and grief.
Show me who you are!

'Do not be afraid. I am!' (v17)
In your presence, I am not afraid.
In your presence, I worship you,
for you are the beginning and the end
alive for ever and ever,
worthy of all praise and glory. Alleluia!

- In your place away from home and cut off from other people, look around you.
- Hold in your mind the vision of Christ the living one from Revelation 1.
- How will you carry that with you?
- How does it change your exile?

Prayer of One Who Feels Crushed

Image: Crushing seeds

In the Old Testament 'crushed' means total defeat, as in David's song of victory in 2 Samuel 22:38; either Israel is celebrating the crushing of their enemies or they are themselves feeling defeated, crushed by God.

Crushing is also the process by which wheat becomes bread, olives become oil, or grain is offered as a sacrifice on God's altar (Leviticus 2:14).

Isaiah prophesies the coming Messiah who will be "crushed for our iniquities" (Isaiah 53:5) but "will not be crushed until he has established justice in the earth" (Isaiah 43:4, NRSV).

In 2 Corinthians Paul describes himself and his friends as being crushed to the point of despair by attack (2 Corinthians 1:8), and yet he goes on to declare that "We are afflicted in every way, but not crushed" (2 Corinthians 4:8, NRSV).

Prayer action

- Put a handful of edible seeds or nuts (e.g. almonds) on a chopping board. You'll also need a rolling pin or large jar.
- Say these Bible verses aloud, and when you say the word 'crushed,' crush the seeds with the rolling pin or base of a jar.

Bring a grain offering of first fruits to the Lord, offer **crushed** heads of new grain roasted in the fire. *Leviticus 2:14*

All was well with me, but God shattered me; he seized me by the neck and **crushed** me. *Job 16:12*

He was pierced because of our wrong-doing, **crushed** because of our evil-doing. *Isaiah 53:5*

We were so utterly, unbearably **crushed** that we despaired of life itself. *2 Corinthians 1:8*

We are hard pressed on every side, but not **crushed**; perplexed, but not in despair. *2 Corinthians 4:8*

- Notice how you feel as you crush the seeds. Watch them split and crumble.
- *How do the verses speak to your experience?*
- *What is the prayer of the crushed seed?*
- Take time to pray, journal or draw your insights and questions.
- Use the crushed seeds or nuts in some baking.

Closing Prayer

Lord of all, I offer myself once again to you.
Accept my sacrifice, like crushed grain on your altar.
Lord, I have felt shattered and disappointed,
attacked by people I trusted,
even by you, O God.
Lord Jesus, you were wounded, pierced, crushed for me.
I did not ask you to, I did not deserve it,
I still struggle to understand it,
but I know in my hurting that you were here before me
and I thank you.
Spirit of God, strength when I am hard pressed,
make me whole when I crumble,
be my courage when I lose hope;

make me into something new, I pray,
that I may again be beautiful and useful in you,
through Jesus my crucified and risen Saviour, Amen.

Prayer of One Changing Roles

The Garment of Praise: *Isaiah 61:3*

Console those who mourn in Zion,
to give them beauty for ashes, the oil of joy for mourning,
the garment of praise for the spirit of heaviness (NKJV)

Prayer action

- Find an item of clothing which reminds you of your old role (perhaps a jacket, name tag or liturgical item).
- Put it on. While you are wearing it name to God the memories and emotions that come to mind about your previous ministry position.
- Take it off. Notice how it feels to take it off.
- Say aloud Isaiah 61:3, as though God were addressing it to you personally.
- Find something which feels to you like a "garment of praise." Put it on.

Write a prayer of praise.

Sing the old chorus: 'Put on the garment of praise' *(by David Ingles)*

Put on the garment of praise
For the spirit of heaviness
Lift up your voice to God
Praise with the Spirit
And with understanding
Oh magnify the Lord!

All you that mourn in Zion
I have authority
To appoint unto you in Zion
Oil of joy that will set you free

Lift up the hands that hang down
Lift up the voice now still
Give unto God continuous praise
Sing forth from Zion's hill

Sing to Yahweh, alleluia!
Worship and praise our God
Praise and adore Him
Bow down before Him
Oh, magnify the Lord

Prayer for Moving from Complaint to Trust

Water from the rock Read Exodus 17:1-7

It was hot and dry.
With cracked lips the people cried for water.
With bitter anger the people complained to Moses about God
and Moses complained to God about the people.
God led him further on into the rocks
and stood him on a hard slope.
Moses lifted high his staff, pointing it to the sky,
and brought the tip down between his feet.
The rock cracked and water spurted out
over his toes, running through dust, pooling in stone.
Moses and his brother and his friends
cried out amazed, scooped and splashed,
drank and – ah! – so sweet so good!
The people came running as the water flowed.
Trust in the Lord, our living water.

Prayer Action

- Fill a bucket with water. Find a hard dry place.
- Take a stick or a stone and mark on the ground, a mark for each complaint you have before God.
- When you have named all your frustration and disappointment, take the bucket and pour it slowly onto the ground. Watch the water splash and flow.
- Play in the water, drink some.
- Mark with the water the things you are grateful for.

Marked by grief

The experience at Meribah left a permanent mark on Moses. Of all the crises during his leadership, this one prevented him from crossing over into the promised land. In the Numbers account (20:1-13) God judges

177

Moses and Aaron as lacking faith and failing to uphold the holiness of God, and at the end of his life Moses deals with the consequences as he stands on the wrong side of the Jordan River (Deuteronomy 32:50-52).

Grief changes us, and not always how we would choose.

Prayer of confession

Lord God, you are good and you are holy.
I confess that I have not always trusted in you with all my heart and mind and strength. I have not always stood with courage, declaring your holiness and mercy.
I stand now in the mercy of the crucified Saviour.
He crossed over death for me,
and in his grace I know myself forgiven and healed.
Spirit of living water, flow through me.
Turn every complaint into gratitude,
fill every lack of faith with your everlasting love.
Through Jesus Christ, Amen.

Praying Goodbye with Children

A creative interactive prayer for families and all ages.

This is written specifically for a minister (or other person leaving) to lead on their last pastoral visit to a family home.

Prepare

- Bring a couple of copies of this page, and a tea-light candle (and matches).
- Gather (preferably together with the children) a basket of flowers (or leaves, sticks or small toys).
- Half fill a large bowl with water and place in the middle of the group. (If there are boisterous young children, you might also want a towel on hand!)
- Sit in a circle with the bowl and the basket of items in the middle.

Begin by explaining that you are leaving. Together with the family, tell the story of your relationship. Remember some special moments. Invite the family to ask you any questions they have.

Light the tea-light candle and float it in the bowl of water. Say a simple prayer to acknowledge the presence of God.

Invite each person to place an item from the basket into the bowl, and to say something they give thanks for. Everyone can affirm together *"Thank you God"* after each offering. Keep adding the items from the basket until they are all floating on the water.

Saying sorry

"Now we have a chance to say sorry to each other, for anything we feel bad about."

You need to begin; apologise for leaving (and anything else you wish to say), *"I feel bad about that because ..."*

Forgiveness

Jesus gave his life for us, so that we might be free and at peace. Friends, I declare God's forgiveness over you and over me. God does not count anything against us. And so we forgive each other, in this family and in our church. We know that we hurt each other, but we learn to let that go, over and over, and to live together in love.

Shake hands with each person, saying *"The peace of God be with you."*

You could sing a song together if that seems appropriate and familiar.

Blessing

Now is a chance to offer any gifts, or words of encouragement. You might like to name for each child the gifts you see in them.

Finish by saying together the Aaronic Blessing:

> The Lord bless you and keep you
> The Lord make his face shine on you
> and be gracious to you
> The Lord turn his face toward you
> and give you peace.
> Amen

Blessing of Closure When Leaving a Congregation or Group – Mary Nilsen

This blessing liturgy written by Mary Nilsen and her family, was published in a beautiful book called *For Everything a Season: 75 Blessings for Daily Life.*[7]

Preparation

When people leave a congregation or group it is sometimes with much frustration, sometimes with little feeling, and sometimes with much sadness. This blessing will help ease the emotions of a painful leaving, whether that pain is anger or grief, and send people on their way with God's blessing. For congregational use it can be done with a small group or with the whole congregation if feasible.

- Fill a blessing cup.

Welcome

For everything there is a season and a time for every matter under heaven.

Welcome to this time for reflecting upon our life together and wishing each other God's blessings.

Prayer

God of every yesterday and every tomorrow, make your presence known to us in this time of letting go and moving on. Wrap us in your love. May the experience of grace during this time we spend together support us in the days and weeks ahead. Amen.

Bible Text

Peace I leave with you. My peace I give to you. I do not give you as the world gives. Do not let your hearts be troubled. And do not let them be afraid.

John 14:27

Reflection

Ask the person(s) leaving to respond to one or more of these statements:

- I am grateful for …
- I am sad about …
- I am leaving now because …

If appropriate have the persons remaining respond, perhaps by sharing ways they are also sad and grateful.

Ritual Action

Leader:	For the joys shared,
Response:	**Thank you Lord.**
Leader:	For the hurts caused,
Response:	**Forgive us Lord.**
Leader:	For new beginnings,
Response:	**Bless us Lord.**

- Invite people to pass the blessing cup saying: *May the peace of the Lord be with you.*
- Give the blessing cup to the person leaving to drink.
- Those who are leaving then respond: *And also with you.*

Blessing

Sing or say the blessing song **'As you go on your way.'** (See music below)

As you go on your way may Christ go with you.
May he go before you to show you the way.
May he go behind you to encourage you,
Beside you to befriend you,
Above you to watch over,
Within you to give you peace.

Songs for Endings

As You Go On Your Way – *John Ylvisaker (song)*

Text: Anonymous. Music: "Rapid City"
John C. Ylvisaker © 1982. Used with permission.

Holy Spirit, ever seeking – *Colin Gibson (song)*

A hymn for the ending of a ministry

CROSSOVER

Words and music © Colin Gibson (2022)

1. Ho - ly Spi - rit, al - ways rest - less, seek - ing what is fresh and new;
2. Bless what now has been con - clu - ded, time to take an - o - ther way;
3. Much be - gun, much un - com - ple - ted, sa - tis - fac - tions hard to find;
4. Yet the Word has been de - liv - ered, dai - ly joys and sor - rows shared;

MAY BE SUNG AS A FOUR-PART CHORUS

through the chan - ges in our liv - ing, may we e - ver fol - low you.
friend - ships made not left be - hind us, car - ried to an - o - ther day.
con - ver - sa - tions on - ly start - ed of the heart and soul and mind.
deep com - pas - sion, love in act - ion, time and en - er - gy un - spared.

In each end a

new be - gin - ning, in each close an op - 'ning door. *Bless* this min - ist -

ry now end - ed, lead us through what lies be - fore.

Words and music by Colin Gibson,
composed for Moving On, used with permission.

May the God of Peace – *Jules Riding and Silvia Purdie (song)*

May the God of peace him – self sanc-tify you – u. May your

spirit, soul and body be kept sou – u – nd. May your

life be who – ly blame less at the coming of the Lord

for he who calls you is faith – ful and true.

He under - stands you. He's close around you.

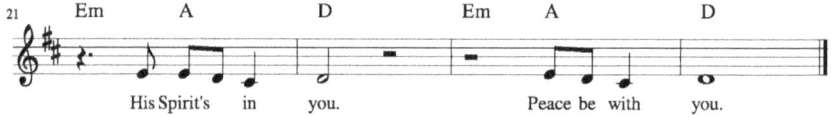

His Spirit's in you. Peace be with you.

May the God of peace himself sanctify you.
May your spirit, soul and body be kept sound.
May your life be wholly blameless at the coming of the Lord,
For he who calls you is faithful and true.
He understands you
He's close around you
He's caring for you
His Spirit's in you
Peace be with you.

May the God of mercy bless and anoint you.
May your mind be opened to his brilliant light.
May your life ring with praises and the joy of the Lord,
For he who loves you will see the journey through.
He understands you
He's close around you
He's caring for you
His Spirit's in you
Peace be with you.

The Blessing, by Jules Riding
Adapted by Silvia Purdie with permission from Jules Riding

The Peace Song – *Silvia Purdie (song)*

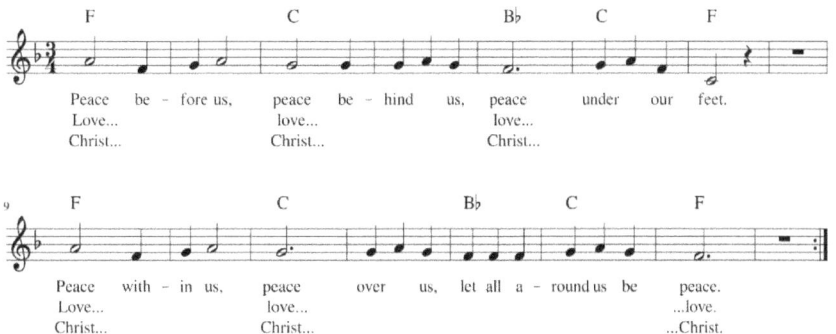

Blessing Song List

There are various musical settings to the Aaronic Blessing (Numbers 6:24-26), including **'May the Lord, mighty God, bless and keep you forever,'** sung to the Edelweiss tune. During the Covid pandemic **'The Blessing'** (from Elevation Music) became a global phenomenon. Kiwi blessing songs include:

'Ma te marie a te Atua' (traditional Māori hymn), *With One Voice*,[8] 679

'Now as we go' (words by Shirley Murray, music by Colin Gibson) *Alleluia Aotearoa*,[9] 99

Beautiful leaving and blessings songs from *Faith Forever Singing* (New Zealand Hymnbook Trust):[10]

'God speed you on your way' (words by Shirley Murray, music by Shona Murray), 29

> *Verse 1:*
> God speed you on your way,
> safe keep you every day,
> give you wing, cause to sing,
> all this we wish and pray.

'It all depends on where I'm going' (words and music by Colin Gibson), 39

> *Verse 2a:*
> It all depends on how I'm choosing
> for the life that is in me,
> but I will never lose the hand of Christ,
> the one who walks with me

'Nothing is lost on the breath of God' (words and music by Colin Gibson), 50

> Verse 3:
> Nothing is lost to the heart of God
> nothing is lost forever;
> God's heart is love, and that love will remain,
> holding the world forever.
> No impulse of love, no office of care,
> no moment of life in its fulness,
> no beginning to late, no ending too soon,
> but is gathered and known in its goodness.

Poems and Psalms by Silvia Purdie

Tipped out

My eyes sting with weeping
body shaken with emotion
from the heavy hand of God on me
Lord save me from me!
Tip me out completely into you
pattern me after your ways of doing things
constant outpouring
and refilling
tears and dancing
lightness of feet
and tender of touch
you walk the weeping way
utterly free from worry
devoid of anxiety
holding these paradoxes
of trust and struggle
perfectly balanced
light as air
strong as stone.
Me and my tears
are scooped up
shaken kindly
wrapped around
turned around
patted on the back
and sent home again.
Was I expecting something else?

My question on pain

OK, so we do the tasks of grief
work through the complications of grief
and threads disentangle
and layers fall away
leaving
a core of pain.

I could do without this, Lord.
Surely I'm done with this by now, Lord.
There is nowhere for the pain to go
but to you, Lord
Jesus, suffering One.
It pulls me to your cross
right inside your pain.
Your heart surrounds me,
beats around me.
So here is my question for you, Lord:
When Thomas put his hand
inside the wound in your side
did you flinch?
Did it hurt?
Did it ache with the memory of pain?
Your resurrected body carried the marks of your suffering
– why?
If they were healed how could Thomas put his hand into your side
into the holes in your wrists?
You are glory on earth.
Your resurrected body was the signpost of eternity
where grief and pain will be no more

(Revelation 21:4).

So why was it not perfect?
"My grace is sufficient for you, for my power is made perfect in
weakness"

(2 Corinthians 12:9)

I know these things, but my pain cries out for more knowing -
Does pain endure?
Will sorrow fade into everlasting joy?
Lord I do not want a washed-out peace.
I want Your body,
punctured and yet whole
beaten and yet glorified
perfect in imperfection
love sufficient
love enough.
I'm not sure that is an answer
but it will do
for now.

Trauma and Recovery

Trauma is static
crackle hiss in the background
assaulting concentration
constantly interrupting
pain as noise
noise as pain
Recovery is silence
growing grass and bird call
as stress splutters and fades
and rest, beautiful rest
comes sweet and welcome

Trauma is unmentionable
look on the bright side
change the subject
don't bring it up
don't mention the war
the elephant in the room
glowers and grumbles at being ignored
Recovery is telling
my story, my truth
courageous honesty
looks the growling memories
in the eye
stare them down
until they shine back
with strength
brave and true

Trauma is stuck
new day old pain
here it comes again
round and round going nowhere
Recovery is endurance
this too will pass
get through, hold on
hang in there

Trauma is hit
after hit
slam
nose bleed black eye
reeling
Recovery is kindness
a touch of care
clean water
kind words
just enough

Trauma is not understanding
no answer for questions
the WHY batters incessantly
Recovery is not understanding
but trusting anyway

Psalm 20: "The Answer to My Call"

To read Psalm 20 you need to decide who is the 'you' and who is the one speaking. Then the last 3 verses are 'we' – who is 'we'? Here is one possible reading, from an understanding of Jesus' role as intercessor. This is Jesus speaking, "Christ Jesus, who died, yes, who was raised, who is at the right hand of God, who indeed intercedes for us." Romans 8:34.

Jesus, Lord Jesus, I hear your Word to me today:
[insert your own name], I pray for you today,
I declare God's truth for you today.
The Lord answers you in your day of trouble
the name of the Lord protects you
help comes from the Holy Place
you are sustained from Zion.

[your name], the Lord remembers you and all you have laid down
the Lord honours the price you paid, burnt in holy fire
the Lord is giving you what your heart desires
the Lord is fulfilling your whole purpose.
Shout for joy, for you are overcoming!
Fly the flag of victory of the name of the Lord
for the Lord is enacting all you have asked for.

You are anointed, you are chosen,
you call and the Lord answers –
his hand opens for you, wait and see!
Some stand on strategy, others trust in their own authority
but you and I, all we have is the goodness of God.
Others will collapse and fall in the day of trouble
but we stand up and stand firm.
Father, oh my Father, we call to you
and you answer us, you uphold us.

Psalm 42: "As the deer longs"

As the deer longs …
hunger and thirst, holy desire
bubbling up from a place hidden beneath
the tasks to do and the emails to answer and the dinner to cook
… my heart
cast down, weighed down, shoved down
out of the way, out of polite conversation
this unbalanced longing that refuses sedation
that leaks as tears for no particular reason
… Why?!
disquieted discounted dissatisfied
deep to deep, the roar of the ocean
calls to the roar of your Spirit within my spirit
 … Where?!
This is You, this hope, this thirst
this knowing of You I call my Help, my Hope, my God
… When?!
battered still by evidence of failure and rejection
pain carried yet in the heart, in the bone
… and deep calls to deep
as by day the Lord commands steadfast love
and by night holy song calls to song
calls up prayer,
prayer to the God of my life.

Psalm 70:14: "Hope Continually"

But I will hope continually
and praise you more and more
I will hope continually
and trust you more and more
I will adore continually
and deepen in you more and more
I will wait continually
and trust you more and more
I will listen continually
and obey you more and more
I will
and invite you more and more
and believe you more and more
I will rest continually
and work with you more and more
You are my hope, Lord God
my confidence from my youth
I have leaned on you from birth
You carried me from my mother's womb
My praise is You, always You

A Theology of Ending

Oh but I do like shiny new things!
Can't we just skip the ending,
go straight to the new beginning?
Surely God is God of the new!
New every morning – Great is Thy Faithfulness!
(It's in our name: New Zealand.
Who knows or cares where the 'old' Zeeland was?)
But God in the endings?
in the crumbling of hope
the breaking of promises
the losing of love –
What is my theology of ending?
I seek the face of God
shiny in morning glory.

But can I crouch with Moses under a rock
and only see the back of God
passing by, disappearing –
Come back, God! where are you going?
Can I stand with Mary and see the back of Jesus
ripped by the whip
splintered by the cross
as they take him down
and carry him away?

How annoying Jesus was,
talking about the endings before he'd hardly begun!
"The Son of Man must die" – just shut up already!
He rotates my theology in my hands
"Look at it backwards," he says
"See the end before the beginning"
"All you build will fall
all you do will be lost.
Only I remain
for I Am
and I love you."
Not very flash theology
but it will do.

Life Calls For Lament – *Malcolm Gordon*

Rev. Malcolm Gordon is a Presbyterian minister who has returned to his Dunedin roots, where he is currently doing a PhD on lament through the University of Otago. He is also an Adjunct Lecturer with both Carey Baptist College and Knox Centre for Ministry and Leadership, especially in topics of creativity, music and the arts, and worship. Malcolm is an accomplished singer-song-writer; music and other resources available through One Voice.[11]

• • •

Who in your life can ask you the question, "How are you?" and get an answer other than, "Fine"? For most of us, in most settings, the question 'how are you?' is just a standard greeting. People in shops ask us, people doing phone surveys ask us, and they all get "Fine." But there are some people in our lives for whom the question means something more. You can even hear it in the way they ask it: "How **are** you?" or "How are you **doing**?" This is someone who wants to know what life is like for me at the moment.

How I answer that question reveals something about my relationship with the person who asks it. The more rehearsed and routine my answer, the more superficial the connection I share with them. There's only a handful of people who can ask me that question and get more than "Fine" in response. I wonder, is God one of them? And is God's community, the church, one of those places where I can answer that question honestly?

Lament is an ancient Jewish practice that involves telling the truth to God, with God's people, even (perhaps especially) when the truth is not pretty. Lament is a significant part of the Bible. Not only are at least a third of the Psalms songs of lament (it is the single largest genre in the Psalter), but Ecclesiastes, Lamentations and huge tracts of Jeremiah, Ezekiel and Isaiah also fall into this category. However, the practice of lament has not really caught on through the history of the Christian Church, except in pockets – until recently as theologians and pastoral leaders have begun to reconsider its place in our worship.

Lament, at its simplest, is the act of complaint in conversation with God. It is built, as Walter Brueggemann would say, on a conviction that 'life isn't right' and that it could be different.[12] Jewish lament audaciously demanded that it was God's responsibility to put things right. It is worth noting just how presumptuous that sounds to our Christian ears, where our default position is to defer to God. However, let's recall the truth that it is only in our **closest relationships** that we can be the most honest. It is the people I know the best who can handle the worst of me. What does it say about our connection with God if we are constantly filtering our experience, forever checking ourselves, continually leaving aspects of our lives out of our worship because they 'don't fit'?

St Athanasius said, "In the Scriptures, God speaks to us. In the Psalms, we speak back." The Psalms, which are part of the ordained Word of God, are a gift to humanity in order to help us grasp the breadth of conversation that God invites us to share with him. Don't miss that: **God** is inviting us into this conversation. It spans from the whole hearted praise of "Bless the Lord, O my soul: and all that is within me, bless his holy name" (Psalm 103:1) to the broken hearted despair of "My God, my God, why have you forsaken me?" (Psalm 22:1) and the vitriolic outrage of "Break the teeth in their mouths, O God" (Psalm 58:6). Not only is God inviting us into this conversation, but God is also providing us with words for the moments when we have none of our own, words that even dare to question and doubt God's faithfulness. We are permitted to say these words – after all, God gave them to us!

If I am honest, and lament demands that I try to be, I do not have to look far to find the feelings expressed in the lament Psalms lurking in my own soul. Following an experience that leaves me wounded and feeling hunted, the line "Break the teeth in their mouths, O God!" does not so much give me ideas as it gives vent to what is already in me! Murray Rae suggests that lament is how we pray all our anger and violence to God, so we don't end up letting it spill out elsewhere.[13] God alone is the One who can bring an end to the war that rages in my soul. Christ takes all the hate the world can muster and dies uttering, "It is finished." So my real choice is not whether to feel these things or not, because I **do** feel them. My only choice is whether to share them with God or not. I can live truthfully, or I can live in denial. I am learning to choose the truth, because it sets me free. Have you noticed the way the Psalms of lament so often turn to praise? **Something** happens as we tell God what it's like for us; **somehow** people are liberated.

In our Christian worldview, the doubt and despair that typify the Psalms of lament implies a loss of faith. However it represented precisely the opposite for our Jewish forebears. Lament was an act that was animated and undergirded by faith. It may not have been pretty, but it was **still prayer**. God may seem distant, or absent, yet the lamenter still cries out to be heard and delivered. A true loss of faith would result in silence, for there is no one there to hear. Lament, therefore does not represent a loss of faith, but a profound **act** of faith, especially in places that seem to deny God's steadfast love.

In our eagerness to defend God, we have to be careful that we don't end up defending evil, giving reasons for why terrible things have happened. Evil is not to be explained. We do not do the work of God when we look for silver linings in black thunder clouds. Often we simply reveal our own inability to sit in the presence of great pain. It is the experience of life in a broken world that seems to reject a belief in a God who cares and can make a difference. It is the person who laments who resolutely refuses to surrender that conviction, despite all the evidence to the contrary.

Some summarising thoughts:

Lament is pragmatic: Of course we all wish we weren't suffering, we wish we didn't endure seasons when God seemed absent, we wish the world didn't seem so dark and full of evil – but faith doesn't operate terribly well on wishful thinking. There is darkness around me, and there is darkness within me. I can either tell the truth about that, or I can lie to myself, to you and to God. But if my faith is going to survive in the real world, it needs to live in the real world.

Lament is faithful: It declares that God exists and demands that God do what God promises to do. It feels risky. God might get angry if we talk to him like that. But do you know what the Psalmist seems to say to that? Good! Only a **real** God can get angry, and only a real God can show up and save the world.

Lament honours God: Without lament we become 'yes men' and 'yes women' to whatever is happening in the world.[14] Without lament we surrender to fatalism; whatever is happening, no matter how awful, must be God's will. Without lament we end up undermining God's sovereignty and God's character. We undermine God's sovereignty because we doubt that God can do anything about what's wrong. And we undermine God's character, because we doubt that God **wants** to do anything about what is wrong. Lament gives God the space to turn up and be God.

Lament moves us through our pain: One of the objections I encounter is that engaging with our suffering will be like Pandora's Box; once we start, we may not ever be able to stop, or regain the control (or pretence) we had previously. Lament is an enacted belief that God is more powerful than our brokenness.

The Road to Emmaus (Luke 24:13-35) tells of two disciples, heart sore, trudging out of the story of redemption, too bewildered to believe the rumour that Jesus might have risen. They lament to the stranger who falls in step beside them, "but we had hoped that he was the one who was going to redeem Israel" (v21). The stranger hears their story, then walks them out of it and into a new one, until they are able to see that the stranger is actually

Christ himself. Lament does not lead us into a dead-end of wallowing, but in conversation with Christ it leads us into an honest dealing with our pain, and out the other side, just as Christ leads us into death and out the other side into life everlasting.

A final pastoral thought. It may be tempting to read this and concede that lament may have something to offer, and the next time something terrible happens you will look into it. By that stage it will be too late. There will be too much bewilderment to learn new songs, and too much anxiety to try to explore a new aspect of God's character and relationship with us. It would be like trying to do a fire drill for the first time when the building is already burning. By then it is too late. In the aftermath of the Dunblane massacre in Scotland in 1996, one minister confessed shortly after, "It was on that Sunday that I realised we had lost the ability to lament."[15] I heard similar confessions from pastors and church members following the Christchurch Mosque attacks. If lament is going to be part of our response to evil and suffering, then it needs to be part of our normal spiritual conversation with God every Sunday, and on many of the days in between. When something terrible happens in our community, or in our country, it put us all on the same footing, united in bewilderment and grief.

And there is someone in that place every Sunday in our congregations, because their marriage is on the rocks, their job is uncertain, their kids are in trouble, or their parents are going downhill. Ordinary life calls for lament. Our own ordinary lives call for it. How are we giving voice to the suffering that would otherwise render these saints silent? How can we resist the work of evil, which isolates us in our pain, and feeds the narrative of God's distance and disinterest? There is a Gospel shaped irony in the truth that it is not in the denial of these doubts, but in bringing them into the loving light of God and God's people that we are freed.

A Lament: a prayer to God when we cannot find God
– *Malcolm Gordon*

I'm right outside your door.
But I have knocked and knocked,
I have rung the bell til my arm hurt
And I have shouted til my voice cracked.
Are you even at home?
Where are you if you aren't here?
I don't know where else to look,
And I'm so weary from the journey it took to get here.
I need to talk for I'm at my wits end.
I need to rest for I am rung out and worn out.
I need you to be here.
I need you.
Where are you if you aren't here?
Come and light a lamp in the window
Come and open the door,
Let your warmth spill over me
Let me stumble over your threshold
And into your arms.
Don't leave me out here.
I feel hunted and alone.
I need more than a memory
Of your kindness and your strength.
I know you can help me
And I believe you want to.
I'm not leaving until you show up.
Don't keep me waiting forever.
And once you've come
I'll tell anyone who'll listen
How you showed up and saved me.
So show up.
Let me feel the kindness
I have heard so much about.
I'm not leaving til you do.
Where are you if you aren't here?

Inside Out – *Ana Lisa de Jong*

(Living Tree Poetry)

We are broken
but we are entirely intact.
We are shattered
but still in one piece.
We are grieving
but still wholly complete.
We are lost
but found.
We leave the throng
and arrive in Him.
We run
but never for long.
We look left, or right,
within and without.
He is always there,
waiting for us to recognise.
We are broken
but held together by love.
Shattered
but pieced together with tender intent.
Grieving
but held from breaking apart.
Lost in ourselves
but never to Him.
Who finds the cracks
and enters them
to restore us from inside out.

Except a Grain of Wheat – *Ana Lisa de Jong*
(Living Tree Poetry)

Except a grain of wheat

fall, catch the current of the wind
and lose all sense of direction
to rest in a place unbidden and foreign,
it remains a single grain.

Yet, unbridled or contained,
and at the mercy of God's faithfulness,
it bears the seed for the new season's harvest.
It becomes new bread.

Yes, I think it is that what often looks like death
or lack of fruitfulness is instead
just the time it takes
for the gift of life to flourish.

And tears and gestures, or words,
the frustrated expressions
from good intents gone vaguely wrong,
or not as we would have determined,

the love that appears to be in vain,
they bear our heart's cries as seed.
While God's purposes he sometimes shields
from our current understanding.

So that just like grain or leaves,
or anything that falls,
we find next season's yield
is often stored

in the remains of the first.
Apparent death just the shedding
of the husk
that brings about new birth.

Endnotes

1   Joyce Rupp, *Praying Our Goodbyes* (Ave Maria Press. Kindle Edition), 64.

2   Rupp, 65.

3   Rupp, 66.

4   Rupp, 68.

5   Rupp, 73.

6   'Thank You, Lord', by Dennis Jernigan, Hillsong Worship.

7   Nilsen family, *For Everything a Season: 75 Blessings for Daily Life* (Zion Publishing, Iowa, 1999). Used with permission from Mary Nilsen.

8   *With One Voice: A Hymn Book for All the Churches* with New Zealand Supplement, Harmony Edition (Collins, 1982).

9   Alleluia Aotearoa: *Hymns and Songs for all churches* (New Zealand Hymnbook Trust, 1993).

10   *Faith Forever Singing: New Zealand Hymns and Songs for a New Day* (New Zealand Hymnbook Trust, 2000).

11   One Voice: www.onevoice.org.nz

12   Walter Brueggemann, 'The Costly Loss of Lament', *Journal for the Study of the Old Testament,* October 1986, 62.

13   Murray Rae, 'Christ in the Old Testament', *Journal of Theological Interpretation,* vol 2.1, Spring 2008, 5.

14   Walter Brueggemann, 'The Costly Loss of Lament', *Journal for the Study of the Old Testament,* 11:36, 1986, 60.

15   John Bell, in Paul Bradbury, *Sowing in Tears: how to lament in a church of praise* (Worship Series, Grove Books, 2007) 3.

Section Five: Tools for Moving On

Leaving Well: 10 Tips

Grief and stress can do funny things, even to normally calm and competent people. It helps to be prepared for the processes of leaving a ministry. If we feel hurt or unfairly treated we have to draw on every ounce of maturity and training and support in order to not make matters worse. What does leaving well look like?

1. **Start to disengage from your role as minister in that place.** Accept that after you announce you are leaving people will start to exclude you from decision making. Start to absent yourself from conversations and encourage others to lead.

2. **Touch base personally with all those in local leadership.** Tell them what you have appreciated about them. Ask them how they have found working with you. Ask them what they need from you before you leave. Pray for them.

3. **Tidy up.** Handing over well means: don't leave a mess. Sort out papers, systems and digital files and hand these over to others in a form that they can fully access and make their own.

4. **Communicate well with your denominational leadership.** Make sure they know what is happening, and draw on regional help with any issues. Steve Jourdain makes the point that ministers have a responsibility to teach their congregation about the denominational processes that will step in after a minister leaves.

5. **Seek out new (and old) supports.** John Daniel advocates cultivating relationships with a wide range of people in a range of contexts, friendships strong and loving in which people can tell us what they really think, based on genuine respect and affection. Don't wait until you need help – invest in friendships over the long haul.

6. **Pay for help.** Our friends and whanau can only take us so far. Professional help in the form of supervision, counselling, coaching or spiritual direction is also required.

7. **Speak well of others.** Even when we are in pain, our ethical commitment is to use our words to build up the body of Christ not tear it down

8. **Choose what conflicts to address and with whom.** The Biblical principles of conflict resolution encourage us to talk directly the person concerned, and involve church leadership. However scripture also provides the option of breaking relationship and walking away from conflicts.

9. **Draw on the Holy Spirit** for power beyond yourself in order to keep bearing fruit of kindness, gentleness and self-control, even when these may feel in short supply. Worship in other places where you can.

10. **Rest.** Take time out. What enables you to come to a place of deep rest? Go there! This is easier said than done in the rush and busyness of leaving and moving, but rest is a vital component in transitions.

What to Say and What Not to Say

Perhaps the single biggest dilemma I faced in the process of leaving a ministry, both during the transition and afterwards, was what to say when people asked me why I decided to leave. How honest should I be? What motivated the question for this particular person? What information are they actually interested in? What is helpful or unhelpful for me to share? To whom was I accountable for what was said or left unsaid?

There is a strong Biblical principle warning against 'over-sharing' of hurtful words:

> "Death and life are in the power of the tongue, and those who love it will eat its fruits." (Proverbs 18:21)

> "A gossip goes about telling secrets, but one who is trustworthy in spirit keeps a confidence." (Proverbs 11:13)

Strongest of all is Paul's warning in Romans 1:29:

> "They were filled with every kind of wickedness, evil, covetousness, malice. Full of envy, murder, strife, deceit, craftiness, they are gossips."

On the other hand there is a strong Biblical principle of honesty, truth, speaking the truth in love, genuine friendship based on open communication.

Once we have done the work of recovery, then it is easy to speak well of each other. True wholehearted forgiveness is won through honest grief, hearing our own anger and confronting wrong-doing and injustice. Once we have come through the inner battles and conquered in the power of the Prince of Peace, the mark of this victory is an ease of speaking with kindness and respect about other people, even those we once considered adversaries. However, this does not mean banning all critique or warning from our speech. Where there are failures in our systems, how do we hold ourselves collectively to account, without condemnation or damage to each others' reputations? How do we speak about each other with both kindness and honesty?

The hard part is what to say when the emotions are still raw. Perhaps it is better to say nothing, to answer the curious question with: "I'm sorry, I'm still in the middle of sorting this, I can't answer you just now."

A real danger is triangulating, especially where the person who has asked the question has their own hurt or grievance against the church. I don't want to hand out ammunition for other people's battles. I don't want to sow dissention or feed conflict. I don't want my words to circle around in the mouths of others and cause hurt.

Rules for communicating when you are leaving

I'm not typically a 'rule' person. However, rules have a time and place, and one of those times and places is when things are mucky and relationships are strained. Grief does not tend to bring out the best in us. Maturity looks like sticking to your principles even when you don't feel like it. These 'rules' may help:

1. Only be fully honest about your pain with people outside the situation.

This may be only people that you pay: your supervisor or counsellor. With everyone in the church and even with your own family and friends, be careful what you say.

2. Decide in advance what information to share with whom.

Talk it through with people you trust and work out what to say to your congregation, to your family, and to wider networks. It's tempting to say more than you intend when someone is persistent and caring.

3. Don't criticise people in writing.

Never write unkind or critical things in an email or text message, either about the person you are writing to (direct) or about another person (indirect). When you decide to confront someone or share hard truths, do it in person, in the same room, in a safe space, when you both have time to be present for the hard conversation. Text messages and emails are too easy to 'share', 'save' and your words will come back to bite you! James's warning about the destructive power of the tongue applies triple to our social media world of instant permanent text:

> The tongue is a restless evil, full of deadly poison! With it we bless our Lord and Father, and with it we curse those who are made in the likeness of God. From the same mouth comes both blessing and cursing. E te whanau, this should not be so! (James 3: 8-10)

4. Never click 'send' when you are angry!

"Rash words are like sword thrusts, but the tongue of the wise brings healing." (Proverbs 12:18)

It is great to write stuff when we are upset. Just don't send it.

5. Be extra careful who gets copied in.

Be very deliberate about who you send emails to. If you copy someone in, write their name into the email with "copied to…"

Practical Pointers – *Andy Piggott*

The Venerable Andrew Piggott makes some practical suggestions for ending a ministry in *Leaving Well: Exploring Aspects of Moving from One Ministry to Another* (a Grove Booklet).[1] A retired archdeacon in the Diocese of Bath and Wells, Andy has been a long-time member of the General Synod of the Church of England.

• • •

Announce the news:

- Take steps to ensure that your news is communicated carefully and well. There is no best time, but the least worst is probably at the end of a service. My advice is to ensure that not only is a verbal announcement made in church, but that something is put on paper so that those who have not heard properly can read in their own time what you want to say.

- There will be some people you want to speak to before news of your leaving reaches the majority. There is no reason not to take them into your confidence, but remember the more people you include, the more likely it is that the news of your leaving will leak.

- Remember that for those with whom you have been working quite closely, your departure may have a disproportional impact. Try to anticipate their reactions and think how best they can be handled, recognising that you may not be the best person to do the handling.

- Please remember to be in touch with your senior colleagues to let them know of your plans.

The final few months:

- Some people can feel this as a kind of limbo period. Try to use it positively. Recognise this could be a helpful opportunity for the church to look back with thanksgiving at what God has been doing whilst you have been in post, and forward in preparation for the new season that lies ahead.

- Stay focused. Switching off mentally and spiritually before we leave will not help us to leave well. Be clear about what God wants you to concentrate on.

- The farewell party may be more necessary for those you are leaving than for you and your family … try to enjoy it.

- Mend fences. Inevitably there will be some people with whom you have not always got on and others with whom there have been difficulties. It is important for your sake, for theirs and for the sake of the gospel that in the process of leaving you try to ensure that you leave in peace. Make time to visit such people and to demonstrate grace, seeking reconciliation.

- Hand over head knowledge. It is crucial to spend time with your key leaders before you leave, talking through the things they need to know. What is stored on your computer that needs to be passed on? Talk about the people you have been caring for. Who will be caring for them when you leave?

- How would we like our successor to find things? What can we do to ensure there is a smooth transition?

- Who might be able to help you by chatting things through, praying for you or holding you to account?

The Role of Presbytery – *Steve Jourdain*

Rev. Steve Jourdain was (at the time of writing) in the process of retiring from a two-decade parish ministry in Palmerston North. For much of that time he has held leadership positions in the regional (presbytery) and national church. I interviewed him about his experience of supporting other people through ministry transitions.

• • •

Silvia: What is presbytery's role in ministry transitions, in your experience?

Steve: To a parish, presbytery often seems distant, irrelevant to their week by week life. So whenever I go into a parish in a presbytery role I always stress that I am "Presbytery with skin on," presbytery coming alongside to support them through this time of ministerial vacancy. I help them to review their life, clarify what kind of ministry they may need, and I offer help or resources for the transition. This is what presbytery does; this is what it means to belong to a denomination. And I have consistently found that congregations in transition become very appreciative of that role. Especially if there is some kind of crisis involving their minister, they are very glad to have an outside agency to support them. Where there is tension, presbytery works with the church council to say: "There are some things that need to be addressed here, before you go looking for another minister."

We also need to be aware that, more and more these days, the people who make up our congregations are not from a Presbyterian background and don't know Presbyterian polity and processes. So it is a good opportunity for a representative from presbytery to front up to the congregation so they can ask any questions they have. It is also important for a minister who is leaving to help their congregation understand what the process will be from there. Prepare your people for the transition; that will help with the grieving.

In our denomination, a pastoral tie is established by the presbytery and is ended by the presbytery. The minister is a member of presbytery, and is ultimately answerable to the presbytery, not to the congregation. Part of our Presbyterianism is that we are a cluster of congregations that form a presbytery, and ministers have responsibilities to use their gifts within the wider church as well as locally.

Silvia: What is best practice when a minister decides to accept another call or resign or retire?

Steve: It is wise to inform your local leadership first. Work with your church council about the best way and the best timing to finish. This is a bit of a hobby-horse of mine. When we are calling a new minister we involve the congregation and the leadership. But when a minister leaves, often they think it's all about their decision and no one else's. So it can come as a bombshell for the church.

I learned about this many years ago at St T's Anglican, when I was a member of the vestry. The vicar got a call to another parish, and he came to the vestry and said: "I've had a call that I am interested in. What do you think about me considering this?" I hugely respected him doing that, and it shaped my own thinking about how to finish. At that meeting he asked us all for our feedback. We were at a time of change in the church's life, and each of us said to the vicar, "We acknowledge that this is your decision to make but we appreciate you asking us." And each person added, "I don't think this is a good time for you to leave, because of what we are moving into together." The vicar thanked us, went away to consider our responses and he came back later to say: "I've decided not to accept this call. I have heard what you've said."

Interestingly, two years later he came back to us with another call, and did the same thing. And all of vestry went around the room and said: "As much as we love you and value you, we think this is an appropriate time for you to leave." And he did.

I am currently working towards retirement. I told my elders of my thinking over a year ahead, and we were able to talk and work through that, and plan together. It is good to be open with the church council and seek their feedback. We talked about 'When is a suitable time to finish?' I explained that, when I announce my retirement, presbytery must establish a Ministry Settlement Board, and then I can have no part in that process. I offered to the council: "If you would like to have conversations with me about the future, and possible people, we can delay my announcement until we have worked through that process." Once it is public, then it is important for me to stay right out of those conversations about the next minister.

The parish leadership is concerned about the responsibilities that I carry which will fall to them after I retire. So I prepared a 'one-pager' on the major events of the year, and I suggested some ways that the elders could keep connection and liaison with the ministry groups in the congregation. They found that clarity very helpful. I think their biggest concern is, 'You don't know what you don't know.'

Silvia: In your experience, what role does presbytery play in supporting ministers through difficult phases towards an ending?

Steve: Ministers and parishes are wise to consult with presbytery when there is conflict and unhappiness. Seek presbytery help if they need an outside perspective, or if they hit a difficulty that they need an external process for. Problems are often worse when people fail to communicate.

There are various ways in which a ministry may end, and each requires something different from presbytery. Some are happy retirement, or when a minister moves on in response to another Call, and may be occasions for celebration. However, any resignation has difficult factors, either personally for the minister or with the parish; you wouldn't resign otherwise. And some endings are the result of major upsets of some kind, where we need heavier processes.

So there is a continuum of presbytery response. At one end is low-key mentoring, a collegial chat that keeps presbytery in the loop with "This is what's going on for me." At the other end is the full weight that presbytery brings to bear, through a legal commission, where there is a serious breach of conduct or a breach of the pastoral tie in some way.

In the middle is our new Pastoral Resolution process. This is the presbytery coming alongside in a difficult time. I have seen examples where it's worked well, and I've seen examples where it hasn't worked.

A formal commission is incredibly expensive, in money and time and lawyers. It is a legal process that is required to make a decision. A commission has to be public; people have to know about it and have the opportunity to contribute. A Pastoral Resolution process can be kept more in-house, confidential to the parties. A commission has to announce a finding, whereas a Pastoral Resolution does not, so you can get parties together and try a mediated approach. I recently was part of one that had an exceptionally positive outcome. It was really great to see that it helped facilitate a way forward, where everybody was heard and got back on the same page. I am aware of other ones that didn't really resolve anything; but it is worth trying before a commission or a resignation.

Silvia: From what you have seen as a leader within these institutional processes, what makes the difference between whether a ministry ends well or ends badly?

Steve: We can't get away from the centrality of relationships. I've been thinking about this quite a bit lately. In any church leadership role you have to love your people. There is nothing more basic or important. So you try to communicate well, to listen in order to understand. You take into account their concerns when you are making your decisions.

In my case, I have said to the elders: "This is what I'm thinking – when do you think it would be appropriate for me to finish? When shall we announce it? What do you need from me as you prepare for this? What process do you want to follow?" We have shared 21 years together of leadership, and I know there's going to be a hole and an extra load for them. So if I love my leaders I will try to make that transition as easy as it can be, while recognising it will be a big change for them.

I don't think there are any different principles for ministry endings. You just apply good ministry principles to the end. Involve your local leaders and support them to the end. As you leave, try not to create additional difficulties for them.

I hope to end pastoral relationships with the congregation well, and to give space for whoever follows me to be able to establish themselves as minister and pastor without me looking over their shoulder. It will have its challenges, because we will stay living in the same city, and we have some deep relationships and good friends within the church. Some people may have difficulty accepting this ending. But my wife and I will not continue to be part of this church. I will make clear that my pastoral relationships will need to end, and also make clear the new arrangements until a new minister begins.

Silvia: When colleagues have come to you feeling deeply hurt or burnt out, what do they need from you as a presbytery person?

Steve: They need personal support as they go through their transition. Ask people what they need, what they would appreciate. Sometimes what they are looking for is a sounding board, feedback, someone to listen. Sometimes they want advice, but mostly they just need support and reassurance. Sometimes they ask, "What do you think my options are?" That is one of the things presbytery can help with: "I find myself in this situation, and I'm not sure what options I have. Can I take Leave? How much? Will you negotiate with the congregation, with the elders, or do I?" Ultimately it is their decision, but they need good information about the options in order to make a good decision. And the parish leadership also needs support: to feel heard and to understand their options.

Personal support is so important. Like any pastoral or crisis care, you want to be there with them so they don't feel alone. As I said to a colleague recently: "I trust you to make a decision. It's not about your family or your church; it is important to consult them, but it's your ministry, and you've got to make the call, in relationship with God, that you think is best. And whatever call you make, we will support you in it."

Silvia: That has been a real part of your calling and gifting to the church. I know I have benefited from that personally, and I'm sure many others have also. You genuinely do care, and that is ongoing. In the church it is easy to be 'out of sight out of mind,' and one of the harsh aspects of resigning is that a lot of relationships just stop. Nobody rings you, it's an odd thing. In the church we're not very good at providing ongoing pastoral connection with people who step outside our boxes.

Steve: I think that's a fair point, and not something presbytery has always done well. You would hope for better pastoral care beyond difficult transitions, wouldn't you?

Silvia: I do hope for that and that's definitely a motivation behind this book.

Steve: Ultimately it comes down to personal relationships. It's being aware and caring enough to say: "Even though you have resigned, I want to let you know that I'm here for you."

Releasing the Pastoral Tie – *David Coster*

Rev. David Coster is an active retired parish minister in Christchurch. His ministry included several years as the Moderator of Alpine Presbytery. In this conversation he discusses church policy regarding ministry transitions, highlighted by a ministry hand-over when I began in a parish after David had retired.

• • •

David: Retired ministers struggle with the transition from being 'in the loop' to being 'out of the loop.' I made the decision that when I retired I would no longer be a decision maker. Those who have to live with a decision should be the ones making the decision.

So, when you became the minister of *K* church, I made certain I stepped back. I said to you: "I'm here if you need to talk about something, but you have got to find out for yourself."

Silvia: What is our Presbyterian polity around this? Why does it matter, do you think, that ministers cease to exercise influence when they leave a parish?

David: I don't think it is written down, but that is our policy. When I left W I was invited back to take a wedding of a young couple I knew well but I said: "Look, I'm sorry. I'm not allowed to do that." The interim moderator is the one who decides, and he took the wedding.[2]

When I left *B* one of the elders was very close to death, and the family asked me if I could come back to take the funeral. I asked the elders and the moderator: "Is this acceptable?" I was invited and so I did. But they set the conditions, not me.

Silvia: So how would you state that as polity? What is our established practice in the Presbyterian Church?

David: Our established practice is that when the pastoral tie is severed, it is severed. The pastoral tie is your spiritual care for the wellbeing of the congregation and its people. When that is cut you are no longer responsible. You have a responsibility somewhere else.

Silvia: A pastoral tie is established at an induction service and is concluded by the presbytery representative at a final service.

David: When you retire or receive a new call, your presbytery and the parish set a date for a farewell. Your ministry finishes on your final Sunday. You leave, and you leave the people behind you. It is not easy. I remember my final day at *W*, when we were driving away, all of us were in tears: the kids, my wife and I were all in tears. She didn't want to go there in the first place, and yet by the time we came to leave we were part of the community.

For the minister, the pastoral tie means that you are the minister. You have a relationship with the people, but they're not your friends, even though many of them have a friendship with you.

Silvia: It is not a friendship, it's not family. It is something which can be started and ended, which is different from a friendship. You don't cut a friendship like that; that would be highly offensive.

David: Yes. Except there will probably be certain people in a congregation that you have developed a friendship with.

Silvia: I wonder if that requires a connection outside of parish life. The pastoral tie is a particularly framed relationship, and for a friendship to outlive the pastoral tie I suspect it needs to have grown in other contexts as well.

David: I think you can have an ongoing personal relationship without it being as the Minister. But it is up to us to make certain that these relationships do not pull us in to interfering in the life of the church.

Silvia: What would you advocate as best practice when leaving a parish?

David: If you are aware that there is a tension for the incoming minister, to my mind, the best practice is to leave. Graciously exit and pay the cost. We have to let things change after we leave. Many churches do change, for better or for worse, and that can be hard to watch.

After I retired, someone in the congregation said, "We'd love you to come back, please keep coming" and I said, "I can't actually do that." "Why not?" they asked, and I said: "Because Silvia is your minister, and if I am there I may impede what she wants to achieve in the life of the congregation. If you like her, you're going to tell me how good she is. And if you don't like her, and there are problems, you are going to tell me how bad she is!" That would undermine your authority and role as the minister.

Silvia: You're describing what I would call triangulation.

David: Yes. It was up to me to make sure that I did not participate in those conversations. The responsibility for not getting into triangulation rests with the leaving minister, out of respect for the incoming minister.

Silvia: So you felt a sense of responsibility to me as the incoming minister, to not undermine my ability to establish a pastoral tie.

David: That's right. We are colleagues. You must have the freedom, without my continuing influence in the background, to exercise your ministry with your gifts and your abilities.

Having a period of a complete break is helpful. After a year or so, you invited me back to take a service or two, which was wonderful. That was your choice. And it was my choice whether I say yes or no.

The Key Role of Church Elders

(Contributor's name withheld)

• • •

前人栽樹，後人乘涼.

This Chinese proverb translates:

"One generation plants a tree, the next enjoys the shade."

To me this shows how one generation in the church benefits from the strength of previous generations, especially how young ministers and youth pastors benefit from the wisdom and godliness of elders and church leaders.

I'm still fairly new to pastoral ministry, and my experience so far highlights the key role of the eldership in either encouraging or undermining a pastor. If a church leadership is strong and godly, then they should have the ability to take on a young or inexperienced pastor. They could then support them, as I experienced, realising that there must be fair expectations on the pastor with grace and patience for them to grow. However, I have also experienced the pain of a ministry ending before I felt called to leave.

It is incredibly hard getting a foot in the door when most churches want an ordained minister with twenty years' experience, but still twenty years left before retirement! I will always be grateful to a Chinese independent church in Australia who took a risk in taking me on as their English pastor even though I had no experience of being a pastor before. I had served as a youth pastor and other ministries, but leading a church while in my late twenties was very different. Mistakes were made and I grew a lot in my first two years of pastoral ministry. The church leadership showed me a lot of grace and gave me time to grow, which prepared me for the challenges to follow. My sermons were initially too much like Bible college lectures, and an elder gave me some constructive criticism, done in a loving way. This was the feedback I needed to make improvements. A career change would probably have been the result if the church had placed unreasonable expectations on me, but the elders supported my wife and I. I will always be grateful to them for giving me the start that I had longed for.

I once discussed with a presbytery Executive Officer (EO), what would be easier: taking over from a pastor who had left the church on good terms, or from a pastor who had left on bad terms? I was of the opinion that it would be easier to follow a pastor who left on bad terms. If people were happy to see them leave, the expectations on the new minister would be lower. However, if everyone loved the previous pastor because they preached great sermons and spent time meeting the pastoral needs of the congregation, the new pastor may not live up to the high standard set by their predecessor.

Many people struggle with change when a pastor retires, and having to get used to a new person. A minister I served with in the Chinese church announced his retirement and that he was heading back to Hong Kong. "I was supposed to die before you retired!" one of the older members of his congregation told him. It was both an incredible compliment to the minister but also a sad indictment on how congregations struggle with change. The next minister had big shoes to fill. I therefore said to the EO that I would much rather follow someone who hasn't set the bar so high.

He replied with his experience and wisdom, "Sometimes that is easier, but often when a minister leaves on good terms they leave the church much healthier than someone who doesn't." I saw this in one church where a minister's contract was not renewed because he did not spend enough time in pastoral care and did not listen to feedback. It took some time for the church to recover. His successor was gifted in pastoral care, and well loved, but there were a lot of issues to sort through. The new minister's sermons were not as good as the previous minister's, but because he spent time with the people they showed him grace.

I was once appointed to a church on stated supply, following a minister whose sudden retirement came as a shock to the church. Even after he left he continued to communicate with some of the elders and had ongoing influence. This resulted in my position coming to an end. Two of the elders told me that they were still talking with him, including sending him copies of my sermons. When I shared this with the interim moderator, he dismissed it. It was then that I knew my time at the church was limited. One elder said that he was never going to vote for me to become the minister of the church, so I could not be approved. When my supply contract ended I tried to leave on good terms with everyone, but it was hard because I did love the people of that church.

That experience taught me the importance of having people on your side. It is one thing for people to say they like you, but it is another for people to fight for you; in this case, to fight for me to stay. If the interim moderator had resolved the situation of the previous minister interfering then I may have stood a chance. Having the right people in the eldership makes all the difference. Their collective decision making has more influence than a pastor's; they are responsible for choosing the pastor, and many other important decisions. Credit for a healthy church often goes to the pastor, but much of it should go to the church leadership. They choose the pastor as well as support the pastor to make the good decisions that result in a healthy church. The congregation is the foundation of the church, not the pastor at the centre – who is expected to grow the church without changing it!

So if your church is looking for a minister or youth pastor, take a look at yourselves first to see if you have the strength to support a new pastor. The church with the interfering predecessor was clearly not ready, because they needed to sort things out before they could move forward with someone new.

If you are a church with a new minister, are you giving them the opportunity to grow and supporting them when they need it? Do you show them grace and allow them to make honest mistakes?

If you are a church with a loved minister who is about to retire, do you have a succession plan? Are you truly aware that the future new pastor will be different to the one you have? Could you support a new pastor as an associate before the current pastor retires, so that there is a period of transition? I have seen this happen a few times, especially in Chinese churches where some ministers give up to two years notice.

Whatever your situation, you need to be asking questions with the knowledge that the best thing for a new pastor, other than a strong relationship with God, is strong and healthy church leadership. That foundation allows us pastors to become the pastors we are called by God to become and the pastors the church needs us to be.

Grieving Congregations and Church Decline
– *John Daniel*

Rev. John Daniel has for many years specialised in mission resourcing and transition ministry in the PCANZ. Originally from India, he now calls Dunedin home. He is also a long-time hockey coach and was recently appointed to the national board of Hockey New Zealand.

I talked with John about how congregations grieve when they experience transitions. What happens as congregations face the possibility of their own ending? What are the grief processes involved in this, and what does this bring out in people? What does 'ending well' look like for a church?

• • •

Silvia: When my husband and I were training for ministry, nearly 20 years ago, our class talked about the organisational life cycle, and tried as best we could to prepare ourselves to minister in a denomination in decline.

We understand what is happening: Presbyterian (and Methodist and Anglican) churches grew rapidly in the post-war 'boomer' years, and since then have followed the life cycle of the generation who were post-war teenagers, who are now in their 80s. It is all quite predictable. As that generation passes away so will the churches that they loved and lead.

Our training for church leadership focused on ways to interrupt that cycle, to attract younger generations, to rescue churches from death. We committed ourselves to nurture new things emerging out of the old. Turns out, this is easier said than done. I wish we had understood more about what it actually feels like for a group of people to experience decline, and the grief that comes with it, and what that brings out in people. I wish I had understood more about the dynamics inherent within churches that undermine new missional initiatives, that protect the church from change, that insulate the church from God's fresh work – and so that make ultimate closure more inevitable.

John: We struggle to deal with grief in the church, especially for the ending of a congregation. When organisations experience decline, and start to face the possibility of demise, there is grief, both individual and collective grief. But there is typically little in our normal Sunday worship that helps us reflect on dis-ease, decline and death. We try not to think about it; we assume that the church is forever.

One day Christ will return and the church will no longer be required. Until then, Jesus calls us to be faithful stewards, to walk alongside one another with grace, and learn the lessons of humility. That is my hope: Christ in us the hope of glory!

Silvia: What are the pastoral, relational and emotional aspects as a church approaches its own ending?

John: The church is an organisation and an organism. Each congregation has shared fond memories, and deeply held attachments to ways of being and the buildings and physical objects that make up church life. When this is threatened by decline or closure this will bring to the fore any unresolved grief from the past. Voices of blame and anger and control can ring loudly in the room. Our collective grief makes it hard for us to do the right thing and to listen to the whisper of the Spirit. I think of Elijah in the cave – it can be easier to focus on the earthquake, wind and fire than listen to the still small voice.

We humans love the comfort of the same, and when we are forced to change we resist it. We cling to the familiar. Having to let go brings anxiety and fear of loss. And if we have eyes to see it, there is also excitement of the new. Each individual will have their own past history of grief, their own experience of death and loss. When people, especially leaders in the church, carry significant unresolved grief, they can project their grief into the church in dysfunctional ways, which can have a significant effect on what happens in the decision making.

Silvia: My observation is that some churches gently let go into closure and accept it somehow with relief and grace. But more often it brings out the fight in people, and unfortunately we end up fighting about things like the organ, or the building, or the money. And in that process the very things which could bring new life or a new beginning are rejected.

John: The hardest thing for me is the disconnect between what a church says it wants and what it actually does when things come to a crunch. Most churches, when facing their own decline, want to attract more people, but it can get a desperate edge. It is anxiety driven, and set up to fail. Our rhetoric and intention is mission, but our systems continually pull us back towards trying to maintain what we used to have.

Silvia: What grief do churches have to work through in order to release energy for the new?

John: Denial is a gift from God. It says that this person needs to be in this safe space for a reason and for a period of time. Denial is part of the process to successfully go through their travail in this situation. It is not helpful to try to force people to grieve, or shake people out of denial. When I come in as a transition minister to help a congregation deal with their grief and face an unknown future, I trust that God's purposes that will enable them to traverse this. My task is to pray for them, to pastorally accompany them, and be present to them. And to then gently tell them a story, like Jesus did. Place that person in that story, in a way that's not blaming or humiliating, in a way that points to the future and hope that the gospel provides for us all. That takes time.

Healthy grieving as a church, as a collection of companions within a discipleship framework requires spiritual disciplines. That means prayer, lament and celebration. It means telling our story, where we have come from. Here is our history. Let's celebrate that. And here is the reality that is facing us. Let's face that.

Silvia: One especially gnarly issue is about ownership. When I hear people's ongoing sense of grievance after a church closure, I often hear their sense of losing what was 'ours.' How did we figure that the church belongs to us? The building, the money in the bank – that we built it, we have rights over it, even if the 'we' ceases to exist. It becomes a tough question of who is 'we': can we release our own little corner of the church into the hands of the wider church? Can we bless others and enable something new somewhere else?

John: As a church we have our institutional responses to congregational decline. The PCANZ has decided that small congregations must be reviewed, and the Presbytery has the option to force a dwindling parish to close. We have also decided to not encourage two struggling congregations to merge. We have found that when two declining congregations combine it leads to even fewer people and even bigger problems. However, institutional solutions don't solve relational problems. We have to address the pastoral issues. A congregation is part of the wider institution but it is a relational organism.

Silvia: When a congregation is in a stage of decline, I notice that they become less connected with their wider community, a more closed organism. It's a 'chicken and egg' situation, we decline because we become less missional and we have less missional capacity the more we decline.

John: Yes, but a tiny elderly church with 12 people over 80 can pray something new into being; I have seen that! By God's grace new things can happen, new points of connection between a church and their community – the Kingdom of God can burst in! Just one person in active service to God following Jesus and doing the thing they have been called to do can create waves that change multiple lives. Mission begins with spiritual practices and a deep sense of surrendering all this to God. It requires an openness, and a willingness to respond to what God might be asking of us here and now, to fulfil our promise to follow Christ.

Silvia: What can the wider church do to enable congregations to grieve in healthy ways?

John: The most important thing is to give people a safe space to express their grief. That starts with us as leaders and ministers. How much have we reconciled ourselves to loss in our life? If we have not addressed our own grief, we are likely to project that into the church in dysfunctional ways. To lead effectively requires that we understand our own deep losses, fears and long held hopes. Ministers are good at supporting other people through grief, but can we talk about our own grief?

Silvia: What is your Biblical framework for grieving?

John: There is a huge amount in scripture about grief. The ultimate story of healthy grieving is Jesus. He knows that there will be loss and he prepares his disciples for that as best he can. He knows he is going to die, and feels all that grief of leaving his human condition with his human loves. We see the tears and the sweat that rolls like blood at the Mount of Olives. And there is the strength to continue on that journey. There is that moment of surrender: "yet not my will but yours be done" (Luke 22:42). There is the terrible grief of betrayal. And then on the cross, the ultimate grief of feeling cut off from God and abandoned. Then there is the sense of completion: "It has finished! I have done it! I've done it." God has accomplished that for which God sent me and I have remained faithful. That is holy grieving, both personal and collective.

From the Centre to the Edge – *Susan Blaikie*

Complex grief in churches is experienced collectively as well as individually. Rev. Susan Blaikie argues that churches in decline need to identify and let go of old assumptions that keep them in 'survival mode.' This also means addressing the fear and grief that goes with leaving the old, while enabling the missional life that the church is called by God to do and be. Susan's Master's research was on how leaders can be equipped to help churches move from maintenance to missional culture. She is currently doing a PhD through the University of Otago.

• • •

Susan: Just like other organisations such as businesses or charities, churches operate with underlying assumptions and shared values that shape their culture; these can often be summarised in the sentence, "That's just how we do things around here." Thinking about congregational transitions and the impact of grief can be better understood with the aid of tools such as organisational sociology. Unlike most other organisations, however, the church doesn't need start from scratch in working out 'how to be church.' The church is unique because it is a 'pneumacratic' or 'theocratic' organisation; the purpose and values of the church are initiated and guided by God Immanuel.

But we can still learn a lot from organisational theory, especially about how churches can start to entrench themselves when they are declining. They can feel unable to share or connect with people who have no church background. The way they gather becomes out of touch with the culture around them. This entrenching is a survival mentality; or as one missiologist calls it, 'museum curator mentality.'[3] Facing decline can get the church into: "We need to do whatever we can to survive."

Silvia: But isn't that counterproductive, because it leads people to do exactly those things which decrease their chances of survival: retrench, focus on buildings, do less and spend less, and fight more?

Susan: Well, ironically, yes, that's right. The purpose of the church is not for its own sake; it exists primarily for the Kingdom of God, to be a sign and symbol of God's Kingdom here on earth. Declining churches can lose that hope and confidence that they are 'salt and light' to **transform** community. And instead, the focus can narrow toward 'attracting enough people to survive.' When I work with church councils, they often ask me:

"How do we make our church grow?" The underlying agenda, which is not said, is: "… so that we can survive."

It can be hard to uncover these underlying assumptions. I've worked with churches who are in decline, and they will often say they are 'missional' because they have a ministry that is community-facing (such as a playgroup, offering food or second-hand shops etc). Often however, they are still primarily operating with 'survival mentality' assumptions; the meaning of 'missional' is narrowed, eroded to 'community facing.' We need deep and on-going teaching around the mission of the church.

The generation of ministers before me (baby boomer or young builder generations) were trained for a church that was the centre of society; a Christendom culture. They were primarily trained to meet the religious needs of the members of their church, and churches were full.

Now we are living in a culture where the church is on the **edge** of society. The centre is now secular, with Christianity being just one of other religions on the edges. But, this is just where the church started. Some missiologists, such as Stuart Murray, argue that the church **should** be in the margins of society; let's not try to re-capture the centre, but embrace being a marginal movement.[4]

The values and assumptions of a marginal church are very different to one in the centre. They are worlds apart. The Book of Order, which was formed for churches operating in the centre of society, isn't going to give you what you need to understand the missional ecclesiology of being a church in the margins. It simply hasn't got the language, let alone the principles, values and roles for marginal movements. To use an analogy, it would be like trying to use a copper wire telephone to connect to the internet – it requires totally different 'language' and hardware to connect. It's a huge paradigm shift.

The good news is that some denominations around the world are navigating this shift. Craig Van Gelder has a great book called *The Missional Church and Denominations*.[5] In the book are real-world examples of where denominations have courageously done away with the equivalent of a canon or Book of Order, and produced one-pagers that summarize what they're about. They have adopted light missional networks with value-based principles, moving away from prescriptive/legalised documents. It's a massive change, as you can imagine, and it takes enormous courage to do that. But we don't have to start from scratch; there is good stuff out there that has already been written and shared.

Silvia: From a theological perspective, where do you see the Holy Spirit? You see God leading the church into these edge spaces of mission; how do you see God at work there?

Susan: You strive to be faithful to what God calls the church to be and do. We are called to be faithful and not successful. Success can be viewed as "the church is growing and we've got more numbers sitting on seats on a Sunday." But what does a faithful church actually look and feel like? In my role as a mission catalyst with the Presbyterian Church, we developed fifty markers of a healthy missional church, and only one of them was about increasing numbers at worship gatherings. The other 49 don't mention numbers at all. Describing missional culture focuses on what we see, do and hear: 'the artifacts of culture.' If we are faithful and seek God's Kingdom above all else, then God will reciprocate saying: "You're on the edge and it's uncomfortable, but – you know what? – you're going to be okay. Because I can equip you with gifts and roles and prophecy, and leaders and apostles and prophets and pastors and teachers and evangelists, and you're going to be fine." If we trust God, God reciprocates, as shown and taught by Jesus. But you can imagine how terrifying and insecure that can feel.

Silvia: What do people need to grieve, in order to be open to that?

Susan: A massive loss of security, and sometimes position and power. It's huge, huge! In one of the churches I ministered in, half the council were desperately wanting to go back to the centre of society. I remember someone saying to me, "The Anglicans have got a church in the centre of the city and we jolly well need one as well!" They desperately wanted to reclaim the centre. "We need the organ. We need this big huge space. We can't lose our building, our history." Their rhetoric was often loaded with grief and even anger. Which is not surprising, because it's hard to let go, when this is how they understand church. But the other half of the council understood missiology quite well and were comfortable being on the margin. They believed that the church is transformative when it is faithful. They didn't see a need to re-capture the centre, and desired instead to invest money and resources in different ways. Not surprisingly, these different perspectives came into conflict.

Edgar Schein, a brilliant organisation sociologist, acknowledges the loss of security, power and position in organisation culture-change.[6] He describes navigating these changes like a seesaw. On one side you have to create enough tension to say, "We can't stay here anymore." But at the same time you also have to create enough support and training so people can find their place in the 'new way.' So churches need lots of training, new role descriptions, and someone to work with them so they can learn how to operate in the new environment. It's important to not to do one without the other; tension and support need to go together, which is a real challenge for leaders and teams.

One of the things some denominations or churches have done is just give out the bad news: "The church is in decline. This is dreadful. We're all getting older. Thank you very much, goodbye!" If churches only hear this side of the story, with little to equip them to the new way of being, they can become numb or immune to the bad news.

Motivating positive change requires both facing the reality of our situation **and** solid training and support for how things will be done in the new. Leadership has the unenviable role of 'holding the tension' on this seesaw of change; generating the tension to keep the change going, and being responsive to feedback, healing and sharing (without diminishing the tension!).

Leading intentional culture change in churches requires a good understanding of organisational culture. Edgar Schein defines organisational culture as having three levels.[7] The first level he calls 'artifacts'; for example, when I walk into a church for the first time, this is what I see, feel, hear or do. The next level Schein calls 'shared beliefs and values.' So if I join a Presbyterian Church, I'll know that ministers work to the Book of Order and there will be elders and probably some kind of Presbyterian liturgy used at services. But Schein says the key thing of understanding organisational culture is the bottom or third level. He calls these 'basic underlying assumptions.' These are unconscious, taken-for granted values which are "nonconfrontable and nondebatable."[8] You know they are there when you question the validity of them. Then they can unleash defensiveness, anxiety and even anger.

Silvia: So that is where the anxiety and anger comes from?

Susan: That's right. A great example of this was when a colleague, a vicar in a suburban parish, tried to get rid of some of the pews. Now this church did not hold a shared value statement that said 'We are faithful because we sit on pews'! They knew that pews aren't essential for being God's people. The vicar followed all the right processes, had a good consultative process with his leadership team, but when it finally came to sharing with the congregation, the request unleashed incredible anger. People went to the press! One person said, "Over my dead body are you going to get rid of these pews!" That is a classic example of tramping on an underlying assumption. For them the pews were a marker of when the church was thriving, when it was successful and growing; to take away the pews was

– rightly or wrongly – to take away a significant part of what it meant to be church for them.

Silvia: What are healthy ways of moving through this? What do people need in order to let go things which are blocking a healthy transition?

Susan: We have to repent; genuinely lament that some of how we are doing church and understanding church is no longer relevant. Being on the margins of our society involves grief. We have to get real. We must face the confronting reality that we are holding onto things that erode our missional life, that are actually working against the church's purpose for the kingdom of God. That is hard. Most people will respond, "Oh no, we're OK."

Silvia: Because that is emotional work, and it's breaking the rules of the collective assumptions.

Susan: Absolutely. And people use the institutions and structures of the church to protect themselves from the painful processes of lament and repentance. What served our old understanding of ecclesiology and missiology provides us with very little language for where we need to be now. And retired ministers can sometimes reinforce this. I have experienced being undermined by a previous minister as I was trying to lead a church in a new way. I don't think she did it consciously or maliciously. But I was trampling on her understanding of what it means to be a minister and her understanding of church. So when people were upset with the 'new way,' they would go to her and ask, "Can Susan do this?" and she would say "Well, no, because the Book of Order says ... "

Silvia: Someone who has held that authority in the past can struggle to release a new person to lead in a different way.

Susan: That's right.

Silvia: We use language of repentance a lot in the church, it is part of our liturgy. But this is kind of a new idea: how do we repent of our own collective ways of being?

Susan: It is understanding that we can be unfaithful individually and collectively. It requires corporate confession and repentance. I am an Anglican at heart, so I'm very comfortable with confession, repentance and renewal. That's the key; I repent to receive newness of life and renewal. It is like forgiveness. Lewis Smeed in his book about forgiveness shares how a vital step in forgiveness is letting go of the pain – including our desire to get even – before we can receive healing. He describes this process of placing all your pain and anguish in your hands, taking one last longing look at it, then opening your hands and letting it spill to the ground like water.[9] When you forgive, you bear the cost of it on your own back. That is why forgiveness is so costly.

It is not too dissimilar for corporate confession and repentance. As a church, we come together to name our unfaithfulness, to lament that we have lost our way, and express our desire to turn back (i.e. repent) to God. Fortunately God is the God of second, third and 750th chances!" He is inexhaustible.

Silvia: But could people hear that as a personal attack?

Susan: Yes. Which is why it takes so much courage individually and collectively. Alan Roxburgh and Fred Romanuk[10] write about how churches that are declining can go in one of three ways. They may have declined to such an extent that they consciously choose to close their doors and offer their assets to others in their missional journey. Or, as we've talked about, they can go into survival model – which means they hoard their assets for their survival, rather than freeing them up for the new. In these situations, churches might end up with beautifully restored or strengthened buildings, but little if any missional life.

The third way is to not give up or withdraw inward, but to discover God's mission anew. To bring into the open the underlying assumptions that are eroding their missional life. To name them, own them, and repent to receive the full life and joy God has for them.

It is very difficult to call the church to repentance. I have tried; sometimes I succeeded and other times I failed dismally.

That kind of work requires the strong support of regional leadership. It's not uncommon in these situations for people in the church to go 'over your head' when they feel their understanding of church is being undermined. I've had two contrasting experiences in this. In one, the archdeacon was incredibly supportive. In another experience, a conflict process was discussed and agreed without any consultation with me, which totally stunned me. When clergy or ministers are leading these kinds of changes, it is important that denominational leadership understand missional ecclesiology and possess and foster the skills to hold the conflict while the transition is being worked through (which can be up to two or three years).

Silvia: We need the ability to hold conflict. To give people the confidence: "It's alright, you'll get through this. Keep working at it."

Susan: Yes. It's an area that most clergy, elders or ministers aren't trained in. If we can't hold the conflict, then we risk falling back to the old ways of doing things. This is where missional leadership comes into its own.

Silvia: What is the personal cost?

Susan: When these transitions don't go well, it can feel awful. There can be a deep sense of shame and failure. The loss of community and family is painful.

Silvia: And seeing the people around you grieving too?

Susan: Oh, indeed. I really feel for people in these conflict situations. It can come at an enormous cost. I hate seeing that. Supporting others through their grief cuts very deeply for me.

I feel for declining churches. What is it like being in a church where your community is shrinking, you see each other ageing, and what you love is not being valued by the younger generations? You desperately want to grow but you're not growing. And then as a church begins to turn on itself you often get increased conflict between each other. But the good news is that we can repent right up to the 12th hour; one minute to midnight!

The letters to the churches in Revelations are great in this context. To me, Laodicea is not too dissimilar to some of the Presbyterian churches stuck in survival mode (Revelations 3:14-22). "You think you are rich, you think you are wealthy, but you're not. If only you stood naked in front of me. If only you repented and took your gold from me, not from the world, then I would restore you." Those letters are powerful. That is God calling churches to repentance; "If you repent collectively, and come back to me, then **I will restore you**. Not by the work of your hands but by the work of my hands."

Silvia: That so much more profound than just: "Try this strategy" or "Learn this tool" or "Do this programme." You are talking about something very different than looking for a 'solution.'

Susan: That is why I love missiology, because there is no programme or strategy. It is a call to the church to rediscover its call and life in God: "What is the purpose of the church today?" The church is a marker, a gorgeous and beautiful symbol of the kingdom of God on earth. Which is so exciting. I love the church. Despite going through successes and failures in church leadership and culture change, I absolutely have faith in the wider church.

Our 'Vacancy' Model is Broken
– *Richard Dawson*

Very Rev. Richard Dawson is a past Moderator of the PCANZ. His experience in national and regional leadership has convinced him that we need to rethink our ministry transition processes.

• • •

Richard: We don't do transitions well in the Presbyterian Church. We rely on an old system which I don't think works for us. Ministry transitions are taking far too long and are basically killing smaller churches. That's what I see: churches just disappear into the ether. If you take away the lead person then there is a massive hole, especially in a smaller church. A larger parish can survive for a while without a minister, but not in a good state. The trouble is that these days people expect so much more of church and what church can provide.

Silvia: Our Presbyterian system is that we don't start thinking about a new appointment until the previous minister has left.[11] Then it is normal to have at least a year and a half gap between one ministry and another. Are saying that model is not helpful?

Richard: It is broken.

We want to encourage the ministries of everyone in the church, and we think that they can continue without a minister. But in fact these long transitions have the opposite effect. It works against team ministry because people get overstressed by running the church and are worn out by the time they get a new minister. That then puts a huge amount of weight and pressure on the minister who is appointed after a long vacancy, because they come into a parish that is exhausted. I remember coming into a parish and people saying: "You've got it, I'm finished!" I had this experience three or four times.

I can understand the need to grieve a relationship which has ended. But too much focus on this can make the parting worse not better. The more we emphasise the loss of the departing minister, the greater the temptation to think that everything revolved around them. The point of the minister is to be the leader of a community's mission, not their own mission. The role of the minister is to lead that church community to be effective missionaries in the society around us. I think the minister's role is vital but it is not the mission. The mission goes on.

Silvia: We seem to consider it a good thing for a parish to have a bit of a breather between ministries. In that 'vacancy' we require a parish to do mission planning.

Richard: It is a very silly idea to do mission planning without the leader there. It's very unproductive; frankly I can't think of anything worse. Then the church says to an incoming minister: "We want a leader, but we have already made up our minds what we are going to do. So you can just keep everyone happy please." I just don't think it works.

It seems to reflect a view that a parish almost starts again with each new minister. It doesn't. We need a far more dynamic longer term view of a parish's life. The parish's life must continue through and past each minister.

Our attitudes discount the importance of the minister: "It shouldn't matter if we don't have a minister for a couple of years." We are stuck on the idea that a minister is just a teaching elder and everything can go on regardless, without a minister. It is just not the case. The minister is now the CEO, the leader. A lot of people don't like that view, but the fact of the matter is that in any community leadership is a priority. Without leadership we see parishes going backwards.

If they can't get an ordained minister quickly, a church might appoint a lay person. There are plenty of people who think they can do the job, and some of them can do a half decent job. But long term it's not the answer. Long term, you need a leader who is trained, who is able to give all of themselves to a parish, and is able to grow the church. I have watched half a dozen viable parishes disappear into nothing because they were left to people who had not been well trained.

We also need to look at our supervision model for new ministers. I worry that newly trained ministers are put in parishes where the expectations are unreasonable, or where the perceived the need for change is not compatible with the needs of the parish.

Our regulations were formed in a Christendom model society, in which ministry had a fairly set job description. We did not have to think hard about how we grew and maintained a church because the society supported that. Now we are in a society that does not think the same way we do. It is fundamentally agnostic if not atheist, and we have to consider how to both interact with our society and preserve a faith viewpoint. Our culture no longer sends people to church. It is a very different context from the one which our regulations were set up for. We have been in this space for ages but our regulations around ministry transitions have not changed.

To start solving the problem, presbyteries need to build up a set of five or six ministers who are professional transition ministers. They can go into a parish immediately after a ministry ends and look after the parish. That's one solution.

The second solution is for the minister to indicate well in advance when they plan to leave, and work in consultation with the local leadership. We can begin the search with plenty of time, so there is not a massive gap between a minister leaving and a minister coming. Ideally there should be some overlap, or at least a smooth transition to continue the missional vision of the church.

I see it as highly important to reform our transition regulations and get real about the ongoing life of our parishes.

Managing Staff Transitions – *Richard Dawson*

Richard Dawson is the Senior Minister at Leith Valley Presbyterian Church, Dunedin, where he leads a team of ministry staff including student, youth, pastoral, administration and outreach positions. I talked with him about transitions between ministry staff, and his role in managing the endings well.

• • •

Richard: There is a constant turnover of staff here, with seven or eight positions. For every good person who resigns there is a bunch of people who grieve and the whole parish grieves. In the last three years, one of our youth workers resigned and became the university chaplain. She was greatly loved by the youth group and they all regretted her leaving. Another person stepped into the role last year, but he left, and all of a sudden I had to find another youth worker. A new person is now leading a very good program; that's been a great transition and she is rocking ahead. All of this takes time and involves things I have to attend to. We don't have an HR manager. It makes my life busy, but if you don't solve these sorts of problems then you go backwards so quickly it's not funny.

When a person flags they are leaving we immediately examine their job description and chat with them about it. We ask ourselves: "Is that what we need?" And if it is, we'll start looking around. We always look internally first. It is a much harder transition from the outside our church. If the worst comes to the worst we'll advertise outside the parish.

My wife has had a long term job as the administrator here; she has resigned and is stepping down. I have had long discussions with our Manager and the Session about how we should replace her. The big question is 'What fits now?' Not 'what was the job then?' or 'what is she doing?' but 'What fits now with where we are as a parish?'

Silvia: When it comes to the actual farewells, what things do you include?

Richard: We build in an exit interview. We build in a celebration for the group that they led. And we build in a congregational farewell, in a worship service, with a prayer, some presents and acknowledgement of the work they have done. We pay most of our staff a salary so we don't believe in giving them a massive gift. They might get a voucher and a box of chocolate and some flowers, that's all.

Silvia: What do you need from a person who is leaving?

Richard: I simply need them to finish on a good note. We have had a couple of real failures in this regard.

Silvia: Were there times of hurt or anger in the exit process?

Richard: Yes; difficult conversations have gone on for months, in one or two situations, to be honest. This is particularly the case when staff members don't agree with your assessment of the situation or your need to make changes. The big thing is to do everything according to the PCANZ Book of Order, and to try to be fair and open.

When you have a significant number of people employed you have every kind of experience you can imagine. I'm not saying we are squeaky clean. But these days I focus very much on team health, and try to keep ahead of the issues with staff members. So I aim to have a good sit-down every couple of weeks with each person on the team to find out how they're going and how they are in themselves.

Youth Ministry Transitions
– Nga Rolston and Gordon Fitch

Ngahuia Rolston is a long standing Youth Enabler for Presbytery Central and prior to that Wellington Presbytery before it merged. She is also a Supervisor and Youth Worker.

Gordon Fitch has been the Youth Manager for the PCANZ for the past 11 years. Born in London to Scottish parents, Gordon has served as a youth worker both in the UK and US.

Presbyterian Youth Ministry (PYM) is the national youth department of the Presbyterian Church of Aotearoa New Zealand. PYM is committed to helping churches foster a culture of Christ-centred ministry and discipleship through coaching, training, resourcing, advocacy and networking.

• • •

Silvia: Youth work is notorious for frequent transitions. How do endings affect youth workers, and young people? What can the church do to promote longevity in youth ministry, and to manage endings well? Why do youth workers leave ministry positions?

Gordon: The biggest reason youth workers leave is financial. Youth ministry does not pay anywhere near enough. PYM has a recommended pay scale, and though it is significantly lower than a minister's complete package (stipend + housing etc), it is helpful when churches opt to use it. However, many churches pay less than the PYM pay scale and we continue to find youth workers who are only getting paid the minimum wage. The PCANZ agreed that all church employees should be paid at least the Living Wage. But even that is very low for people with a university degree or ministry qualification, especially when they get to the next stage of life and want to get married or buy a house. So we see youth workers choosing other careers, or ordained ministry, more on the basis of pay than a sense of calling. We have some amazing youth workers around the country who have stuck at youth ministry for the long term, but they tend to have other forms of income.

Nga: Youth workers often feel unable to talk about money; they feel bad asking for more pay. They come to us after they have already decided to leave, and we hear that they did not feel financially supported, but by then it is too late. And these people are doing incredible work in such an important role. In my experience churches are not great employers. PYM has put together an Employment Kit for youth workers, to try to address these issues and enable youth workers be well supported and to stay longer.

Gordon: Churches also need to support their youth workers in other ways. Youth leaders need to feel prayed for and spiritually supported. They need time and space for reflection, and ongoing training and development. Sustaining youth ministry requires good management, and celebrating the ministry so that the leaders feel appreciated. Churches need to share responsibility for the youth ministry, not just hand it all to the youth worker.

Nga: The youth workers who don't leave are the ones who feel listened to, and feel like they are part of the ministry of that church, with a strong voice. Those who move on leave because they were in a silo and did not feel part of the ministry team.

Gordon: When churches see youth ministry as a hole to be filled, this sets up an unhealthy environment. People inevitably leave, because the ministry is not prioritised and they are only employed for a few hours a week. It does not set up the church well, and young people end up disengaged rather than engaging in church and faith.

Silvia: How do youth ministry transitions affect young people?

Nga: It is very tough on young people to lose that relationship with a youth pastor. I have seen significant drops; a third to a half of a youth ministry can disappear overnight when a youth pastor leaves. Some young people just leave, disappear, shut off contact completely. Young people can take a long time to be open or to trust a new youth pastor. They might push boundaries, play up to see how the new leader will engage them. Or they might love it and thrive under the new youth pastor.

The most helpful thing is for the youth ministry to not totally rely on the employed youth worker. The model we promote is that the youth pastor facilitates other people in the church to step up and support the young people. A healthy youth ministry is where the youth worker builds up a community wrapped around the youth. So when he or she leaves, that community is still there, only one person changes.

Gordon: When a youth worker's role is seen as a programmer or entertainer, then it 100% relies on that person, and when they leave there can be a mass exodus. But when you understand the role as facilitating a ministry, it can continue to thrive even through transitions. Our best youth ministries are those with longevity, whether they have paid youth workers or volunteer teams: people who sustain relationships through time.

Genuine, stable relationships are so beneficial to young people. When there is a different youth leader every year or two, a young person may roll through 3 or 4 youth leaders who are trying to input into their lives. That can be quite negative for the faith journey of the young people. In any transition there is a danger of conflict or uneasy situations that can impact negatively on young people.

Nga: Youth workers do not always leave a church when they finish in their job. This can lead to a difficult transition. If you are staying in the same parish, a plan needs to be put in place to ensure there is good communication between the old leader and the incoming new leader. It can be very confusing for the young people, who see you as a person not as a role: "You've been part of my world for so long, and now you're not, but you're still around. How does my relationship work with you?" We need to work hard in open dialogue between all those involved to negotiate ongoing relationships.

Silvia: What have you seen as the effects on youth workers when they have experienced bad employment practice?

Nga: When it goes badly it is tough. I have seen it break people. Their whole world crumbles. They doubt everything. They become unsure about the church, and how God fits in to everything. It can take years of counselling and hard work to claw themselves back, to regain their identity, who they are. For those who do come back into ministry, how do you get into a healthy place where you can give back to people again?

Youth pastors, and also ordained ministers in my observation, are not good at setting up healthy holistic lifestyles. They work like running a marathon instead of putting things in place to take care of themselves and know when to take breaks or step back or ask for help.

Local church councils don't always have the skills to manage employees well. Bad management leads to conflict; and youth workers often don't realise what is happening until it's too late, and by then it is really unhealthy.

Gordon: Some people who leave badly walk straight into another church, because they need a salary. That is not positive for the next church.

The grief is complex. When you work in a church the people you work with are also friends. Even if you keep your boundaries well and take your agreed days off, when things get hard in a church environment it affects you intensely because it is intertwined into your life.

Nga: If you have a partner and kids if also affects them and their relationships. When a youth worker leaves a role and leaves a church, that is really hard on the spouse and kids, because they have built their world in that community. It is very confusing for kids; why are they leaving the children's ministry and all the friends they have connected with for so long? There is grief for the youth pastor leaving this role that has been so important for them, but there is also the grief of their family. It is a lot.

Silvia: What helps a youth ministry to end well?

Nga: A really special farewell is a vital part of a good ending. It is important that the young people, and the families of the young people, are given the opportunity to farewell the youth worker. I have seen beautiful cards, written messages, video messages. Farewells include the chance to share. Youth workers value those reflections because they want to know that the time, the effort, the aroha that they have put into the work has been worthwhile. They invest so much of themselves in supporting the young people and their families, and that needs to be acknowledged as meaningful. That's the most precious part of an ending.

Even when things haven't gone well, it is important that young people and their families are able to share that also. Ending well is when everything is shared and aired, and everyone can go away feeling peaceful and settled, because they have been able to reflect together and express that gratitude.

Gordon: Think about all the different relationships that need to be included in an ending process. Obviously this needs to involve the young people and family members, as well as the church leadership and wider community relationships.

Communication is another important part; clear communication with the church about why the youth worker is leaving, so people are not confused. It may be emotional for a whole range of people. The young people could be quite upset, and the church needs to find ways to continue those conversations.

Having a slow transition is good; a period of time for everyone to get their head around it. A sudden ending is especially hard on teenagers, like hearing that Bob has just left already and you won't ever see him again! If there can be some points of connection after the ending of the position, this is very helpful for young people.

Nga: I would agree that a long ending is helpful. To have time to process things in supervision before I finished in a position enabled me to finish up really well. I was able leave in a space of peace.

In youth ministry we often talk about transitions between age groups, as young people move from primary school to intermediate, to high school and beyond. We know that those transitions are very important. This conversation has highlighted for me that the transition out of a role is also very important. We need to resource youth workers more for how to do that in healthy ways. I don't know that we have focused on that as a national team.

Silvia: How does PYM continue to look after youth workers after they have finished an appointment?

Gordon: If you are leaving a ministry job you lose support systems such as supervision. It is worthwhile reflecting on how we as a wider church can support youth workers when they leave their role. Presbytery people are able to continue the relationship, and Nga does an exceptional job with this. This benefits our youth workers in practical ways, and keeps the door open to coming back into ministry.

Nga: Absolutely, that is a big part of my ministry. It is important to me that I don't discontinue my relationship with these leaders. It is a 'win-win' for both of us to keep them connected in with our network. It is not specifically in my job description but it is vital to how I work, that relationships continue even when people change jobs.

This is how we work as youth ministry in the Presbyterian Church. We build a community together across our regions and nationally. We create this amazing network of youth pastors who connect and support each other. Peer support is massive. We are concerned for ministers in the church generally and want to encourage good self-care and mutual support, not just for youth workers but for all those in ministry.

Silvia: It would be great if built into employment contracts for youth workers was some kind of exit package, with some options such as paying for a couple of extra supervision sessions, or counselling, or career advice.

God Goes and God Stays: Children and Change
– *Robin Humphreys*

Rev. Robin Humphreys leads the Children and Families Ministry team in the PCANZ. Born and bred in Raleigh, North Carolina, USA, she was ordained into the Presbyterian Church of USA. Robin married a Kiwi; Paul works as National Leadership Facilitator for Scripture Union. They now live in Christchurch with two dynamic girls. Robin has worked in teaching, camping, youth and children's ministries and brings a passion for creativity, storytelling and cultivating teams.

• • •

Silvia: How can we help children learn about grief in healthy ways, particularly when people they love leave?

Robin: In the church community, children develop connections with other people who come to represent God to them. Hopefully, that includes the minister, and children's ministry leaders. When someone like that moves away, there will be a loss for the child. Just like with any grief or transition, we help children through that by giving them a safe space and a listening ear. It is helpful to acknowledge the big feelings they are experiencing and to model that all feelings are "okay." There is no emotion that we're not meant to feel. If children name their feelings and experience, it is best to repeat back to them what you hear them say. The skill of open, reflective listening is good for any age, and particularly for kids.

Another way to help children learn about grief is to encourage children to physically map their feelings or draw a picture to show, for example: "How are you feeling about so-and-so leaving?"

We want to journey with them and give them skills to move through these 'goodbyes' that are a natural part of life. Therefore, it does not help to hide the truth of these situations from children. We share that so-and-so is leaving and what is happening in a straight and direct way. It is important to also think about the timing of when we share this news with them. We want to give them time to process, but not too much time for younger children as we don't want them worrying about something that is going to happen way in the future. We can frame this as a "goodbye" for now – a defined moment.

The leaving could be physical or it could be a change of role, someone who is retiring or transitioning out of children's ministry. We have so many wonderful children's ministry volunteers who have spent their lifetime helping with Sunday school. It might be that Miss M will still be around, but she will no longer be in her role.

When a significant person is planning to leave the church community or their role, help children to prepare: "This person is so important to all of us. We will miss them when they are gone. How can we honour them? What shall we give them/make for them?" Invite children's contribution in how the community will say "goodbye." I think it is important for all of us, the person leaving as well as the children and families, to be invited to make meaning in that moment. We need to intentionally create time and space for this to happen as we acknowledge the person who is leaving.

Creating 'healthy goodbyes' means preparing the ground and being straightforward with children about what is happening. It means listening and reflecting back, allowing them to express their feelings around it. And then contributing to the goodbye, marking the moment in a ritual action, such as giving a gift. Active meaning making is so important, for children and for the rest of us too.

Silvia: What do you mean by 'active meaning making'?

Robin: I think it is key for us to affirm, in simple ways, the truth that we know and hold to. I find that using something tangible is enormously helpful. We might choose an object, often from nature, and give children an action to do, together with strong simple words that name what is happening and where God might be in all of this.

Our family had a transition recently and I involved the children in a ritual around this. I realised that they did not understand the bigger picture of what was going on for us adults, but I knew that involving them physically in an active prayer was key to make meaning for them. And I hope that this sets them up with skills for life; they might look back and have a memory of gathering petals and putting them in a bowl. For children something tangible is really, really helpful. We need good prayer rituals to help us to say our goodbyes.

Silvia: Have you seen adults trying to protect children from sadness and pain? Sometimes that leads to more confusion and makes grief worse.

Robin: Yes, we do. We worry that children can't handle grief. Sure, there are situations, particularly around death, when it is helpful to shield children from some of the specifics. However, acknowledging the finality of endings is important. We don't want to 'fluff off' loss with statements like, "It will be okay." That is not what children really want to hear, because this feels hard and heavy and sad to them. And along with that we bring the message of reassurance: "I am here with you in this."

Just last Sunday our church was commissioning some missionaries leaving for overseas. On the way home our youngest daughter said, "Today was a sad day." And I said, "Oh. Tell me more about that. Why was it sad?" She replied, "Because they are leaving. They are going far away." There was a lot going on in her mind and heart at that moment. I wondered how she could even understand anything about this far-away place. However, at its most basic level it shows that even a three-year-old has the understanding that there is sadness in saying goodbye. To me it was a happy day, but I wasn't going to say to her, "Well, no, it was a happy day." We don't need to cover up and hide children's feelings. We don't even need to try to cheer them up. We need to give them safe space, reminding them we are with them and even inviting them to share more, for instance: "What do you mean by 'it was a sad day'?"

Silvia: When she said "This was a sad day," how did that help her to process grief?

Robin: Just naming it and having an emotion validated by somebody else. Then a little later, sitting at the table for lunch, she said, "When I become a church person, I want to go to that place faraway and stay with them." I could see her working through her grief. There was a progression there, that helped her look forward rather than stay stuck in the sadness. When we are allowed to grieve, for however long we need to, whatever we need to grieve about, then, after that, we are able to look forward into the future and see that there is something good ahead. There is a bit of hope there. Our role is then to help cultivate that hope alongside the child.

Silvia: That is a very beautiful example of redefining our relationship with the person who has gone.

Robin: It is so helpful for children to be a part of the action. At church last Sunday she understood the sending that was happening; she knew what was going on, even though she has no idea where the faraway place was, and she was part of the wider church family experiencing the love of God in that moment.

Silvia: Have you seen children express grief in other ways? It's sweet and easy to say "I feel sad," but how else might children show grief?

Robin: Withdrawing from social normal daily activities that children would typically want to be involved in is one way that grief could be expressed. A change in behaviour is another indication, whether that is being less involved or more expressive – it could go either way. Anger or acting out can also be part of grief. I personally have seen more examples of withdrawal. What's important to remember is that children may express grief in as much or even a wider range of emotions than adults.

Silvia: Do you see children struggling to love again, if someone they have loved has gone?

Robin: There is such a range of possibilities here, it can change as children get older and of course it depends on each individual. Young children have a tendency to accept and love again easily. Older children might reflect on how a relationship they have lost has been foundational for them, and wonder how they could connect, trust or love again with a new person.

Silvia: This is related to our theology of children's faith development, the importance of human relationships and the experience of being loved and treasured. We learn about God in a relational context. What happens when attachments get broken?

Robin: Children benefit greatly when they are reminded regularly that God loves them, that they are a beautiful child of God. We can never say that too often. A sense of belonging is key for all of us and is magnified for young ones. Belonging and love is so critical in how we handle loss and transitions. But children can handle more than we think they can.

There's a lot going on in children's ideas of God. To give another example from my own house, my three-year-old declared recently, "God can hear me!" She already has a concept of who God is and how God works – and it speaks into my life regularly! The spirituality of children is something that we often overlook.

A child can know that God is going with this other person, and that God is staying here. Especially if their relationship with God is connected to that person: God is going with and God is staying, and God is everywhere, all at the same time. It is kind of crazy when you think about it, but kids probably understand it better than we do!

Communicating with children involves simplifying – not simplifying a truth, but simplifying the wording around a truth – instead of trying to explain away pain or blanket children with words. "God is going with and God is staying"; to me that is a helpful framing of the difficulty of loss and understanding where God is and how God works. That can help in the transitions.

Silvia: Children learning from observing the way the adults around them handle grief. Hopefully we are good role models for our kids, that we can let ourselves feel sad and grieve, and hug – even in Covid. How do you see the Covid pandemic changing the way children and families relate with the church?

Robin: Here we are, in a pandemic. There is no "blueprint" for how we are to navigate this space; whether for individuals, families or the church. It is giving us all a shake-up. One area that is affecting the way children and families relate with the church is the drop-off of direct engagement (which could also be true for other age groups). If young children and their families were attending regularly before the pandemic, they have now experienced a big gap of regular attendance of Sunday gatherings. This "gap" of engagement affects children, families **and** the church. Many churches have been asking: 'How do we stay connected to the families we aren't seeing regularly?' There is an opportunity here that I pray the church does not miss.

Another way the pandemic is changing the way children and families relate to the church is that it might just be expanding children and families 'definition' of the church. There is great potential here. My girls ask on a Sunday morning, "Are we doing church online or are we going to church?" They don't mind either way, they accept that this is the way things are. Maybe children are better than adults at the agility required in this time of pandemic! It certainly affects them, and it is hard for them in many ways. But particularly in relation to church and how we meet, we are now in a looser space. We are in the midst of redefining what church is, and that can be beautiful. Change is happening; we are laying new foundations that in the end might be very helpful for us and especially for our children and the generations to come. It is making room for what we need in order to move into even more transition ahead. We would be wise to let the children lead us.

Silvia: What do you hear from around the country from leaders with all the changes they have been forced to adapt to?

Robin: The reality is that exhausted leaders have been caring for exhausted families. Leaders are not super-human. They need care while they give care. Sometimes we have responded well to these needs as a church and sometimes we have not. I hope we will take our learnings about how to care for our leaders into the next season of our church life. For some leaders, it is important to note that this time of constant adaptation in the ministry space has been a place of excitement for many. We can hold the exhaustion with the excitement of doing things differently and the creativity that flows from that into other areas of life.

Silvia: Is there grief for children in being separated from others, particularly older adults? While we are still in pandemic, older people have to be very cautious about being exposed to COVID. It is much harder to have intergenerational contact.

Robin: There has certainly been sadness and loss from all generations as we have lived through these times of minimal contact. Parents have missed the spiritual and practical input into their children from the older generation. Older people have missed the joy and energy gained from young children and others. Maintaining contact in both age-tested ways such as posting letters and in newer ways such as connecting via FaceTime or Zoom calls has helped us all. Kids love to receive things in the mail! And adults do too! It still amazes me how my youngest daughter (having last seen my parents when she was 6 months old) has been able to bond with them over FaceTime over these years. I know it has been a life-line for me, for my parents, for us all!

Silvia: What Bible stories might help children deal with grief?

Robin: There are so many stories in the Biblical narrative that can help in these times. The desert stories seem like a great place to start. In the desert there is a sense of God being near to the people and the people being near to God, no matter what else is going on. In Godly Play we say, "God came close to Moses and Moses came close to God." Those powerful Old Testament narratives are key and we can help weave these narratives into the lives of our children. These desert stories contain themes of transition, loss and change: the Exodus story, Sarai and Abram and their whole journey.

Certainly, the New Testament has plenty to say about grief as well. If we look at the 'lost and found' parables, there is pursuit, an unyielding pursuit to find the 'thing' that is lost. In these times, we might feel lost but God is not lost from us. We also experience Jesus' own lament and grief around the death of his friend Lazarus.

One of the real key insights of Godly Play is the importance of 'I wonder' questions.[79] It is not even a question, it's a statement that invites a response, and any response is a good response. In children's ministry we are not looking for a 'right' answer from our children. We are genuinely interested in what they think.

As we reflect on a Bible story we might say, "I wonder how this person felt," to invite children's response. When we ask children questions we need to be ready for whatever children say and accept whatever comes. As adults we are invited to have a genuine curiosity, an authentic receiving. Children help us to discover our wonder again and we are richer for it!

Silvia: That is very different to what Sunday school used to be; adults were 'teachers,' and children were there to memorise.

Robin: Memorising Bible verses can actually be helpful when we are in times of loss and/or transition. Psalm 23, for instance, is a wonderful thing to repeat and memorise as a family to bring us through hard times. To be able to pull out those phrases in everyday life is very helpful, to remind us that God is right here with us, through change and sadness, and out the other side.

Farewell Gifts

I put it out on Facebook: "Tell me about your best and worst farewell gifts." My friends were quick to publicly post wonderful examples. However, several people messaged me privately, and asked for anonymity, as they shared painful experiences of parting gifts which felt inappropriate or careless. After three years of part time voluntary ministry, one friend was given a $100 book voucher when he left. Another was given "a pottery candle holder which is one of the ugliest things I've ever seen. It felt like a last minute thought, that somebody found in the back of their cupboard!!" These gifts seemed to 'add insult to injury,' and compound the grief of ministry transition.

Lovely Gifts

"Leaving St S's, the Sunday School gave us a cushion cover with all their names on. Sadly it is no more as it was so well used it fell apart. And the congregation gave me a milk jug and sugar bowl, which I love to use for special occasions. Another time I left a position I received a lovely gift voucher for a local day spa – a real treat!" (Leanne Munro)

"Reg was given a beautiful painting of the Soren Larsen sailboat in light of his love of sailing. It was extra special as the artist was part of the congregation." (Dianne Gilliam-Weeks)

"After my mother died I received her Royal Doulton dinner set, which was beautiful but a very 'busy' green. At morning tea at church one day I commented that it was lovely to eat off fine china, but the pattern was a bit much. A parishioner commented, "What about mixing it with some white?" When I left, this person was invited by the parish to go out and buy me some matching white dinner plates. I love them and I use them every day." (Kay Webster Stevens)

"I was given a large framed photograph of the Castlepoint lighthouse from a Session Clerk, who is a very good photographer. The church wanted us to remember that the region has great beaches – it was intended as a reminder of the time we had shared in the area. Little did he know, the photo was taken from the very spot where I had proposed to Amy, who is now my wife! God definitely helped in their choosing of that photo to give to us." (Alec Wallis)

"Den has received very thoughtful and meaningful leaving gifts from all the parishes in which he has ministered. The most meaningful involved a commissioned piece of art from a local artist – a beautiful korowai – and for me a beautiful wooden platter made from the wooden floor of the old church; not to forget the photo book recording our time spent in the parish. We felt very honoured and appreciated." (Jenny Flett)

"After leaving a youth ministry job in Gore I was given a recipe book with recipes from many of the congregation. It stemmed from me constantly asking for the recipe whenever anyone brought baking for morning tea! So personal and cherished!!" (Karo Wilson)

The best gift our family received was from the wonderful folks in Wainuiomata Union Church, who sent us down to Dunedin to train with an enormous quilt of many colours. Each member of the congregation had created or added their name to a square. The patterns included cats and Thomas the Tank Engine which our boys loved. We still use it and it has not faded.

Principles and Questions

What these examples have in common is a sense that the church knew them and valued them; the gifts reflected that. A farewell gift needs to say 'we know you.'

Gift suggestions:

- A framed photograph or artwork of the local area is always an appropriate gift, especially if there is a connection with the artist.

- Another 'go-to' option for a gift is a large pottery or wooden bowl. A salad is an excellent metaphor for the church! Being locally made and unique makes a gift special.

- A beautiful woollen blanket is also universally appreciated (especially if the person is moving south!).

- A leaving gift may 'tell a story'; such as our quilt, or a photo album. Creating a printed photo book by uploading photos online is an easy and attractive gift.

The church may also wish to include the spouse and children. Mavis Duncanson shared that "It was lovely that our children were given gifts. But the gendered nature of the toy garage for our son and toy clothesline for our daughter could have been thought through a little more!"

Should we discuss the gift or keep it as a surprise? I would encourage conversation ahead of time. The departing minister may have a particular need or idea for a gift, such as an book they would not otherwise be able to buy.

Should we give money, or a voucher? My advice is to always give a tangible gift. If the congregation wishes to further bless a departing minister, it is important to ask the family what kind of voucher would be most appropriate. However, in some cultures cash is given, and money can be a thoughtful gift. Kay Webster Stevens suggests that "everyone has something they just can't quite justify in their budget. If I am giving cash I say, 'I am giving you this, not because I haven't thought about, but because I have.'"

Margaret Garland shared that "I was given pounamu, and a cash gifting on the understanding it was to help fill the space of retirement. I bought a weaving loom and I am working on a tapestry that I intend to give back to the church, in time."

Ministers are also free to give the church a parting gift. "I gave my church in Auckland a piece of Oamaru stone that a candle could sit on, when I left to come to Oamaru." (Rose Luxford). Diane Gilliam Weeks donated "many of my most formative books for the church library" when she retired. Chris and I gave our congregation in Dunedin a large wooden cross as a thank you gift when we left. However, be wary of giving a gift with strings attached. Ministry happens in the present moment, and we cannot attempt to leave a lasting memorial behind. If you give a painting for the church lounge, will you be offended if you come back a few years later to find it was sold at the fair?

What is the tradition and culture in your church? My army chaplain husband Chris describes the military culture of farewell gifts:

> "In the army, people move every 2 or 3 years. Each Unit has its own 'moving on' gift, normally in the form of a plaque, which is individually engraved with name and dates of service. When you finally leave the military there is a party, and a farewell gift can be more individual – which depends on how well liked the person is! There is a tradition of Officers giving a framed artwork to the Officer's Mess when they leave."

If a church is able to establish a policy about gifts this can help prevent feelings of injustice, such as in this situation (name withheld):

> "During my ministry the church gifted a pastoral care worker with a tremendous blessing of a week-long holiday when she left. But I received a pocket knife from the church as my parting gift. I felt a tremendous amount of grief in leaving, even though I knew that God was leading us on as a family and into a role I felt a strong calling for. The same church I had seen bend over backwards for other people showed my worth to them with a $20 pocket knife. And not even a letter from the leadership. I recognise in hindsight that they were hurt by me leaving after only two years, but I felt very saddened by the ending."

Career Coaching – *Josiane McGregor*

Our traditional expectations of ministry being a life-long calling are increasingly challenged by changing social norms. Alistair Mackenzie's research predicts that young people today can expect to have 20 different jobs during their lifetimes and go through five major career changes. How does ministry find a place in a more fluid understanding of vocation? What can the church put in place to better support people leaving ministry roles?

A friend of mine shared with me her experience after several years of ministry as a workplace chaplain. As she began feeling that it was time to move on, she asked her employer for support with re-training, but was told that no such support would be available. This left her feeling that the organisation did not value her as a person, and had no investment in her ongoing wellbeing outside of her function as an employee.

As a Presbyterian minister I am blessed to be entitled to Study Leave. Every time I have put together an application for study leave, someone at Parish Council inevitably asks, "How will this benefit the parish?" Churches expect to directly benefit from any training undertaken. A longer view of people's careers would support our ministers and lay staff in responding to how God may be leading them. This could include access to career coaching.

I talked with Josiane McGregor who is a career coach, currently working for the New Zealand Defence Force. One of the benefits for my husband in being an Army Chaplain is the military's commitment to his career as a whole, with training that leads him on beyond his current role.

• • •

Josiane: I have worked in career planning my whole adult life. I developed a strong sense of social justice early on, and I have worked a lot with people with significant barriers to employment. I didn't know what I wanted to be when I grew up so I just helped everybody else!

Silvia: What is career planning?

Josiane: We look at your career as a whole, not just this job. It's about who you are, your hopes, your personal situation, your family and other considerations, as much as it is about education and the jobs that you do. When you join the church, or the military, you may think it will be long-term but you should plan for not being there, because everybody leaves eventually. The future is never quite what you expect, and it's helpful to look beyond your current situation.

We used to talk about 'climbing the career ladder' – the traditional method of getting promoted and earning titles. This is good for highly specialised careers where you expect to become an expert; it's an explicit structure in which progression is clear. But now we talk more about the 'career lattice,' with diverse pathways. Rather than working your way **up**, you learn multiple new approaches and put them into practice by working in different teams. Collaboration happens more naturally, across departments. It benefits both the employer and the employee as it keeps people from staying in jobs too long, and allows others to grow. You're less likely to get bored and export your talent, and it develops you as an adaptable and resourceful employee who responds positively to change. This is the future of work: you identify what you want to learn next, and you go where you can grow your skills and connections.

Silvia: Our expectation of a lifelong commitment to one particular model of ministry is a 20th century model. It's just not going to work in the 21st century. How does career coaching help?

Josiane: The model that underpins my work is called SODA: self-awareness, opportunity awareness, decisions and actions. I talk about understanding yourself and your skills. Then we consider possible opportunities you may have in the future: 'What might I do when I leave?' Look both within your current field but also wider at something quite different that you might want to do. This helps you to identify the gaps in your experience, in your networks, in your education and skills. Then incorporate these into your career plan: 'Where are the gaps? What can I do now to mitigate those gaps, so that when I do leave the transition is more seamless?' This enables you to make decisions and take action. That is the SODA model.

Silvia: When working in a job, including ministry, there may be little encouragement from that organisation for training that might lead you outside that context.

Josiane: Employers fear that people will leave if they start exploring their options. But actually, exploring what else is available and doing a range of learning all adds value to the job you are currently doing. Also, if you retire at 65 and you are fit and healthy you could go on to work in a new role. Retirement can be a long time.

Silvia: What would you encourage the church to do, as a good employer, to look after its people?

Josiane: Professional development is important. Each organisation has an interest in their staff development, and provides training that directly impacts their work. But I also encourage external training, from outside your organisation. Opportunities for lateral learning are important to develop people with larger skill sets. Give people opportunities to gain experience in other areas. Broader skill enhancement adds to your own future as well as whoever you work for.

Silvia: How would career coaching benefit those in ministry?

Josiane: A career conversation with someone who is not involved in the church, who is neutral, who looks at career in a broad context, who would talk to the person about their skills, about what they want to learn, about what they understand about themselves, and what's available to them in the world. Yes, that would be awesome.

Silvia: Parish ministry can be all encompassing and it's easy to lose touch with other professions. If you've been a minister for a long time you are likely to feel that your skills are not well valued in the business world: 'How else could I earn an income?'

Josiane: A session with a career practitioner would enable you to unpack your self awareness: 'Who am I? What am I good at? What's my expertise?' And understand that as a professional, not just as a minister. Ministry is where you have done much of your learning and career growth, but that set of skills is far bigger than the role you are currently in. Coaching gives you a sense of where your skills might fit if you did transition out of the church, or chose to combine ministry with other part time work. The grief of a transition is minimised when people understand that they have skills that meet criteria for other employers and industries. That is the work that I do.

Career planning significantly enhances people's employment. It helps people feel that they are in control of what happens to them. When things feel out of our control, that is when things become pretty bad for people.

Silvia: The alternative is feeling stuck, and we don't work well when we feel trapped. We don't want people to stay in ministry because they are afraid they don't have alternatives.

Josiane: Sometimes we need that uncomfortable space to push us to look sideways. But early planning is definitely better, to maintain a sense of being in control of your career over your whole life.

We have a questionnaire that we have developed for long serving personnel that asks: 'Do you want a career beyond Defence? What does retirement look like to you?'

Silvia: The church could develop a tool like that, to get ministers thinking about these things. And then contract career professionals to offer support to those who are struggling with these questions. I think that would be fantastic.

Josiane: Best practice suggests that you should start planning at least two years in advance of a transition. Just as we all have performance appraisals, we should also talk regularly about professional development. Every few years people should be having a discussion with a career practitioner to say: "This is what I've been doing. These are the skills I am developing," and refining your career plan. You might never leave ministry, but if you understand your worth in a wider skill context you are more focused in your current work. That is what I see.

Silvia: You also support people as they are leaving a role. That can be a difficult time.

Josiane: Loss of identity is huge. When people exit the military we talk with them about loss of identity, managing different workplace environments and expectations. We do one-to-one coaching. We do workshops and webinars, in key areas like strategic job search, interview skills; how to use LinkedIn; how to update your CV and target it specifically to each situation.

Silvia: How might we access a career coach?

Josiane: As part of the Covid response the Government set up Connected to help people with career advice and retraining. This offers a free service. Website: www.connected.govt.nz

Careers New Zealand is part of the Tertiary Education Commission. This is aimed mainly at school leavers. Website: careers.govt.nz

The Career Development Association of New Zealand (CDANZ) is our professional body; that gives the credibility that underpins individual practitioners. Website: https://cdanz.org.nz

Debrief and Re-brief
– Rachel and Damon Fitzpatrick

Damon and Rachel have moved through part-time and full-time church ministry into interdenominational learning communities supporting those in ministry. "Our call is to work with those in transition, moving into, out of or between ministries."

• • •

Moving in and out of ministries is like moving house. When you move you need to sort through what you take with you, what to leave behind and what to throw away. When you do it well it is easy to set up in your new home: you've got what you need and you've dealt with the things you didn't need. But if you are rushed or can't decide what to do with certain baggage, you tend to bring it with you so you can deal with it later. The extra boxes sit around unopened. You have to keep shifting them when they get in the way. Maybe you open a box only to be discouraged to see what's inside, because you meant to leave that stuff behind. Perhaps those extra boxes trip you up; they might even trip up others who come into your new place. Some boxes may have been with you, unopened, through several moves, because you weren't ready to deal with what was inside. And sometimes in the rush of transition you leave behind things you had hoped to take with you, and you feel the absence keenly once the dust has settled.

When finishing ministry or moving onto a different ministry, it is possible to continue carrying the hurt of broken relationships, or the weight of expectations about what we felt our ministry should have looked like or what it should have achieved. Sometimes it means leaving behind friendships or support networks, the absence of which is heightened as we face a pile of emotional boxes to unpack, sometimes with little idea where to start.

After we left youth ministry we were very blessed by a week-long personal debrief, which we did at the Piringa Trust, north of Auckland.[12] This allowed us the space to reflect on the previous 16 years of ministry, to explore and process those things that we wanted to carry forward. Debrief allowed us to articulate those things we wanted to lay down, and to face the next phase of our life in a healthy manner. The model has been used particularly with missionaries returning from overseas, but we see huge potential to benefit people moving out of or between other forms of pastoral ministry – an area where support is often lacking.

You may have spent a significant time in ministry drawing out and listening to other people's difficulties, but how is it different when the boot is on the other foot? Those around you are not sure how to relate to you once you have decided to step out of that ministry role or they know that you are leaving. When you have got your 'ministering hat' on you can help other people express those things, but it can be hard to step back and see these things in your own life. Debrief is an opportunity to be on the receiving end of the power of sitting and listening.

Debrief is a personalised bespoke process, not a set plan or '10-step programme to success.' What people choose to share with us shapes the path the debrief will take. Sometimes there are no answers to our questions, or no clarity to articulate the answer. Debrief is a process of listening to situations and providing the appropriate in-context guidance that reveals an answer. There are different tools that suit different people and their needs; debrief may not be everybody's cup of tea, counselling or another practice might be more appropriate. And the timing needs to be right. Some people might not want to do a debrief straight away after finishing a ministry, and need space to breathe or rest. To get the most out of debrief requires mental space and emotional energy.

So how do you know when debrief is appropriate? Perhaps you get that feeling "I didn't expect leaving ministry to be like this" – that is a good indicator that there's something you need to look deeper at. Another sign is when you find yourself reacting disproportionately to something. You have a 'moment' (whatever that looks like for you) and you think, "Why did I do that?" It's like tripping over that extra box and thinking, "What is that doing there?!" Things may feel unresolved. You know that you have left and the ministry is finished, but part of you is still back there, still holding on; you might find yourself feeling, "I still want to be engaged but I've left and I can't." These are signs that you need to work through some things.

You may find yourself being uncertain about the next steps. You may be asking questions like "Who am I now? Where to from here?" Ministry was once a predictable career path with an expectation of permanence and stability, but our society no longer supports this. Lots of churches are struggling financially, perhaps also with shrinking numbers. Pastors may need to find other part time work to support their role, and their church work can feel undervalued by society. Debrief can also be very useful for helping discern future direction

Our call is to provide support to those who are in ministry transition. To journey with you and help you reflect on where you have been and where you are going. To help you both unpack the past and discern the future. This is particularly important when your previous clarity of calling feels broken. We believe it is good practice for anyone to stop and evaluate before moving to a new ministry. Our dream is for all ministers and pastors to be able to take some space between ministries, to debrief and replenish.

We would love for all churches to allow for debrief. Churches need to ensure that ministers are not burnt out or unable to contribute fully in their next role. This requires churches to view themselves as part of God's kingdom which is so much bigger than that one congregation. When a person is leaving, that means a commitment to allow this person to be whole as they go on to their next ministry. The exiting church could provide for a debrief retreat before a person finishes. Or the church calling a pastor could say, before he or she starts: "Take some space before you come, to sort whatever was."

Unfortunately the financial pressures of ministry can be a big factor causing people to overlook debrief. Churches are often broke, so pastors are often broke. This may mean there is very little time or space between roles. We see people going from one position to another not able to take time in-between, purely for financial reasons. Often leaving a pastoral position means giving up your house, so you have to go wherever you can get a house. The financial pressure forces a choice that might not be the right one.

The nature of ministry is to be connected to people. The length of service and the depth of relationship and connection can add to the difficulty of leaving. Long term youth pastors, for instance, connect deeply with young people, families, and the wider community. To finish in ministry is to break those connections, or at the very least change those relationships significantly, and that's hard.

Additionally, ministry affects the whole family – particularly if the family have been contributing to the ministry. When one spouse leaves a ministry, the whole family leaves behind the connections and friendships they have made in the church. The degree of the family's contribution to the ministry and the pain of this separation on other members of the family is not always acknowledged. We would definitely encourage couples to do a debrief process together. It is a very important time to focus on who you are as a couple and as a family; and it may be appropriate for children to join in too.

When people go into a new ministry it's all about the call; it's about God, it is this amazing spiritual time. But when you leave there's a tendency for it to be very business-like: tick the boxes, do what you have to do. We focus on God on the way **in**. On the way **out** we revert back to business models, the typical questions like: have you used all your leave, how soon must you start paying rent if the church owns the house, or move out to make way for the next pastor? This is particularly a struggle when you leave without knowing where to next.

In the church we have a clear understanding of God calling you to something new but we don't understand God calling you to wait. Our societal norms take over and people ask, "So what are you going to do? How are you providing for your family?" When we left youth ministry we were very clear that God did not want us to go straight into another ministry. To say this outright was a conversation stopper within the church. But conversely it was a great conversation starter with people outside church who saw it as practicing what we preached!

As a society, we are not good at waiting. Our fast-paced life-style only aggravates the difficulty. It is hard to manage our frustration, and uncomfortable to sit in a space of not knowing. Everything around is asking: "What is the next thing? When is the next thing?" Some people might be comfortable 'waiters,' but from our conversations with others and our own experience, when you have been a leader in a congregation, setting direction and planning to see the church thrive, to stop is difficult. To wait is difficult, and we either can't take the time or don't make the time to wait in the between spaces. The cumulative effects of that can catch up to us – rapidly and unexpectedly. In contrast, an important Biblical idea is to leave the land fallow every few years. Take time to figure out what God is doing in your own life before you move on. Scripture values feeding into the land, and feeding into yourself, before you start producing fruit again.

While we were struggling with this personally we heard a sermon on Psalm 119:105, "Your word is a lamp unto my feet and a light onto my path." The preacher explained that in Bible times you would have a very small light and you'd swing it back and forth on a rope. The light cast from this lamp would literally only light the very next step as you walked. That was truly how it felt. We know what God wants us to do, but the path is not well signposted.

A whole bunch of assumptions get caught up in that too: about who God is and what he should do, about what the church should provide, or how leaving should look. And adding to that are the assumptions from others. Debrief creates space to honour that experience and stay in it. Talk to somebody who can bring an outside perspective about where you are moving from and what you are moving towards. That gives you the freedom to express yourself and the freedom to feel things that you try to avoid feeling. Particularly when the leaving has been hard, and you may be fragile. Otherwise there can be a tendency to avoid dealing with the things that are hard because you need to hold it together for the next thing. Having somebody else to help carry that, to hear that, is really important.

Debrief helps people uncover things they have not acknowledged. Sometime it takes someone outside of ourselves to say: "Yes, there is real hurt and pain left from your time in ministry. And there is a way past those feelings. I will help you put yourself back together again after you have fallen apart."

For people going through transitions, it can be a very lonely time. You may feel disconnected from those around you, those who you are leaving behind, without yet being connected to the people in the place you are moving to. One very helpful thing someone said to us was:

> There are other people on this trail. Some of us are ahead of you and some of us are behind you. You can't necessarily see other people on the trail because of the twists and turns of the past. But they are there.

Despite how it may feel, we are actually not alone on the path. God is with us and he has placed others before us and behind us. The call of debrief is to get people around the bend and onto the straight; where they can again see other people, others who are also doing this work of building God's kingdom.

• • •

> Lord, thank you that you go ahead of us
> – that we are not alone.
> Light the path before us to reveal the next step,
> lift our heads, to see where you are.
> Lead us to a place where you are at work,
> and call us to join you.

Journaling as a Grief Practice – *Henry Mbambo*

My study leave focus this year is on journaling. Journaling is a tool I have learned, rather than something that came naturally. In my culture we don't write; we tell the story and tell it again. I have come to learn that both writing and talking are very helpful.

Journaling is about honesty; we face our grief and loss with honesty. The Psalms of lament are a kind of journal; there is a lot of honesty, even frustration with God. When you honestly tell God what is happening in your life, you can come to a place where you say to God: "Yes, this has happened, but I know that you are still God, even in this situation."

Writing helps me to remember and to grow. As I write on a piece of paper I am also writing in my heart and spirit. My journaling involves prayer. I trust that God is in my thoughts as I write, sometimes in a scripture that comes to mind. There are promptings in my heart and spirit. Those promptings tend to be confirmed, by my wife, or someone that I meet on the path.

I hear God as I notice what is happening, the way events come together. These become sign for me that God is in this. The noticing happens, for example, when I go out to walk in the bush, which I tend to do quite often. I notice things in nature, and if I meet people, the greeting can trigger something in my silent conversation with God. Journaling creates space where I am open to the leading of the Spirit.

A Bridge from Here to There – *John Hornblow*

Rev. John Hornblow has compiled a manual for journaling through a ministry transition. This is available for free download at the *Moving On* page on the Conversations website:

https://www.conversations.net.nz/moving-on.html

John advocates for the importance of journaling:

• • •

Making a good transition is possible, but is not necessarily a given. Dealing with both the external factors and the internal complexities of a transition is always challenging. The more thought given before and throughout the transition the better the outcome. Rush into a transition or think you know it all and the chances are high you will have more conflict, damaged relationships, and have lost opportunities for personal growth that cannot be retrieved. That outcome can be avoided. Time given to considering questions, such as those in the Transitions manual, will maximise the possibility of a really good transition for you and others impacted by your transition. This guide was developed from my own experience of many personal transitions and over three decades of coaching others through their transitions. I pray that it will guide you to intentionally reflect, think, pray, dialogue and decide so the outcome can be satisfying for all involved.

Supervision and 'Space for Grace' – John Daniel

Rev. John Daniel works as a ministry supervisor and trainer within CAIRA Pastoral Supervision, based in Dunedin.[13]

• • •

Supervision Process

Supervision is a vital tool for enabling our transitions. Ministry transitions, by their very nature, are not easy to talk about with other people. Within the ministry context there are issues around confidentiality. And once a minister has announced that she is moving, other people have their own emotional reactions to that news. I don't want to burden my own family, especially when there are problems associated with the transition. I don't want that to poison anyone else's relationship with the church. So supervision is very important.

Silvia: How do you see your role as a supervisor in helping people in transitions?

There is change all around us. Transition is about what is happening within you, and how you move from where you have been to where you need to be. Supervision is a way to process the changes and allow them, through God's grace, by the Spirit's urging, and your own experience and reasoning, to move to that next place. From the ending to the beginning of the new, the transition sits in the middle.

Transition is like Lent or Advent. These are waiting periods during which we attend to the transition within us, as we address our involvement in the changes around us. Change is not just external. Change is also internal, and bodily as well. Transition significantly affects us psychologically and spiritually. Healthy transitioning is being able to say "It is well with my soul" as we go through change.

What does it take to get to that place with a supervisee? As a supervisor I'd say, first is insight. Second is identifying previous experience that can help them with what they are going through. Then it's about helping the supervisee find their learning.

Insight is key: 'Transition is a Thing!' Do they realise that they are in transition? There can be a level of denial, or lack of awareness, and this can catch us out and impact on the people who rely on us. Transitions can bring out in us either faith and trust in God, or a sense of abandonment.

An insight I would be looking for in a supervisee going through transition is learning from their past. They have been through transitions before: "What did you learn from that? How can you apply that here? What does this transition mean for you?"

Your supervisor knows your situation and your perspectives and your history, as much as you have divulged. That's the rub in supervision: we are reliant on a relationship that is strong enough to be dialogical. I need enough information to be able to help the person going through the transition. If I know you well and you have shared with me, then I can say: "Well, Silvia, remember your past, this is where we you've come from – we have discussed this – now how does that apply? What can you take with you to this transition?" This becomes a touchstone, to say: "I've been here before. I can get through this by God's grace, with resources that God is giving me in this."

The next thing is the practical implications: "Where do I go from here? I've got the insight, I've identified connections between my past and my present as I go into the future, and I've got some information from my supervisor about these things to join the dots. Now I'm in a place where I'm a bit more confident and at ease. Now what do I do with all of this?" The challenge at this point is: what is this person's capacity? What is the person's ability to deal with change? In their past, how have they dealt with this? Has there been a meltdown? Has there been a loss of self-esteem? Have they destroyed relationships around them on their way? Different people deal with change in different ways.

The supervisor can go deep and ask: "So what is troubling you about this situation? What are you uncertain about, that is making you anxious, that you need to talk about?" We can get to the root of that, and ask: "How does this reflect God's love for you? What does Christ's life and work and witness teach you as you go forward? What wisdom do the scriptures give you? What is the Spirit urging you in the depth of your soul?" And finally, and really importantly: "What are you going to do about it? And how can I hold you accountable?"

It is not the supervisor's role to give advice. Even if the obvious decision is staring at me, and I think I know what the person should do, it is not for me to advise. My telling them what I can see so clearly, which they can't as yet, would rob them of that that insight and sense of agency. They need the confidence to know that they can do this. They have the resources. They have a direct line to God and I am not it! I'm one of their companions, albeit a very specific one. But they need to have their confidence and sense of agency built up so they can decide for themselves, discern for themselves, and then determine their way ahead.

Then they keep going, albeit one foot at a time, maybe one inch at a time, but still progressing. Sometimes it is a step back in order to step forward. There is a wonderful French proverb: when you come to a chasm in your path, you have to take a couple of steps back in order to leap forward.

The biggest insight is that, as a minister, God is actually there for me; not only for my parishioners or the people that I serve, but God is there for me. That engagement at a deep spiritual level helps them regain a foothold and gives them confidence to take a leap, even if it means stepping backwards first.

Companionship

None of us is always at ease with transitions and change, but as a supervisor I can say: "This is your life learning. This is your current understanding of the nature of God and God's people. And in this you have a companion in myself as your supervisor." In previous generations our companion would have been a friend, extended family, someone within the community, but these days we have professionalised that relationship into supervision.

Our primary companion is God, and we have Jesus as an example, Christ's Spirit within us, the scriptures to guide us, and God's overall involvement in this process. As best we can in our Christian maturity we trust that process. We can trust the process and trust God with that process. And trust ourselves, which we can find hard to do. Supervision is bridging all of that and connecting the dots to bring them to a place of confidence for this phase.

But it can't be only in supervision that we are having these kinds of conversations. I would also encourage every minister to have close friends, people you can trust, people who know you. I call these people my 'Rabbis.' For me this includes my wife, some members of my extended family, old friends, a previous minister, people that I've known for a long time, as well as my supervisor. They are rare people from diverse backgrounds and strengths; a wide cluster of people enables me to 'pick and choose' who I call on. These are people who know me well, who can speak the truth in love; people who can kick me in the pants and say, "John, what were you thinking?!" and I know they mean well. At the same time, they can affirm and hold me through a troubling transition. They will weep when I weep and laugh when I laugh. I expect my 'Rabbis' to unfailingly love me as best they can, knowing that we are all human and we all stuff up at times. It is so helpful to have others encourage me in what I can work on, from knowing me.

Silvia: It's a good challenge for people in ministry to make sure that we invest in those people that we do trust and who know us. It is such a common experience to feel isolated and lonely in ministry.

Absolutely right. Even with companions we can still feel isolated and lonely; that's the reality of ministry and we come to accept that. We look at the life of Jesus and think, "Golly gee, if it should happen to Jesus, why not me?!" If we don't experience those times of carrying the cross, if we don't experience the loneliness, if we don't experience the crucifixion in some small way when we need to let go, and the sense of the resurrection as well, then ...?!

Anger

Silvia: And if there is hurt and anger?

That is unfortunately all too common. There is a mixture of emotions in those situations of inherent conflict. I expect that in our supervision we will already have worked through some of this. If I had not identified that hurt, and suddenly just as they leave – 'Bang!' – maybe I lacked the perceptiveness or observation to see this coming. Or maybe they were very good at hiding it, as some of us are! We are good at acting and making believe everything is OK when it is not.

Sometimes a person just explodes this onto me: "I'm very angry about this!" This needs to be a well held space. They need to know that I am not going to judge them; that I am listening and I'm hurting with them. I am angry alongside with them, without indulging myself, or getting too close. I have a sense of distance, emotionally; empathizing with them, but without getting into the pit with them, because that would not be any help and would be unprofessional. It is listening it out and asking good open ended questions so they get it out of their system as best they can.

I reassure them that it is absolutely legitimate that you should feel angry; it would be inhuman not to. If I perceive that the supervisee is in denial, or if they are not seeing things, or if there is something more pathological going on, then it becomes a process of truth-telling to the supervisee. I have to be very careful with them because they are in a vulnerable state. I respect and dignify them and their transition, and hold them in that space. Conflict and anger can need distance in order to work through. I reassure my supervisees that I will accompany them on that journey.

It is space for grace. That is a good space where God allows room for us to be grow. God honours us by leaving space in creation for re-creation, and we are involved as partner in this; even when it hurts; especially when it hurts. This is the space where we take agency. There is Christ in that space, calling out, saying, "Eli, Eli… God, God, where are you?! How could you have abandoned me?!" This is space for grace, in which we are enabled to act faithfully, on the basis of past experience with God. That is really important space as we leave, when we are angry, when we are hurt, and when there needs to be forgiveness. The supervisor needs good self-management to hold the space for grace, and allow the spirit to intercede for us. It is allowing God, in God's grace, as God always does, to have the biggest say – if we can pause to listen.

It's hard to listen when anger is shouting loud, and our hurt and pain is screaming out. Supervision allows that to happen; let's shout and yell; shake our fist at God, even at the supervisor. I recognise if transference going on, but I don't want to get into countertransference. When a supervisee is angry at me it might trigger me. This is an explosive situation made for trouble, and it needs to be dealt with in a way that is thoughtful and honest. We can say, "I think we need to take a breather here."

This is a really special space, where finally a person has opened up and they are honest and they are vulnerable. So we leave this on the table. It may be a bulbous mass or an angry lightning strike that's continuing to spark, it's sitting on the table. We say, "Right, let's acknowledge that, and let's take a breather from this." Literally I pause and take a breath, and allow the person to shake their shoulders or whatever. But not before they have been able to expel this, like a sneeze!

Ethics

Silvia: What are the ethical issues when a ministry is ending?

One thing that came very clear to me with my own transitions, knowing that I was going to leave, was that others must increase and I must decrease. I love John the Baptiser for that; the sense of humility; forward looking and not clinging to the status he had been given. He risked losing all the people surrounding him, who were now heading off to see this new person. The ethics of that situation come from a sense of humility, from a place of knowing: "I am not it. God is it!"

When I leave a community, I remind myself that these people are Christ followers, and the next person who will come alongside them to help them is the person who must now rise up. I must gently and intentionally take steps apart and away from the situation. It is not emotionally unhooking; that is an unhealthy image, I think. Emotionally, we love people and they love us, otherwise we can't do our jobs effectively and it's superficial. But in terms of the ethics, in transition, in leaving, we need to be able to let go. Letting go, pulling back, becoming smaller so that people may reimagine things in your absence.

There are practical and intentional things we need to do to deal with our own emotions, our sense of loss or insecurity. Even if we do not yet have another thing to go to, we need to say, "God will look after me in this, as God has in the past." God sees the big weave; I see only my little bits. A weaving has dark threads as well as light threads. I only appreciate the light threads, when in fact the dark threads create the possibility of seeing the light threads. Without them the weave would be uniform and would not have the beauty in it.

Letting go is a challenge. As we prepare the ground for the next person, we know that good things will be said about that person because of the foundations that I have laid. This is not easy because we live in a competitive environment. Ministers often compete for many things, including people's affections. Part of the supervisor's job is to help them see that competition is not a healthy thing.

There are some things we need to be ethically strong with. We have to accept that people may not always speak well of us. We have to act ethically even knowing that we might attract some criticism. Accept that we can't be well thought of in every way. There are areas we are weak in, and these may be talked about when we have gone. Leaving well includes intentionally saying and doing things for the sake of others. So we can leave knowing that ethically, morally, spiritually, in following Jesus, we have picked up that cross and have carried it, as we walk through the transition and leave.

Preparing for Retirement – *David Coster*

Rev. David Coster reflects on his own experience of retirement, informed by his study leave research on the subject of ministers and retirement.

• • •

Retirement is a big change; rather than the giver, I am now the receiver. So I go to worship and I sit down as part of the congregation. I have to say, that was one of the hardest things: "I should be up there, up the front!" Now I sit with my wife. It took me quite a while to get used to it, it was jarring for several months. It is a very different role to be a member of the congregation. I am there putting out chairs and making coffee, I am washing dishes. Sometimes the minister asks me, "Can you help?" and mostly I say yes.

When you retire there is a great freedom, because you have the freedom to say "yes" and the freedom to say "no." The presbytery asked me to take on a task recently and I said no. I am doing another task and I don't want to have two things on my plate. I don't even need a good reason to say no! The older I get, the more I appreciate having the time to do what I want to do. In ministry you never get a Christmas, you never get Easter off. This Easter, we went to the Marlborough Sounds and didn't go to church. We were out on a boat. Did I feel guilty? No. Did I miss church? Yes.

There is an adjustment that has to take place to our self-image. Who am I? A lot of retired ministers struggle with that, because their whole identity has been Minister. Some retired ministers are quite bitter and angry at the way the church treats them and how they have been side-lined. They are no longer attending presbytery and being a decision maker. I would say to them: "Change happens. Get used it."

Presbytery is not the bad guy. It was decades ago that the church decided that retired ministers no longer have a vote on presbytery unless they are exercising a role as a presbytery appointment. Having a vote at presbytery is a symbolic thing, and some people feel, "Don't take that away from me!" Grief can get side-lined into blame, or trapped in bitterness. I see people who want to hold on to the anger of being isolated. It's a grieving for the loss of power and status. It is also a grieving for the whole model of church that they gave their lives to, that sustained them. Now they feel abandoned by it.

Presbyteries can support a little, but it is our personal relationships with our colleagues that is the important thing, for spiritual support. It's over to me now, how I engage with presbytery. I don't go to some presbytery events, partly because much of what they are talking about no longer relates to me. It's not so relevant, because I no longer need all the things that they are talking about. In a sense, I'm on the sideline. I'm no longer on the on the playing field. I'm an observer.

In my Study Leave I interviewed a range of retired people. Those whose life was more expansive, involving groups and friendships outside of the church, seemed to adjust better to retirement than those whose life was fully occupied in the church. Their identity and sense of self-worth was not inextricably linked to who they were and what they did. They did not view themselves or their ministry as being indispensable.

I found that those who had spent some years planning for retirement adjusted to it much more successfully than those who had not. Those who did little planning wished that they had been better prepared. Other than making provision for retirement housing, issues of preparation for retirement differ little between ministers and non-ministers. Preparation and planning are the key components. Ministers who had not purchased a home pre-retirement felt greatly disadvantaged financially. Many were dependent on their spouse providing housing capital.

To prepare well means beginning to ask: "What am I losing? And what am I retaining? What am I going to do after?" For me, Rotary took on a far greater importance. My wife and I bought bikes and go riding. We meet friends for coffee. You have to create in your own mind and heart a new identity that doesn't involve being a minister. As a presbytery moderator I had a supportive role, working through with ministers what the future may be. And that was a privilege. There's a lot of privilege in ministry. That is part of what you lose.

To retire well one has to plan well. Support in long term planning is an essential element of wellness and wellbeing in retirement. Retirement seminars for ministers and spouses are, I believe, an essential component of the Church being a 'good faith' employer. It needs to cover topics such as adjustment, letting go and disengagement. The church used to run workshops, and I would like to see that happen again. We need a resource for ministers approaching retirement, that covers a range of aspects, financial, personal, spiritual and practical.

A Retiring Offering – *Margaret Garland*

Rev. Margaret Garland is a Presbyterian minister based in Dunedin who has retired from full-time parish ministry. She takes the term 'retirement' lightly, preferring to acknowledge that ministry continues but in different ways: "Creativity blossoms, questions continue, conversation go deep and pastoral is deeply embedded – forever."

• • •

This psalm was written as I approached retirement. The words helped me find a fresh perspective at a challenging time, as I was ending a very precious and grace-filled ministry. It helped me to recognise that ministry in God's service was mine from the moment of baptism and will continue into the future – albeit expressed in other ways. It moved me from a focus on the things left undone, to the rich and fruitful journey that is ministry in all its wondrous tapestry. May that journey continue for all of us in blessing and in love.

• • •

There is nothing new under the sun, say I.
It is just retirement, people do it all the time.
Why dwell on it, say I.
You are unique in my eyes, says God.
It is a moment on our journey together.
Shall we honour it together?
It is good to give thanks, say I:
thank you for opportunity and trust
  thank you for commitment and passion
    thank you for learning and growing
      thank you for the opening of heart and mind
        thank you for giftings and grace to endure
          thank you for encounters and encouragers.
You are welcome, says God, for each moment of thanksgiving
is a blessing to be shared.
It is good to lament, say I:
for doubt that has paralysed
      for opportunities lost
        for shallowness of insight
          for lack of courage
            for failing to trust your promises
              for moments lost to memory.
You are well loved, says God, for each moment of lament
binds us more closely together.
It is good to celebrate, say I:
      the friendships and the companions
        the achievements and the failures that were steps on the way
          the laughter and tears of relationship
            the shaping and refining
              the ah-ha moments
                the family alongside on the journey.
You are the celebration, says God, for each moment of love,
grace and truth is a light to the world.
Shall we continue on our way, says God?
I am looking forward to the journey yet to come, say I.
I hope you are as excited as I am, says God.
I pray so, for there is much yet to do…

A Happy Ending – *Anne Thomson*

Rev. Anne Thomson is currently Moderator of Southern Presbytery, based in Dunedin. In this chapter, Anne reflects on the experience of being farewelled from a multicultural parish.

• • •

Silvia: How did you come to finish your ministry at T Church?

Anne: I finished because I decided that it was the right time for me to finish. It was a slightly unusual circumstance, because I had been the Associate Minister. I had previously had a bad experience of the ending of an associate ministry, while I was a lay leader in a different church. This memory stayed with me. All through my 11 years as an Associate Minister this was a live question in my mind: how would this ministry come to an end? What would happen when the Senior Minister was called somewhere else? It was my expectation that when one member of a team leaves, that is end of the team. So I had long ago decided that when the Senior Minister left, I would leave. But when it actually happened I thought, "That's ridiculous us both leaving," especially when I didn't have anywhere to go. So I chose to continue until the next Senior Minister was appointed.

So, when the *T* Church congregation agreed to call a *G*, I told the Session I was leaving. And I wrote in the parish newsletter that I would be finishing a few weeks before his induction. At any time during my ministry when anyone asked me I had told them that was my intention. And yet when I did resign a lot of people were surprised, even people I was sure I had already told. I put it in the newsletter so that I couldn't back out! I was still reasonably convinced it was the right decision. But part of me was thinking, "Ah, but it would be such fun being in ministry with *G* and I would be so helpful to him!" I was just second guessing myself. Once I'd told everyone that I was leaving, then I really was leaving!

It was entirely my own decision. I had heard too many stories of messy situations where an Associate Minister had stayed on, and how that can split the congregation; some people want them to stay and some don't. I did not want that for myself or for the parish. I was quite sure that I was not called to be the Senior Minister; I wasn't looking for that. Also, because it is a multicultural parish, I felt it was really important for them to have a Pacific minister in the team; in which case they needed me out of the way.

When I resigned I did not know what was happening next for me: "Have I leaped into a void?" But the uncertainty was fairly brief, as I started with university chaplaincy the following month.

Silvia: What do you remember about the grief you felt?

Anne: There was grief for me, the grief of knowing that I would miss these people. I felt grief for those relationships that were changing, even though the change was inevitable and proper. When a ministry finishes there can be some ongoing contact, but any contact has to be in a different context. On the whole, the ministers I know are clear about that. Congregational members are not so clear about it. My grief was the grief of letting go of what had been, the ministry I'd had and the context in which I ministered. It was the grief of saying goodbye.

My final week at *T* Church was very special. People were very kind. There was also the excitement of *G* coming and a new ministry starting. The parish was looking forward. It made for an easy transition for them. It is a multicultural parish, with three language congregations, and that added a real richness to my farewell. On my final Sunday I chose to preach at all three services, rather than have a combined service, so that I could say goodbye to each congregation individually. Then the Kaikai in the evening, which was great fun!

Silvia: What did you learn about the ways different cultures say farewell?

Anne: Each congregation said goodbye in the way that was appropriate for them. Several of the Pākehā congregation dropped me a card or wrote me a letter, which was lovely. That is one way we say our thanks and farewell; Pākehā are more likely to express that in writing and use words.

I asked for my final farewell to be a Kaikai. This is a Cook Island cultural practice, used for 21st birthdays, weddings and farewells. It is a feast. One of the delights of my time at *T* Church was being involved in those events. I set the terms of the parish function by saying it was going to be a Kaikai, which the Samoans understood but the Pākehā folks were not familiar with.

The gift giving that is part of the cultural expression of farewell for Cook Islanders is so distinct, so different, so generous. That is who they are and how they operate. I knew that Kaikai involved giving gifts, but somehow I had not expected it to happen for me. It took us by surprise. You sit there in the middle and they literally pile bedding on top of you. It's astounding.

As the guests of honor, my husband and I were seated in the middle of the room. The gifts are brought out one by one in a whole procession of mostly the younger woman. I had seen this happen at other events, so I knew what was going on. There were sheets and pillowcases and duvet covers and bedspreads. Their bedspreads are beautiful works of art, quilted bedspread using Tivaivai patterns. Tivaivai are the appliqué quilts that Cook Islanders make. These are brightly coloured, with flower and leaf patterns repeated across the whole of the quilt.

So you sit there it piles up and piles up on top of you, with the occasional pillow as well! And then you have to extricate yourself from it, and they pack it all down and give you this huge pile to take home. It is absolutely the most extraordinary experience of abundant generosity. Being enveloped by love. If I had never seen it before I would have felt overwhelmed and embarrassed by the over-abundance of it. But because I had seen it a number of times at different celebrations, I understood what was going on.

A similar thing happens at an unveiling of a headstone, though the other way around. For Cook Islanders, you go to the cemetery one year after the death, and the headstone is covered with layers of tablecloths. They are removed one at a time, and given to honour those who have supported the family through the year of bereavement. When the headstone is uncovered, the inscription on the headstone is read aloud. It is an incredible way to mark the passing of time. A year on you are moving into a different stage of the grieving; the living are getting on with living. It is a tangible way say 'thank you' to the people who have been with you through that. I think it is just brilliant.

Laying on the cloths at a Kaikai is, like an unveiling, an honouring of the person at an important point of life transition. The gift giving is also about provision and preparation. The gifts are useful stuff for the journey, for where you are going next in life. That makes sense to me, both for celebrations and farewells.

Silvia: How did you experience God in your ministry ending?

Anne: God was in God's people; and in the love that was shown in all that was done. And in the generosity and the esteem and appreciation that came through the speeches, cards, gifts. I had a real sense of being part of the people of God in this place. And thankfulness that God had put me there for 11 years.

Silvia: Theologically we understand that God takes us through times of loss and pain, and leads us through into healing and hope. You're describing a situation with not a lot of pain, but still some loss. God is always able to work, even through our worst experiences in ministry.

Anne: I have been involved in another ministry ending that did involve a lot of hurt, and it took a long time to find where God was in that. There was not much hurt in the leaving of *T* Church. The pain was the pain of grief rather than pain of hurt. It was a natural pain. If you did not feel the pain of having to say goodbye, if it wasn't sad that you were leaving, then that really would be sad! If you couldn't wait to get out, that's sad. To feel loss makes sense to me. No matter how good the next thing is, you still have to say goodbye to the last one.

Silvia: When we do it well, as you are describing, blessing and gratitude comes through it. Hopefully when ministers leave, we leave the people of God grateful for our presence and equipped in some way. And we ourselves leave blessed and richer for that experience of serving God together.

Anne: Very much so. We trust that God continues to be with them, just as God continues to be with the one who leaves. We continue to be held in God's care and to be used by God and part of God's people, even though we move apart.

The Risk – *Ana Lisa de Jong*

(Living Tree Poetry)

> We risk our hearts.
> We risk our tears.
> We risk the breaking of our shells
> when we engage.
>
> When we step beyond
> our private worlds,
> extend the width of our territory
> for love's sake,
>
> we take a leap of faith
> that knows not where it will land,
> or if it will be better off
> for the chance taken.
>
> Yes, such a penetrating beam is love
> that the vulnerabilities which surface
> keep us half engaged
> and half restrained.

Is love worth it all, we ask?
But love, in love's rushing tide,
often leaves no time
to contemplate.

But before long asks for an exchange,
a melding of two hearts,
a transaction in which
each are enriched.

Yes, we risk our hearts,
we risk our tears,
we risk the brokenness of our shells
at loves behest, and for love's sake.

The losses that we fear
through trusting a feeling,
and following it through
to its consummation,

may come, eventually.
The flipped side of a coin
reveals
that nothing stays the same.

But all things take on
the hue of that in which they've been infused.
Love is a leap, a dance,
a chance worth taking.

We lose, but love's residue
is inscribed upon our hearts.
Nothing is fully lost,
when love has been our intent.

Endnotes

1 Andy Piggott, *Leaving Well: Exploring Aspects of Moving from One Ministry to Another* (Cambridge: Grove Books, 2014), 14-24, used with permission.

2 In the Presbyterian church, when a parish's minister leaves the presbytery must appoint an interim moderator – normally a neighbouring or retired minister – to have oversight of the parish until another minister is called.

3 Milfred Minatrea borrows this term from Darrell Guder. He uses it to describe when churches move their focus and resources almost entirely on the spiritual preservation of their members. Milfred Minatrea, *Shaped by God's Heart; The Passion and Practices of Missional Churches* (San Francisco, CA: Jossey-Bass, 2019), 9.

4 Stuart Murray, *Church after Christendom* (Milton Keynes, UK: Paternoster Press, 2004), 155.

5 Craig Van Gelder, ed., *The Missional Church and Denominations: Helping Congregations Develop a Missional Identity* (Michigan: Grand Rapids, 2008).

6 Edgar H Schein, *Organizational Culture and Leadership*, 4th ed, (San Francisco, CA: Jossey-Bass, 2010), 300-303.

7 Ibid., 24-33.

8 Ibid., 28.

9 Lewis B Smedes, *The Art of Forgiving* (Canada: Ballantyne Books, 1997), 7.

10 Alan J Roxburgh and Fred Romanuk, *The Missional Leader: Equipping Your Church to Reach a Changing World* (San Francisco: Jossey-Bass, 2006).

11 I note that the Book of Order does require that a Settlement Board be appointed "without delay" (10.4 (1), PCANZ). However, in practice the process can be delayed and drawn out.

12 Piringa Trust: https://www.piringa.org.nz.

13 CAIRA supervision: https://caira.org.nz.

Moving On: A Conclusion

Therefore thus says the Lord God, "See, I am laying in Zion a foundation stone, a tested stone, a precious cornerstone, a sure foundation: 'One who trusts will not panic.'"

(Isaiah 28:16, NRSV)

"… the household of God, built upon the foundation of the apostles and prophets, with Christ Jesus himself as the cornerstone; in him the whole structure is joined together and grows into a holy temple in the Lord."

(Ephesians 2:19b-21, NRSV)

I entered Christian ministry as Christendom was breathing its last. Those who founded my denomination, the Presbyterian Church of Aotearoa New Zealand, believed they were building on the cornerstone of Jesus Christ an institution which would stand firm through every storm, a symbol of stability. I inherited a church built to last, which is now in fundamental transition. Jesus Christ is still our cornerstone, but how do we "trust and not panic" in the face of wave after wave of change – decline, aging, pandemic, climate disasters, generational change, new technologies and genders? *Moving On: Grief in Ministry Transitions* began life as a very personal reflection on a ministry ending which left me shaken. It has grown become a multi-dimensional exploration of what it takes to minister in a church and world in constant uncomfortable transition.

At the heart of this book is a particular moment in time: when a ministry appointment comes to an end. The work grew and grew as others courageously shared their grief stories with me. The chapters of *Moving On* reveal the lived experience of ministry in the presence of loss and grief, not only personally but collectively as church. We have dived deep into emotion and theology, re-evaluating systems and cultural norms.

Ministry in the church creates deep bonds of affection and a strong sense of belonging in community. Those who minister the Gospel of Christ – in word and sacrament, pastoral care, mission or youth work – invest themselves in their work wholeheartedly. Good intentions of inclusion, love and mission are affirmed week by week by the community in worship. However, these good intentions can be violated by experiences of abuse. Trust can be betrayed, and disappointment can harden into rejection. When these lead to the ending of a ministry, grief is complicated. Where these cause spiritual hurt, spiritual healing is required. Even when a ministry has gone well, leaving still involves multiple loss, not just for the pastor but also for their spouse and family.

Transition is difficult, made all the more so because of high expectations of resilience. Marsha Frame's study on relocating ministers quotes one participant who acknowledges the irony that although ministers are "supposed to deal caringly and effectively with the grief of others, we fail to apply what we know about grief to ourselves," and concludes that "the most pressing need was for assistance with grief and loss."[1] *Moving On* provides such assistance through applying theory and research on grief to the experience of pastors in difficult ministry transition. It advocates for taking time to attend to the complex tasks of grief, and provides a range of resources and insights about recovery. It addresses institutional, systemic and practical aspects of ministry endings. It suggests biblical and theological resources to connect us into the Gospel story; this is important because loss, especially traumatic loss, threatens to tear us out of God's story.

Ministry is not just a job. To honour the wholeness of heart and soul, contributors and I have provided a wealth of prayer material. When we are at our lowest, we struggle to find words to pray. When words are not enough, we need actions to fully express ourselves to God. My prayer is that God may meet you there, and speak to you through the stories of others, through poetry and litany, and through your own heart.

Loss is part of life, the cost of love. Grieving is a space between what was and what will be, and it can be a strange no-man's-land, a wilderness. The faith challenge is to place oneself fully in the knowledge that 'I am where I am meant to be.' The loss of a ministry role and a place as pastor in the people of God is a death, and grieving for this death can go unrecognised by others, but the Holy Spirits reminds us of the One who sees and hears, who comforts and heals and calls us on.

We do Jesus a dis-service when we cast him as the cornerstone of institutional stability. Institutional stability is crumbling (and not just in the church), bringing with it a host of challenging human experiences and transitions. Christ the Cornerstone is our constant presence and guide, a living stone, not set in concrete. Through all the changes of life, may Christ be your rock and your light.

Go in peace. (Numbers 6:24-26)

The Lord bless you and keep you; the Lord make his face to shine upon you and be gracious to you; the Lord lift up his countenance upon you and give you peace. *(NRSV)*

God bless you and keep you, God smile on you and gift you, God look you full in the face and make you prosper. *(The Message)*

Mā Ihowa koe e manaaki, māna koe e tiaki:Mā Ihowa e mea kia tīaho tōna mata ki a koe, māna ano hoki koe e atawhai: Mā Ihowa tona kanohi e whakaara ki a koe, māna ano e tuku te rangimārie ki a koe. *(Paipera Tapu)*

Book List

These books are recommended by contributors, and/or are in the Hewitson Library collection.[2]

Thomas Attig, *How We Grieve: Relearning the World* (Oxford University Press, 2011)

Lynne Baab, *Nurturing Hope: Christian Pastoral Care for the Twenty-First Century* (Fortress Press, 2018)

Lynne Baab, *Sabbath-Keeping: Finding Freedom in the Rhythms of Rest* (IVP Books, 2005)

Lynne Baab, *Two Hands: Grief and Gratitude in the Christian Life* (independently published for paperback, kindle, and audiobook, 2021)

Elsa McInnes, *Shattered and Restored* (Castle, 1990, reprinted 2003)

Elsa McInnes, *A Grip on Grief: Youth face to face with loss* (Castle, 2001)

Marjorie Tuainekore Crocombe, et al., *Polynesian Missions in Melanesia from Samoa, Cook Islands and Tonga to Papua New Guinea and New Caledonia* (1982, Hewitson call number: BV3675 P65)

Norman B. Bendroth (editor), *Transitional Ministry Today: successful strategies for churches and pastors* (Rowman & Littlefield, 2014)

Norman B. Bendroth, *Interim Ministry in Action: A Handbook for Churches in Transition* (Rowman & Littlefield, 2018)

Helen Bent, *Celebration in times of grief and sorrow* (Grove Worship booklet W234)

Judy Brizendine, *Stunned by Grief: remapping your life when loss changes everything* (ReadHowYouWant, 2013)

Tim Conder, *The Church in Transition: the journey of existing churches into the emerging culture* (Zondervan, 2006)

J. Russell Crabtree and Carolyn Weese, *The Elephant in the Boardroom: Speaking the Unspoken about Pastoral Transitions – How to Handle Pastoral Transition with Sensitivity, Creativity, and Excellence* (Fortress, 2020)

Michael K. Girlinghouse, *Embracing God's Future without Forgetting the Past: A Conversation about Loss, Grief, and Nostalgia in Congregational Life* (Augsburg Fortress, Publishers, 2019)

Alister Hendery, *The Grief Walk: Losing, Grieving and Journeying on to Something New* (Wellington: Philip Garside Publishing, 2020)

Alister Hendery, *Earthed in Hope: Dying, Death and Funerals – A Pakeha Anglican Perspective* (Philip Garside Publishing, 2014)

Margaret Holloway, *Negotiating Death in Contemporary Health and Social Care* (Policy Press, 2007)

Lucy Hone, *Resilient Grieving: how to find your way through devastating loss: a practical guide to recovery* (The Experiment, 2017)

John Hornblow, *A Bridge from Here to There.* This manual for journaling through ministry transition is available for download: https://www.conversations.net.nz/moving-on.html

Lolomilo Kamu, *The Samoan Culture and The Christian Gospel* (Methodist Printing Press, Apia, 1996)

Raeburn Lange, *The Origins of the Christian Ministry in the Cook Islands and Samoa* (Macmillan Brown Centre for Pacific Studies. Hewitson call number: PQX LAN)

Elsa McInnes, *Shattered and Restored* (Castle, 1990, reprinted 2003),

Elsa McInnes, *A Grip on Grief: youth face to face with loss* (Castle, 2001)

Alistair Mackenzie, *Soul Purpose: making a difference in life and work* (NavPress, 2004)

Milfred Minatrea, *Shaped by God's Heart; The Passion and Practices of Missional Churches* (Jossey-Bass, 2019)

Stuart Murray, *Church after Christendom* (Paternoster Press, 2004)

Mary Nilsen, *For Everything a Season: 75 Blessings for Daily Life* (Zion Publishing, 1999)

Wayne E. Oates, *Grief, Transition, and Loss: a pastor's practical guide* (Creative Pastoral Care & Counseling) (Augsburg, 1997)

Roy M. Oswald, James M. Heath and Ann W. Heath, *Beginning Ministry Together: the Alban handbook for clergy transitions* (Rowman & Littlefield, 2003)

Lachy Paterson, Murray Rae, Hugh Morrison and Brett Knowles (eds.), *Mana Māori and Christianity* (Wellington: Huia Press, 2013)

Andy Piggott, *Leaving Well: Exploring Aspects of Moving from One Ministry to Another* (Grove Books, 2014)

Alan Roxburgh and Fred Romanuk, *The Missional Leader: Equipping Your Church to Reach a Changing World* (Jossey-Bass, 2006)

Joyce Rupp, *Praying Our Goodbyes* (Ave Maria Press, 2009)

Lewis B. Smedes, *The Art of Forgiving* (Ballantyne Books, 1997)

Edgar H. Schein, *Organizational Culture and Leadership*, 4th edition (Jossey-Bass, 2010)

Kathleen S. Smith, *Stilling the Storm: worship and congregational leadership in difficult times* (Rowman & Littlefield, 2006)

Mua Strickson-Pua, *Matua/Parents* (Pohutukawa Press, 2006)

Steve Taylor, *First Expressions: Innovation in the Mission of God* (SCM Press, 2019)

Steve Taylor, *Built for Change: A Practical Theology of Innovation and Collaboration* (MediaCom, 2016)

Steve Taylor, *Out of Bounds Church? Learning to Create a Community of Faith in a Culture of Change* (Zondervan, 2010)

Wayne Te Kaawa, *Hihita and Hoani: Missionaries in Tūhoeland* (Westprint, 2008)

Craig Van Gelder (ed), *The Missional Church and Denominations: Helping Congregations Develop a Missional Identity* (Eerdmans, 2008)

William Worden, *Grief Counseling and Grief Therapy: A Handbook for the Mental Health Practitioner, 4th ed.* (Routledge, 2010)

Ana Lisa and her Poems

Ana Lisa de Jong is a contemplative poet and author, known for her prolific writing. She is inspired by the power and wonder of words and the myriad of ways they speak to us, and by the Eternal threaded through the natural world. She enjoys connecting with her readers and creating collections to gift to others. Ana Lisa shares her poetry widely on Facebook and at livingtreepoetry.com.

Copyright Information

The poems in this book by Ana Lisa de Jong are used by permission and are from these sources:

"Transition": from *Joy instead of Mourning – Words for Winter*, copyright Ana Lisa de Jong, Living Tree Poetry (Humanities Academic Publishers, 2021).

"The Work of Grief": from *Beauty for Ashes – Words for Autumn,* copyright Ana Lisa de Jong (Humanities Academic Publishers, 2021).

"Heart Songs", "Remains of the Day", "Inside Out", "Except a Grain of Wheat": from *Heart Psalms – Songs of the Heart*, copyright Ana Lisa de Jong (Lang Book Publishing, 2018).

"Long Shadows", "The Risk": from *Gifted*, copyright Ana Lisa de Jong (Living Tree Poetry: Humanities Academic Publishers, 2020).

"This Heart", "I Cried", "How Good" are previously unpublished.

To read more of Ana Lisa's poetry, or to make contact with the author regards books or use of her work, visit: livingtreepoetry.com

Endnotes

1 Marsha Frame, "Relocation and Well-Being", 426.

2 Hewitson Library is the library of the PCANZ, at Knox College, Dunedin. Anyone may apply for membership (via email): https://hewitson.mykoha.co.nz.

www.ingramcontent.com/pod-product-compliance
Lightning Source LLC
Chambersburg PA
CBHW051307140626
46546CB00020B/213